Haynes

Fly
Fishing
Manual

Acknowledgements

I am indebted to Magnus Angus for his invaluable advice, guidance and photography, and to John Symonds for his illustrative expertise. In addition, I'm lucky and grateful to have had access to the photographic skills of Helen Barrington and Charles Jardine, plus the unique entomological close-up photographs of Cyril Bennett.

I'd also like to thank saltwater fly-fishing pioneer Colin MacLeod for his contribution, Dave Southall for his tenkara knowledge, and Dominic Garnett for his assistance on the coarse fly-fishing side.

I'd like to mention all those people who have helped me and contributed during this project's development: Anthony Steel, David Wolsoncroft Dodds, Andrew Mactaggard, Malcolm Greenhalgh, Oliver Edwards, Ally Gowans, Allan Liddle, Roger Dowsett, Kevin Muir, Ben Dixon, Doug Gilbert, Uwe Stoneman, and Laura and Sarah Graham for Banjo duties.

Special thanks to Mike Duxbury and Dave Graham for going fishing with me, and allowing me to photograph them, Lee Cummings for casting demonstrations in adverse conditions, and Fulling Mill for providing the flies.

Last, but not least, Bonnie Maggio, not only for her artistic eye but also for – along with Callum and Zoe Strong – providing the encouragement for me to take on this project in the first place.

Credits

Author:	Mark Bowler
Project manager:	Louise McIntyre
Copy editor:	Ian Heath
Page design:	James Robertson
Photography:	Magnus Angus, Charles Jardine, Helen Barrington, Bonnie Maggio, Callum Strong, Trevor Booth, Andrew Herd, David Wolsoncroft Dodds, Tomas Kolesinskas & Mark Bowler
Illustrations:	John Symonds

Dedication

To my dad Les and my mum Beryl for their constant guidance, their love of the outdoors, sport and adventure, and – despite not being fishers themselves – patience beyond the call of parental duty.

First published in November 2016

British Library Cataloguing in Publication Data
A catalogue record for this book is available from the British Library

ISBN 978 1 78521 074 7

Library of Congress control no. 2015948114

Published by Haynes Publishing,
Sparkford, Yeovil, Somerset BA22 7JJ, UK
Tel: 01963 440635
Int. tel: +44 1963 440635
Website: www.haynes.com

Haynes North America Inc.
861 Lawrence Drive, Newbury Park,
California 91320, USA

Printed in Malaysia

While every effort is taken to ensure the accuracy of the information given in this book, no liability can be accepted by the author or publishers for any loss, damage or injury caused by errors in, or omissions from the information given.

Front cover: Chris Rownes with a beautiful river Test brown trout. *Photo: Charles Jardine.*

Haynes

Fly Fishing Manual

The step-by-step guide

Mark Bowler

CONTENTS

Introduction

When first asked to write this book, I deliberated about it long and hard. To put together a book that covers all aspects of fly fishing – "for the beginner, but with something for the more experienced fly fisher" was my brief – which is an onerous task for such an involved, wide-ranging topic.

However, one over-riding thought drove me: I have spent my life pursuing all types of fish, initially as a coarse fisher, but latterly - ie, the best part of 40 years – only with an artificial fly. During this time, fly fishing has produced some amazing experiences for me: not only have I caught many memorable fish, but also this passion has taken me to the most beautiful parts of UK and Ireland (indeed, the world); I have had string of enviable wildlife encounters; met some incredible people (all 'brothers of the angle'); and every session has been a voyage of exploration and discovery. I've enjoyed every single minute of this fascinating experience. Even now, as I write, I know the trout at the bottom of the

lane will be rising to blue-winged olives and then sedges as the evening light fails, and I can't wait to finish writing this section, so I can have a cast for them. The draw of a chuckling summer river on a warm night with just the trout, owls and maybe an otter for company is irresistible.

This book was written for a number of reasons. Firstly, because when I was learning to fish there was no basic manual to use as guidance or reference. My friends and I learned from our peers, or from snippets of useful information gleaned from articles. Most of what we learned was from trial-and-error (hours of trial, mostly error); as a result much of the information in this book is gleaned from that toughest school of all – hard-won experience. This is the book that I was searching constantly to find.

Secondly, because I edit a national fly-fishing magazine, and have done for over 25 years, I get constant phone calls and emails from friends asking for advice about tackle, venues, tactics and, on more than one occasion, a call from

the middle of Blagdon Lake enquiring about fly choice for the day. If for no other reason I can now, at least, point them to this book and help a lot more others at the same time. More importantly, however, I hope it will help anyone out there to understand the basics, the essential detail, and some of the intricacies of fly-fishing – the fascination for which has consumed me for four decades and will continue to do so, such is its all-consuming, ever-changing appeal.

So, my main aim is primarily to introduce other people to this absorbing and rewarding sport, so they, too, can experience it for themselves. However, I also think it is important for all fly fishers to realise that once the basic skills have been acquired, then the world becomes a different place, no matter where you travel. Learn to cast a fly and your journey has only just begun: trout, salmon, carp, sea bass and countless other fish are all accessible to you, from the south coast, to the Scottish Highlands, to the wild western lakes of Ireland and far, far beyond.

Fly fishing technique and technology has developed so much recently that, apart from game fish, the traditional fly fisher's quarry, many species of coarse fish and sea fish now fall within the compass of the fly fisher. Today, it doesn't matter where you live or visit – there will be the potential for you to fly fish on your doorstep. All you need is a source of clean, natural water, plus a rod, reel, a line and a few flies. I don't claim it will be able to give you all the subtle nuances of every species, tactic and location – that's the role of the monthly magazine I edit, *Fly Fishing and Fly Tying*, but I hope to pass on the essential skills, and hope this book can act as a reference for broadening and furthering your journey.

A fly-fishing permit is a ticket to access locations, waters and banksides few others ever see or experience. It is a privilege that only those lucky people who happen to be fly fishers are party to. Welcome to our world.

See you on the river bank one day and "Tight lines".

THE FISH YOU ARE TRYING TO CATCH

Modern fly fishing is a diverse and varied sport. Today, the fly fisher can just as easily be casting a size 18 dry fly to a shoal of roach on a canal, as pitching a size 2 popping lure into the crashing waves on a stormy beach in his search for an Atlantic sea bass. Granted, most fly fishers will still encounter fly fishing through the traditional channels of trout and salmon fishing on our clear-water streams, small stillwaters and reservoirs, but over the last couple of decades the face of fly fishing has evolved, through both technology and a certain amount of pioneering spirit, into a wider-ranging, more varied approach.

As a result, when a newcomer considers his choice of tackle to get him started he or she needs to consider first the species most likely to be encountered, and then where the most likely fly fishing opportunity/ies might arise. Today, one doesn't need to live on a chalk stream, by a salmon river or alongside a trout reservoir in order to access prime fly fishing; it's available everywhere across the UK; in fact, wherever there's water clean enough for fish to swim and live in it.

Thus, before going ahead and purchasing a rod, reel and line, plus all the other paraphernalia associated with fly fishing, it's important for the budding angler to consider the likely species they're going to tackle.

Salmon *(Salmo salar)*

The 'king of fish'. To catch a beautiful, bright silver salmon is often seen as the pinnacle of a fly fisher's ambitions. And why not? These beautiful silver creatures, possessing immense power and stamina, run to legendary sizes – a spring salmon might touch 20lb, 30 if you're lucky.

Salmon don't feed when they return to their rivers of birth from their feeding at sea, thus persuading one to take a fly is a mystery in itself. Various theories cover aggression, a dormant feeding instinct, curiosity, or perhaps a territorial response. *Salmo salar* (the leaper) is well known for leaping up waterfalls to gain access to the spawning streams, but sometimes salmon give themselves away by leaping in the river. However, a leaping fish is not a guarantee that it will be caught... 'a leaping fish is nae a takin' fish', as the old Scots proverb says.

The British record is 64lb, and has stood for over 80 years. This massive specimen came from Perthshire's River Tay, and was caught by a woman, Miss Georgina Ballantine, as was the second-largest ever to be landed – a 61lb fish from the River Awe.

Key characteristics
- Usually associated with our cleaner, wilder rivers of Scotland, Wales, Ireland, and north-west, north-east and south-west England. As a result, salmon fishing tends to take the angler to the wilder parts of Britain and Ireland.
- Life cycle begins in the gravels of a river's tributaries, where eggs are laid in the winter. The young fry, or parr,

can live in the river for one, two or three years before they change their trout-like parr markings, 'silver up' and become tiny salmon smolts and begin their migration downriver to the sea, usually in late spring.
- On entering the sea, the salmon smolts migrate into the north-east Atlantic, searching for the rich feeding grounds off the Faroe Islands and Greenland.
- At sea, they eat sandeel, shrimp and capelin (a small fish) and grow far faster than in the river (a salmon feeding at sea can pack on a third of its own weight in one month).
- Some smolts, having spent a full summer at sea, return to the rivers of their birth the next summer as grilse – generally now weighing between 3lb and 8lb (1.5–3.5kg).
- Salmon spending two, three and even four summers feeding before they return to their natal rivers between January and June are called 'springers'.
- Salmon use high water to enter the river – *ie* high tides and/or spates (high river levels after rain).
- Having entered freshwater, the salmon then ceases to feed, existing on the body reserves it has built up at sea, making its way up the river (running), and lying in pools for days, weeks, even months.
- Salmon are most likely to take a fly when they're freshly into the river; straight after they've assumed a new lie after running or after a spate; and also towards the autumn, when they become more excited and aggressive as their spawning season (generally mid-December) approaches.
- Salmon take on different colourations as they stay in freshwater. Having entered the river as a shining silver fish, this coloration gives way to a more pewter sheen after a week or so, which gives way in turn to a

reddening tone, with males becoming redder still as they approach spawning.

■ The majority of salmon die after spawning, but a few thin, post-spawn fish, known as kelts, manage to return to sea and feed for another summer before re-entering the river to spawn a second time.

Tackling up

The basic salmon set-up is a 15ft, double-handed rod matched with a #10 line. On smaller rivers, a 15ft rod can prove cumbersome and a #10 line too heavy, so double-handed rods of 12 to 14ft, taking lighter lines of #8 and #9, are more suitable, easier to handle and more dextrous. For small rivers, and for fishing off a boat, a single-handed 10–11ft (#7–8) rod will be eminently suitable, although today double-handed 'Switch' rods, of 11–13ft and taking lines down to #6 offer improved line control and easier Spey-casting.

Sea trout *(Salmo trutta)*

Sea trout and brown trout (see below) are, in fact, the same species.

The juvenile sea trout undergoes a behavioural and physiological change that sees it silver-up as a smolt, just as a salmon does, and migrate down to the sea, where it grows quickly; adult fish return to their river of birth from late April through to September, depending on the river.

Sea trout are found in similar rivers to salmon, but don't require such high waters to enter a river, though high tides and spates enable easier access for them. Like salmon, but unlike brown trout, sea trout rarely feed on re-entering freshwater, although some rivers do have sea trout that 'feed' to a certain extent (see 'Sea trout on a dry fly' in Chapter 11).

Sea trout are ultra wary and easily scared. They're nocturnal – running the river at night – but can be caught during the day.

■ Sea trout returning as fish of ½lb to 1¼lb are known locally as finnock, juniors, herling or whitling.

↓ A sea trout … fresh in the river from the sea.

■ Like salmon, they're more likely to be caught soon after entering the river, *ie* within days of arriving from the sea.

■ Sea trout return to freshwater as beautiful, sparkling silver, spotted fish, but the longer they stay in the river the darker hues they assume, becoming dark grey, almost black, at spawning time (late November).

■ Unlike salmon, sea trout return to the sea after spawning, to feed again in the sea and return the next year to spawn.

■ Sea trout often give their position away by jumping, frequently at dusk.

■ The fishing season for sea trout finishes in September.

Tackling up

A standard outfit for most sea-trout rivers would comprise a 10ft rod taking a #7 or #8 line. Some anglers might like the extra line-control and power of an 11ft rod, particularly when fishing from a boat, but this is always compromised by the extra weight for continuous casting. Switch rods taking light lines (#7) are becoming popular. For low water and small hooks on small rivers, a 9–9ft 6in rod (for a #6 or even a #5 line) is adequate, but casting in wind can then become more difficult.

Brown trout *(Salmo trutta)*

Brown trout can be caught during the day, especially from March to late June, and then again in September. In July and August they're more active during low light – evenings and early morning – and on dull, overcast days. However, in the north (Scotland), once brown trout start to feed they tend to be active all summer.

Brown trout feed on aquatic invertebrates, small fish, snails and terrestrial insects that blow into the water. Cold-blooded, they're torpid during the depths of winter, but feed with increasing intensity from 7°C up to their optimum water temperature of 12–15°C. Upwards of 17°C they become increasingly lethargic and feed less, typically during high summer. A typical wild brown trout would weigh ¾lb; in small streams and lochs they may be much smaller than this, but in bigger rivers and lakes they can grow far bigger. A 1¼lb wild fish would be considered 'good', and a two-pounder

↑ Wild brown trout.

↑ Rainbow trout.

'excellent'. Although slow-growing, the brown trout is known for its longevity and, given adequate feeding, can grow to a large size: the British record currently stands at 31lb 12oz.

■ Wild brown trout are solitary fish, and territorial. Dominant fish take up the better stations in rivers and lochs where shelter and food is in the best supply.

■ Brown trout are found all over the UK and Ireland, living in many of the upper reaches of our cleaner, faster-flowing rain-fed streams and chalk streams. They're also found naturally in Welsh tarns, Scottish lochs, Irish loughs and English lakes.

■ They can take on a wide variety of colourations, mainly influenced by their environment. Colours can vary from silvery, chocolate spotted fish to yellowy golden hues with red spots and the pewters and dark greens typical of Scottish lochs.

■ They spawn in late November/early December, the fishing season running from March to September.

Tackling up

Typical outfit for brown trout would range from a 10ft #7 rod for wilder waters to a 6ft #3 for tiny, enclosed rivers.

Rainbow trout
(Oncorhynchus mykiss)

Not a native fish to the UK or Ireland, the rainbow trout originates from the USA but has now become the most widely stocked fish for fly fishing in Britain. It's quick growing, easily farmed, and its free-rising nature (ie it'll readily take surface fished flies) makes it highly popular with fly fishers. Its name comes from the magenta stripe that runs along the entire length of the body, combined with its blue-green back and iridescent blues and lilacs in the scales, all on a background of silver.

Like brown trout, rainbows will feed on aquatic invertebrates, snails, small fish and terrestrial insects. Unlike the brown trout, the rainbow prefers to cruise in pods or shoals, cruising upwind in lakes. Also, they tend to move at a certain depth – from just under the surface to many feet down, depending on the water temperature, the light and

the food available. They're more tolerant of light than browns, thus are more accessible to the angler during the high summer. They're catholic, opportunistic feeders, and once in a fertile lake they can grow quickly. The British record is 24lb 14oz.

■ Rainbows don't spawn naturally in Britain, apart from a very small number of isolated rivers, such as the Wye in Derbyshire.

■ Rainbow trout are spotted, even on the tail (which easily distinguishes them from salmon, brown trout and sea trout).

Tackling up

A typical rainbow trout outfit comprises a 9ft 6in #6, with a 9ft #5 for dry fly fishing and a 10ft #7 for sunk lines and boat fishing.

Grayling
(Thymallus thymallus)

A wild river fish often – but not always – found alongside the brown trout, as they share similar habitats (although there are no grayling in Ireland, and none further north than the Tummel in Scotland). Characterised by its large, sail-like, vermillion-infused dorsal fin and forked tail, the grayling also

↓ Grayling.

sports an adipose fin. This short, vestigial 'comma' of a fin between the tail and dorsal fin is also present on salmon, sea trout and brown trout; thus the grayling has also become known as the 'fourth game fish', and has enjoyed increased popularity with fly fishers over the past two decades, probably due to its purely wild status (it isn't farmed or stocked).

Grayling caught on fly range from ½lb up to 3lb, which represents an exceptional fish. The British record is 4lb 4oz. An average fish would be ¾lb to 1lb.

- Grayling are a shoal fish, feeding on similar items to brown trout, in particular aquatic invertebrates.
- They possess a down-turned mouth, adapted for bottom-feeding. However, they'll also take flies off the surface.
- They're less wary than brown trout.
- Grayling tend to shoal with the onset of winter. The best grayling fishing is generally assumed to be October into November, and the season continues through the winter.

CLOSED SEASON

Grayling are classified by the Environment Agency as a coarse fish, along with pike, perch, carp, chub, dace, roach and rudd. In England and Wales the closed season for coarse fish on rivers is 16 March to 15 June. Privately owned lakes can also have their own closed seasons.

Tackling up

Grayling fishing is similar to river fishing for trout, but due to their smaller size a 8½-9ft #4-6 would be more than adequate, the heavier line weight assisting with casting leaded nymphs. They're also susceptible to Euro-nymphing, so specialist long, light-line rods are suitable too.

Pike *(Esox lucius)*

A solitary fish in general, in Britain and Ireland this apex piscine predator is found in lakes, rivers and canals, although many northern Scottish lochs don't hold pike. Built for power and acceleration, pike are torpedo-shaped with a powerful tail (caudal) fin. A pike's mouth is designed for catching its prey, with a set of sharp, biting teeth and rows of backward-inclined hinged teeth on the roof of its mouth that fold down when clamped on to the prey fish, preventing its escape.

The pike's markings – overall dark green with banded markings on the side – are designed to camouflage its presence close to its prey, as it often uses 'structure' – weed beds, sunken logs, lily pads, drop-offs etc – to stage its ambushes.

The British record is currently 46lb 13oz.

- Pike eat all manner of coarse fish, mainly roach and bream if available, but will also eat trout.
- Big pike often predate on their own young and also frogs, and are infamous for taking ducklings.

↓ Built for power: the pike.

(Kletr)

- A young 'jack' pike runs between 2lb and 6lb and will be a handful to land for the pike fly fisher. However, huge (usually female fish) can be located, especially in stocked rainbow trout fisheries.
- On occasion pike will gang up to 'herd' and feed on shoals of baitfish. When this occurs more than one fish can be taken from the same area.

Tackling up

Due to the size of the flies used and the wire trace necessary, outfits range from tip-actioned 9ft #8–#10 weight rods coupled with either floating or sink-tip lines.

Perch *(Perca fluviatilis)*

↑ The striped and spiny perch.

The distinctively dark-striped perch with its green back, orange fins and spiny dorsal fin is a worthy and magnificent prize on a fly, and can be found in shoals in both rivers and lakes. A predatory fish-eater with a large mouth, perch also feed on aquatic invertebrates. Often located where small baitfish live, such as weed beds and lily pads, frequently in deeper holes and underwater ridges or around 'structures', such as bridge pilings, mill pools, bushes and boat moorings. A giveaway sign of perch activity is baitfish scattering at the surface as the perch attack from beneath. Perch feed all through the year. The British record is 6lb 3oz.

Tackling up

A 9ft 6in #6 or #7 weight rod will cover all options for perch, from fishing nymphs to casting small weighted lures and sinking lines. Although predatory, a wire trace is not required for perch.

Carp *(Cyprinus carpio)*

Carp are a popular sporting fish of British lakes, found everywhere but north of Scotland's Central Belt. Known for attaining large individual weights, carp on fly can be caught from ½lb right up to 40lb. The British record rod-caught carp stands at 68lb 1oz.

Strongly built and powerful, carp are more commonly found in muddy-bottomed, reed-fringed lakes typical of English country estates, or canals and gravel pits, and have

(Jack Perks)

↑ Mirror carp. Can grow to very large sizes.

become common in smaller coarse fisheries. They feed mainly on aquatic insects, particularly the midge (*chironomid*).

- There are two main varieties – common and mirror carp. Both are bronze in colouration. The common sports an even coating of diamond-shaped scales and rounded fins; the mirror carp has bronze, leathery skin covered with irregularly sized scales in individual patterns.
- The carp is generally a bottom feeder, but will sometimes feed on the surface.
- Occasionally found in slow-moving rivers.
- In mainland Europe there are some shallow carp lakes where fish can be stalked with flies and caught on sight-fished nymph imitations.

Tackling up

Depending on the size of fish sought, either a 9ft #6 or 9ft 6in #7 or #8 rod should cover most presentation options. Carp are strong fighters, so a stiffish rod with back-bone (medium to fast action) should be used to help subdue the fish quickly.

Chub *(Squalius cephalus)*

The chub is a silver or tinted bronze-sided, stockily built cyprinid with a large mouth and reddish anal and pectoral fins. Chub are a shoal fish that are most comfortable with overhead cover afforded by undercut banks, tree-roots, bends, log-jams and obstructions and overhanging trees. A catholic feeder, chub will eat anything from aquatic invertebrates to slugs, small fish and crayfish. Often found in slower reaches of trout rivers of England and Wales, chub

↓ The shy chub.

caught on fly will range from ¾lb up to 3lb–4lb and more, the British record being a hefty 9lb 5oz.

- Izaak Walton's 'fearfullest of fishes', the chub is extremely wary and shy, retreating under cover when threatened by unexpected movement.
- Chub are distinguished from dace by their larger size and scales, and also the convex edge of their dorsal fin.
- Chub can be fished for throughout the year.

Dace (Leuciscus leuciscus)

(Svet Pavlova)

⬆ The silver dace.

Sleeker and with more graceful lines than the chub, and more silvery looking. It's smaller too – a 1lb dace is a specimen (the British record is 1lb 5oz).

Dace are a shoal fish of smoothly flowing water, which feed on small aquatic invertebrates. Also found in estuarine waters, they're busy fish, taking and ejecting flies quickly. Due to its shoaling habit, more than one fish can be caught from a shoal. They can be encountered in rivers in England, Ireland and Wales, but rarely in Scotland.

- The fins tend more to olive and yellows than to red, and the dace has a concave dorsal fin when extended.

(Kondor83)

⬆ The red-finned roach.

Roach (Rutilus rutilus)

Found in slower-flowing reaches of rivers, the roach is a silvery fish with reddish, rounded fins, a bluish or green back and a reddish tinted eye. Similar to the dace and rudd, the roach is deeper bodied and has redder fins than the dace and distinguished from a rudd by its mouth shape, the rudd's lower lip being inclined upwards. Also found in ponds, lakes, canals and rivers, it's found everywhere bar the north of Scotland. It's a shoal fish, found usually on bends, in pools and on slower glides. It feeds on aquatic invertebrates.

Due to its shoaling habit, more than one fish can be caught from a shoal. A roach of ½lb is a decent one, a 1lb fish a good one, a two-pounder a specimen. The current British rod-caught record is 4lb 3oz.

Rudd
(Scardinius erythrophthalmus)

Another shoal fish similar in looks to the roach, but with redder fins, an upturned mouth and a more golden-hued body. Rudd are rarely found in rivers, usually inhabiting lakes, ponds and canals. They feed on small aquatic invertebrates, in particular the pupae of midges.

⬇ The lake-dwelling rudd.

(Kuttelvaserova Stuchelova)

↑ The European bass.

Due to its shoaling habit, more than one fish can be caught from a shoal. A surface-feeding fish, rudd are often found living alongside carp, and are commonly seen swimming just under the surface. A rudd of 6–8in is a nice fish, a one-pounder is a very good one. The current British rod-caught record is 4lb 10oz.

■ Rare in Scotland.

Tackling up for coarse fish

Most of these fish require refined nymph or dry fly techniques, on light tippets (2–3lb), so a shorter, lighter-weight, softer-actioned rod is required (eg 9ft #4-5). These coarse fish don't run big, but can provide good, absorbing sport on light tackle. A #3 would suit the fish's size, but the length is important and will depend on the water being fished. If it's open and windy a 9ft #5 would afford better casting control. Chub, being more weighty and powerful, would require a #6 or #7, 9ft–9ft 6in outfit and stronger tippet (5lb breaking strain).

Sea fish

Fly fishing around the UK's coastline is still in its infancy, but becoming increasingly popular. The tides and coastal winds dictate when and where the fly fisher can ply his skills along our rocky coasts, beaches and estuaries, which will generally be during the warmer summer months when fish come in close to the shore to feed. A factor to bear in mind is that the sea, being a massive body of water, takes time to heat up in summer, but then holds its warmth far longer than rivers or inland lakes. Thus the fly fisher's season might only begin in a warm May (in the warmer south), but continue to fish well into November. Of course, equinoxial gales may put an end to the fly fisher's plans!

Bass *(Dicentrarchus labrax)*

The 'wolf of the sea', the silver bass, with its spiky dorsal fin and large mouth, is now found all around the coast of Great Britain and Ireland. Bass feed voraciously on a huge variety of whatever the coastline provides – marine worms, crabs, shrimps, small fish, sand eels – and will venture close into the edges of the sea in order to locate their prey. A shoal fish when smaller – ½lb to 2lb (school bass) – they can become more solitary when they grow larger (3–6lb), the British rod-caught record being 19lb 13oz. Bass are typically found around rocks and reefs but are also contacted in estuaries and off beaches. Highly valued as food, the British size limit was recently increased to 42cm in order to protect stocks, as the species is notoriously slow-growing.

Their spiky dorsal and razor-sharp gill plates mean landed fish must be handled carefully to avoid skin lacerations.

Sea bass can be caught throughout the summer months, more commonly in the latter half.

Mullet

Probably the most visible of our saltwater fish, mullet are shoal fish that feed at the surface. In calm conditions their tail tips and dorsal fins break the surface en masse, usually at water outflows, such as rivers and estuaries, or even sewers, and particularly from power stations.

Mullet 'graze' on filamentous algae and will also take small worms, maggots and shrimp, but they are notoriously difficult – but not impossible – to hook on fly. The sporting potential of these fish must not be underestimated, due to their immense power and express acceleration. The south coast and north-east coast of England and the coast of Ireland is generally thought to offer possible mullet sport, whereas the west coast of Wales appears to be difficult.

↑ Thick-lipped mullet.

↑ Thin-lipped mullet.

Preferring warmer sea temperatures, mullet are pursued during the warmer months and are more common on the shores of southern England and Wales than in the north, but they can be found on coastlines countrywide.

There are three types of mullet in the UK: thick-lipped, thin-lipped and golden grey.

Thick-lipped mullet *(Chelon labrosus)*

The clue to identifying thick-lipped mullet is in their name – they have a thick upper lip that's unique to the species. This has the consistency of a Michelin radial and often requires pliers for the removal of fly hooks.

↑ The upper lip that gives the thick-lipped mullet its name.

The largest-growing and most widespread of UK mullet species. The current UK record (any method) stands at 14lb 2oz. Thick-lips are relatively slow-growing and a fish of 6lb is likely to be 20 years old. The main fishing season for thick-lips extends from May until October and the species occurs around the majority of the British coastline, with the exception of northern Scotland.

Thin-lipped mullet *(Liza ramada)*

This is the second-largest growing UK mullet species, mainly occurring in the south and west of the country, and the current record stands at 7lb. Thin-lips show a more pronounced predatory instinct than thick-lips and are more inclined to chase a retrieved fly. Thin-lipped mullet don't possess the bulky upper lip found in thick-lips and are generally of more streamlined shape. They're easily identified by the presence of a black spot at the base of the pectoral fin. Thin-lipped mullet are related to flying fish, which perhaps explains the noticeably long pectoral fins.

Golden grey mullet *(Liza aurata)*

The smallest-growing of the UK mullet species, with a rod-caught record of 3lb 8oz. Golden greys visit our shores between May and October and are quickly becoming a cult fish amongst saltwater fly fishers. Golden grey mullet are fish of wide, sandy beaches that cruise close in on the breaking waves, searching for shrimp as the waves break. Golden greys are similar in appearance to thin-lipped mullet but have the distinguishing feature of a gold thumbprint on each gill cover.

The preferred habitat of the species is the relatively warm, shallow waters of sandy bays, sand bars and the long sandy beaches so common in Cornwall and South Wales.

↓ The golden thumbprint on the gill cover is the giveaway sign of a golden grey mullet.

↑ Pollack.

Pollack *(Pollachius pollachius)*

This copper-coloured, cod-like fish, which inhabits the deeper, rocky, kelp-lined shores of the UK, is a powerful predator of small fish. The pollack has the infamous habit of diving to the bottom of the sea when hooked and burying itself in the kelp, and is a worthy adversary. Possessing a large head and mouth, pollack ambush their prey at the weed fringes as the baitfish move in and out with the tide.

Pollack are plentiful off the rocky shores of the UK and are most easily located off parts of the coast where rocks plunge deeply into the sea – lighthouse points and headlands are features synonymous with pollack, but they'll also enter small rocky bays, sea lochs and even brackish water.

The fly fisher will often encounter juvenile fish (½lb to ¾lb) when fishing around weed, but bigger fish (up to 5lb) can be targeted by using sunk lines and fish imitations off deeper water. In bright, sunny conditions pollack tend to take better as the light fades, at dawn and dusk.

Most commonly sought with fly during the summer, especially during the latter half.

Mackerel *(Scomber scombrus)*

Most holidaymakers' image of summer fishing off the coast, this brilliantly silver fish has an iridescent blue back, etched with repeated, dark, wavy markings (which gives rise to the cloud formation name of a 'mackerel sky'). Mackerel are frenetic, fast swimmers with an oily flesh similar to their distant relative the tuna. Large shoals move northwards as the summer heightens, chasing the shoals of whitebait, brit, sprats and sand eels. Sometimes baitfish can be seen scattering at the surface as the shoal chases them from underneath. Diving birds such as gannets also give away their position. Mackerel are best targeted from a boat, as they tend to roam in open water, but sometimes on higher tides they'll range into the shoreline and offer the fly fisher a chance of a cast or two in bays, off rocks or off piers.

They're likely takers of a fly if it can be presented to them, and are energetic, rod-thumping fighters. A fresh mackerel makes superb eating too, but be aware that there's a UK minimum size limit of 12in (30cm). A good fish weighs 1lb, an exceptional one 2lb. The UK shore-caught record is 5lb 11oz.

Mackerel, a distant relative of the tuna.

(Evlakhov Valeriy)

KEY FISH CHARACTERISTICS

When targeting a species it's important that the angler understands the biology and characteristics of the fish being hunted in order to assess their approach, and maximise their chances of catching it.

Fish vision

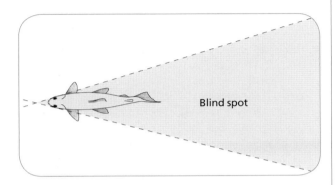

⬆ Trout eye position on head (viewed from above to show 'blind spot' behind).

The more an angler understands the biology of a fish the more he or she will be able to predict its behaviour and calculate how it'll react in certain situations.

Although fish are sometimes labelled as 'educated', this is generally down to the fish's acute awareness of danger – one of the key factors in an individual's survival.

Fly fishing is about triggering a response from the fish. However, a fish that's been alerted to danger is far less likely to respond to our flies than one that's relaxed in its environment, as danger and the instinct to survive override all other behavioural patterns, such as feeding, curiosity and territorial issues. Most fish that we cast a fly to are hunted from the day that they're born: by mammals, such as otters

or seals; by birds, such as kingfishers, ospreys, cormorants, herons and mergansers; and by other fish, such as pike, perch and bass. Man simply represents another threat, and is treated in exactly the same way. Thus it's important that our quarry is unaware of our presence. So, how do we prevent fish knowing that we're there?

A fish's eyes are very different to ours. Apart from predators, like pike, their eyes are to the side and top of the head rather than at the front, like those of humans or any other predator. Prey species, like most fish, need to be aware of predatory attacks, thus their eyes allow them to see all around – to the side, below and above. However, fish do have a 'blind spot', and this is directly behind them. Thus a prey fish in a river – trout, dace, roach etc – can be approached from downstream much more easily than trying to approach it 'head on'. Fish usually face head into the flow on a river; thus the river angler is best advised to locate his prey in clear water by moving upstream and making casts from its blind spot rather than approaching the fish from upstream, straight into its field of vision.

A fish's eye is a sophisticated organ, honed by millennia of evolution. In almost all cases it can be assumed that if you can see the fish, then it will be able to see you. It's actually worse than this for the angler: because of the fish's eye design, and the refraction of light in air and in water, a fish can perceive what's happening not only in the water but also above it, and even quite some distance back from the bank (see diagram). This is called the fish's 'window', and it means an angler standing on the bank on the skyline is perfectly visible to the fish. This image alone may not alert the fish to danger. However, if the image moves, then that's the signal for the fish to switch to high alert and probably go off the feed ('off the take'). Study a heron stalking its prey – it moves with slow, deliberate and patient motion to get into position to make a deadly strike on the unsuspecting fish. The angler must think in the same way, otherwise the fish will have fled before you make your cast.

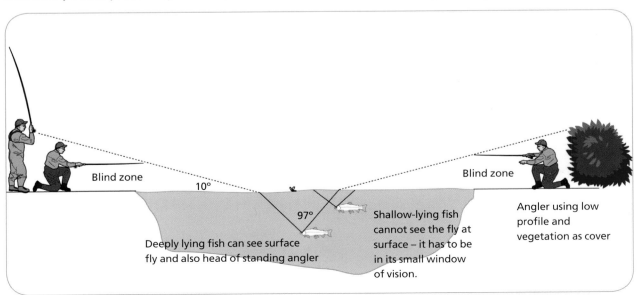

Blind zone

10°

97°

Deeply lying fish can see surface fly and also head of standing angler

Shallow-lying fish cannot see the fly at surface – it has to be in its small window of vision.

Blind zone

Angler using low profile and vegetation as cover

(Cristina Annibali)

⬆ Keep low, move slow and stalk like a heron.

Keep low, move slow, use any background vegetation or structure to break up your outline and disguise your silhouette.

Many fish, such as trout or salmon, are uncomfortable in bright sunshine. In such an uncomfortable environment these fish tend to go into deeper water, or look for cover. However, some coarse fish, like rudd, carp and pike, enjoy being in the sun, and can often be seen 'basking' in the surface layers.

In addition to their eyes fish have a 'lateral line', a series of sensors that let them feel vibrations through the water. This, too, serves as an early warning system for approaching danger through this 'distant touch'. Unfortunately for anglers, sound waves travel through water eight times better than they do through air. Whilst it's unlikely fish can hear voices, a heavy footfall or a noisy, clumsy, rushed and unthinking approach can result in a sudden lack of fish in the water into which you're about to cast. Go quietly, tread carefully and take your time to get into position.

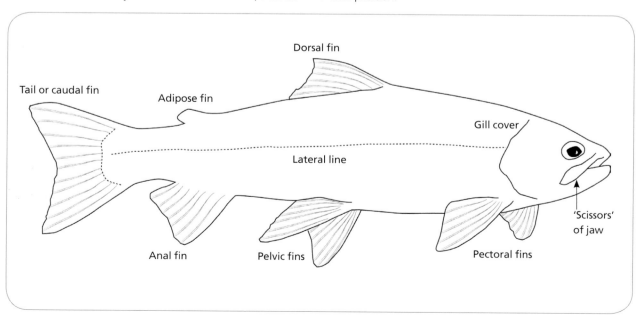

Dorsal fin

Tail or caudal fin

Adipose fin

Gill cover

Lateral line

'Scissors' of jaw

Anal fin

Pelvic fins

Pectoral fins

Temperature

Fish are poikilotherms, or 'cold-blooded', meaning their metabolism is governed by the ambient water temperature. Thus in very low water temperatures fish are inactive, almost torpid, lying on the bottom and scarcely moving. Apart from being reluctant to move, they also tend to feed very little. However, just like a reptile warming itself in the sun, once the water starts to warm after winter so fish become more active. A spring salmon requires temperatures of 6°C and above in order to have sufficient energy to negotiate (*ie* jump) weirs and waterfalls. It's for this reason such obstacles are referred to as 'temperature barriers', and fishing upstream from them is generally of scant reward until the river warms beyond this temperature.

Each fish species has an 'optimum temperature' at which they move and feed at their most efficient. For trout and salmon this temperature is 15°C, for coarse fish, like the carp, it's 20°C and for sea fish, like the mackerel, it's 12°C. At such temperatures fish are at their happiest: 'on the fin', looking for food, eager to chase food and rise from the bottom to the surface.

Water temperatures can get too high, however. Trout and salmon (ostensibly cold-water species) become uncomfortable in temperatures of 20°C and over. In addition, warm water carries less oxygen, thus rendering the fish torpid. Coarse fish prefer warmer water, and can withstand far higher water temperatures than salmonids – up to 28°C – before they start to become uncomfortable and stressed. This explains why, in the height of summer, trout-fishing in a southern English lake can be very difficult, yet fishing for rudd or carp is still good. However, pike, perch and roach prefer temperatures that are lower than other coarse fish.

Optimum temperatures govern when fishing for feeding fish is likely to be best, so it's worth being aware of water temperatures when you venture out. Hand-held digital thermometers can give an instant water temperature reading, and therefore give you clues as to fishes' behaviour.

⬇ The salmon uses its ability to leap waterfalls to access high spawning grounds.

(Mark Caunt)

CHOOSING THE KIT TO SUIT

Ready for anything: A variety of fly-fishing outfits mounted on a car rack.

The angler who spins or casts floats or leger weights uses a combination of the weight on the end of the line and the long lever of the rod to project the lure across the water. The fly fisher relies on the same principle: but the fly usually has no weight in it – it is, literally, a featherweight. In fly fishing a combination of the rod and the long, flexible and slender weight of the line combine to cast out the fly. The rod is the lever and the line follows the track to the tip of the rod, because, in essence, it's attached to the tip. Because the rod is long, a small movement of the hand through a few degrees can cause a large movement of the rod tip. It's this rod-and-line combination that's so important to the fly fisher in making his cast.

Choosing a rod and fly line

The fly line is just as important as the rod, and it's essential for a beginner to ensure that their line and rod are matched in order to be able to cast easily and properly.

Matching the rod to a line is straightforward: each rod has a marking on the butt (just above the handle) that indicates not only the rod model, and length, but also an AFFTA line number. AFFTA stands for American Fly Fishing Trade Association, and it's this body that sets the industry standards for fly lines (calculated by the weight of the first 30ft – minus the level line at the tip – of fly line). For instance, a typical #8 line will weigh 210 grains (13.6gm) over its first 30ft, whilst a standard #4 will only weigh 120

grains (7.7gm) over the equivalent length. This number on the rod butt refers to the rod maker's recommended line weight that's required for that particular rod to cast, and all fly lines are marked with the equivalent AFFTA number on the box in which they're packaged.

Thus, a 9ft #6 rod can be matched by purchasing a #6 line, and this same line would suit an 11ft 3in #6 rod too.

However, how do you know which rod length and line-rating to choose?

Which rod do I need?

The best way to choose a rod is to consider the fly size that you're most likely to be fishing, and the species you're hunting. The reason for this is that the fly size determines the leader strength (ie the strength of the fine nylon, or cast, that links a fly to a fly line), which in turn affects the line-rating which, as we've seen, governs the rod choice. Thus when fishing for small trout on a tiny brook, using small dry flies down to size 18, then the leader is restricted to just 3lb or 4lb breaking strain, maximum. A line rating of #3–#4 would suit, thus a matching rod of a short length, say 6–8ft, would be suitable. However, fishing for salmon with heavy brass tubes and heavy nylon requires a selection far higher up the line scale – AFFTA 10 or 11. To match such a line we're talking about selecting a rod of 15ft or even 16ft. To get an understanding on the type of rod to suit each species, study Table 1:

⬇ The writing on the rod butt indicates that this is a 9ft 6in rod, designed to take an AFFTA-rated #6 line. It weighs 2⅝oz and it is tip-actioned.

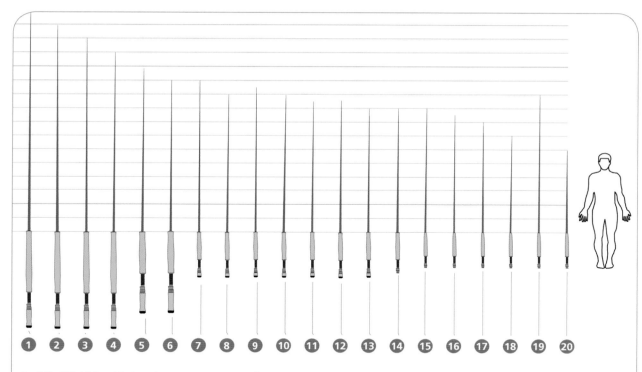

1 | 2 | 3 | 4 | 5 | 6 | 7 | 8 | 9 | 10 | 11 | 12 | 13 | 14 | 15 | 16 | 17 | 18 | 19 | 20

1 16ft #11-12 Double-hander
Salmon on large rivers.
Shooting heads/sunk lines

2 15ft #10 Double-hander
Salmon on large rivers

3 14ft #9 Double-hander
Salmon on small to medium rivers

4 13ft #9 Double-hander
Salmon on small rivers

5 12ft #8 Switch rod
Grilse, Sea Trout, saltwalter

6 11ft #7 Switch rod
Grilse, Sea Trout

7 11ft 3in #7 Single-hander
Sea Trout, loch-style boat

8 10ft #8 Stillwater boat
Grilse river, saltwater, Pike

9 10ft 6in #7 Stillwater boat
Grilse river

10 10ft #7 Stillwater boat
Sea Trout

11 9ft 6in #7 Stillwater all-purpose
Perch

12 9ft 6in #6 Stillwater, large rivers
Saltwater nymph

13 9ft #10 Big Pike, Pollack

14 9ft #9 Pike, Saltwater big flies

15 9ft #5 Small Stillwater, larger
rivers, nymph, dry

16 8ft 6in #5 Medium to small rivers, dry
& nymph

17 8ft #4 Small rivers
Trout, Grayling, coarse fish

18 7ft #3 Small streams
Dry fly and nymph

19 10ft #2 Euro-nymphing
River rod

20 6ft #3 Small, tree-lined streams
Coarse fish

↑ Rod size and handles (all relating to an average man's height).

↓ Three rods of the same line rating.

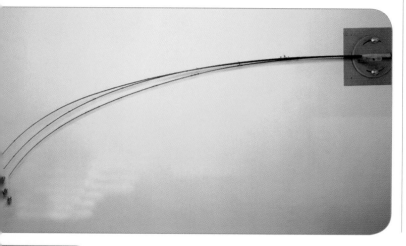

Rod actions

A fly rod needs to bend to assist casting the line and to help cushion the runs made by a hooked fish, yet it also requires an inherent stiffness to help control the fly line as it's being fished. Today, most rods are built as a tapering tube of carbon-fibre.

Every rod has an 'action', which describes how the rod flexes as it's being cast. These can best be described in three different terms: tip action, middle to tip action and through-action.

The photograph shows three different rods rated for exactly the same line weight being stressed by exactly the same weight. The weight suspended from the tip shows differences in action and stiffness. Note the way the rod bends for each: the top rod is a fast-action – the tip is pulled down to almost vertical; the lower rod is a more through action, deeper bending rod (this is a sensitive, modern river rod). The rod in between is mid-action.

In addition, the recovery rate and stiffness of the material used in the rod's construction will affect the way it casts and handles fish. Basically, this is classified as fast, medium and slow.

What does rod action mean to the angler?

Drawing an analogy with cars, at the top end of the scale would be a fast, tip-actioned rod, the Formula One car of rods. This is the rod best designed for casting distance, big flies, and across or into the wind. However, it requires skill to cast with it, and it also requires perfect timing to get the best out of it. It produces tight loops of line on the back and forward casts that cut across or through the wind, and due to its fast action its line speed is high, which aids distance. Get it wrong and it stalls or ends up in a tangle.

At the opposite end of the spectrum is the slow, through-actioned rod – the classic car of the range. It still requires skill to get results, but it will fall far short of the performance of the Formula One fast, tip-actioned rod. Everything about the casting action has to slow down, and the resultant casting loop is wide, which means it's easily affected by the wind and distance casts are difficult to make. However, the result is aesthetically pleasing, especially where presentation (turnover and how gently it alights on the water) of the tip of the line and the attached fly are concerned.

For the beginner and intermediate fly fisher, a middle to tip-actioned rod – the family hatchback – is the best option. Today's models of such rods are powerful enough for most types of fishing, produce a good casting loop to combat wind and bushy flies, and are designed to fish both long and short casts. They also have enough 'feel' within the blank to help the caster improve his timing for longer casts.

Rod handles

There are a number of different styles of rod handle – usually built from rings of sanded cork glued on to the blank. On the end of the handle is the reel seat, to which the reel is attached. Reels seats range from polished wood to metal, to graphite, to plastic. On double-handed and switch-style rods the reel seat fits in between the two handles.

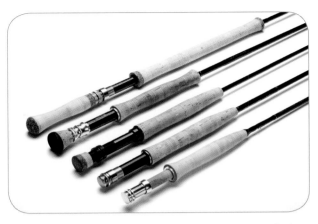

↑ The double-hander (far left) is finished with composite cork; the single-hander with extension butt next to that sports a full wells grip; the next two rods are furnished with half-wells handles; and the rod on the far right has a half-wells tapering to a cigar end.

Choosing a fly line

Fly lines not only provide weight for casting, they're also, through their design and manufacture, implicit in the tactics the fly fisher can employ. Fly lines have a continuous, level core of braid or nylon, coated with plastic. This coating can be designed to have different densities, to make the line float, or sink, or sink rapidly. This is applied to the core in varying amounts over the length of the line – usually 27m to 45m. This coating process means the profile (tapering) of the line can be altered to suit different casting and presentation styles (ie it can be tapered to cast and shoot big flies long distances, or designed to land tiny flies delicately at short ranges – see Figure below). The density of the line can be

↓ Fly-line profiles – ranging progressively.

	Level line
TO FLY — TO REEL	
	Double taper (Long taper)
	Long belly line (Weight forward)
	Medium/fast taper (Weight forward)
	Short taper (Weight forward big fly taper)
	Standard shooting head
	Large diameter short taper (Skagit)

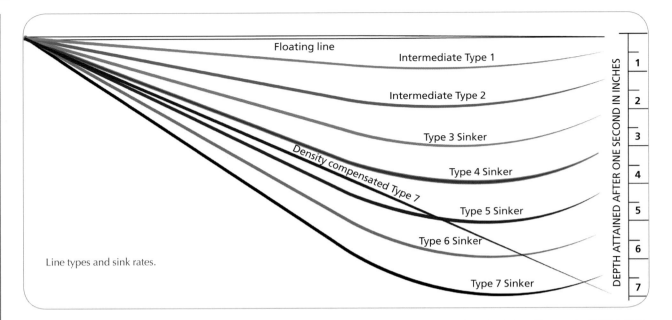

Line types and sink rates.

varied too. For instance, the majority of the line can be made to float but its tip might be coated to sink.

Which fly line?

Again, when choosing a fly line you need to consider the type of fishing you're planning. For instance, for most styles of river trout fishing a full floating line (aka 'floater') is suitable for most requirements, but for fishing deep for pollack you might want to think about purchasing a full fast-sinking line. The diagram above illustrates the types of line that are available, from a full floater to a fast sinker, with a wide variety of sink rates in between. Note how, due to the profiling of the line, it'll sink faster at the 'belly' than at the thin tip. This can aid a sunk-line presentation (see 'The Sweep', Ch 8), but more often than not an angler requires his fly at the line tip to be fishing deepest. Hence, 'density compensated lines' are produced, which allow the tip to sink at the fastest rate.

Interpreting a fly line's code

There are many different types of fly line made today, so understanding their make-up can be confusing. However,

AN INTERMEDIATE SINKS!

The term 'intermediate' fly line came about when it was first designed. Being neither a floater nor a sinker, the intermediate sank, but only very slowly, hence its name – it was neither a floater nor a typical sinker, so it became known as an intermediate at that time. However, it's important to realise that any intermediate will sink (eventually) to the bottom.

the best way to understand what the line does is to interpret the code on the box.

The top box code in the picture indicates the profile is a weight forward (WF) to suit a #5 rod, and it's a floater (F). The box tells us the whole line length is 98ft (30m). The weight of 14gm refers to the AFFTA line-classification used to measure fly lines (ie the front 30ft/10m of the line).

The box code of the line underneath indicates that this fly line – WF 5 F/I – is an AFFTA No5 (#5), weight-forward (WF) profile line with an intermediate sinking section on the end of a floater (F/I). As well as informing us of the line's length (105ft/32m) the label also tells us that there's a colour change from pale green to optic green.

The lower box's label tells us that this line is a #7 weight-forward profile with a sinking tip 7ft in length. In addition, the sinking part is a clear Type 2 sinker.

Backing

Fly lines are only made up to a maximum length of 45m, so if a big fish should be hooked in open water or on a big, powerful river extra line is required on the reel's spool in

↑ A reel should be loaded with thin backing behind the fly line.

Types of reel

There are many types of fly reel on the market. Unlike other types of fishing, the reel comes third in the list of importance, the rod and fly line being far more important for an angler. Some reels are simple, ratchet-checked mechanisms (below right), while others are sophisticated, aesthetically pleasing cage-designs with variable, high-tech, sealed disc-drags (below left). The basics for a reel are: it holds all the fly line and the backing; it doesn't rotate and lose line whilst casting; and it balances the rod in both weight and size. Most reels can be altered to suit left-hand or right-hand wind.

reserve. This extra line is strong (20–30lb BS), thin, and called 'backing'. Backing is typically made of braided nylon or braided polyester and joined to the rear end of the fly line. The amount of backing is determined by the reel's spool diameter and width. The length required varies from 30yd (30m) for a small trout or grayling through to 200yd (200m) or more for large salmon or saltwater species. Most reels will indicate not only which lines they're designed to accommodate but also the amount of backing they'll hold along with the fly line (for instance, #7 line plus 100yd/100m backing).

Should I wind with my left or right hand?

Single-handed casting is made with the stronger hand, right or left, wielding the rod. Many anglers, like the author, cast with their stronger (right) hand and wind the reel handle with their left. However, a good number of anglers will cast with their (stronger) right hand, but switch the rod over to their left hand and wind in with their right when they've hooked a fish. There's no right or wrong here: whatever is most comfortable and convenient for you is the correct way.

Reversing a reel

Due to the fact that fly anglers wind in with either hand, most (but not all) fly reels are designed to be converted from right- to left-hand wind and vice versa. For a fairly typical modern reel (1) this is easily – and most commonly – effected by releasing the spool (2), easing the sealed drag off the internal spindle (3), flipping it over (they have one-way bearings) (4) and reassembling the reel (5&6). For other reel designs, check the instructions on reversing at time of purchase.

FLIGHT CHECK

Before loading all the backing and fly line, double-check that the reel's drag operates with line being pulled OFF the reel, not as you wind it ON TO the reel. If it doesn't you'll need to reverse the drag.

Is a drag necessary?

We need a check, or drag of some sort, to prevent the reel spilling off line during the cast, but apart from this a variable drag isn't necessary for trout, grayling and the smaller coarse fish. 'Hand-lining' a fish to land it (pulling the line in to coil on the ground, whilst slack is prevented by trapping the line under the rod-hand index finger) is acceptable. However, many anglers – including me – like to play fish 'off the reel', utilising the finely tuned, high-tech disc-drags that are available today.

Leaders and tippets

The rod and matching fly line work together to deliver the fly to a chosen distance, but in order to catch a fish the fly requires to be joined to the tip of the fly line by a length of thin, less obtrusive monofilament fishing line – the 'leader'. There are different ways to attach a leader to a fly line (see Chapter 4), and there are many conformations of leaders that include different strengths, diameters, lengths, tapers, droppers (short tag-lengths of monofilament to which extra flies can be attached) and tippet sections (the final, finer lengths of monofilament to which the fly is attached).

There are three common types of monofilament leader material: nylon, co-polymer and fluorocarbon. For a given diameter nylon tends to be a little weaker, but it's also tough, possesses some elasticity and knots reliably and securely. Of the three types it's the one least prone to tangling and suits beginners.

The breaking strain (BS) of a given thickness co-polymer is typically higher than simple nylon, finer in relation to strength, more pliable, and it can also stretch, though it can coil after stretching. It's a shiny, slippery material, so care needs to be taken when knotting to avoid the knot sliding undone and co-polymer knots should be tested thoroughly before fishing.

Fluorocarbon has a similar refractive index to water (so it tends to be less visible in water than the other two) and it's more dense than nylon or co-polymer, so it sinks more readily. It's a stiffer material, resistant to abrasion, but it can be quite brittle too, so can be weakened by knotting. Thus a fluorocarbon knot is best tied carefully, and lubricated with saliva before tightening to avoid friction damage.

Three different leader materials: nylon (left), fluorocarbon, and co-polymer (right).

Inset: a 9ft tapered leader, which graduates in diameter from a thick butt to a fine tippet over its length.

SETTING UP YOUR OUTFIT

Assembling the rod and reel

→ Push the rod sections together firmly, but don't force them.

↓ Check the reel fitting and rings are all aligned.

For ease of storage and transport, rods are made of two, three, four and even up to seven sections. They're easily assembled by pushing the male section of the rod into the female section. There are two things to concentrate on here: first, there's no need to jam or screw the two sections tightly together (otherwise you may have trouble separating them later); and second, the rod rings should all be aligned, along with the reel seat recess in the handle. Some rods have markers on each section to assist lining up the rod rings.

Setting the drag

If the reel has a variable drag, loosen this off so that the line can be pulled off the reel easily, and thread the fly line through the rod rings. Once the rod and line is set up, the drag should then be tightened sufficiently for a fish to pull off line without breaking the nylon cast, yet not be so loose that, if line is stripped off it, the reel spins and 'overruns' causing a 'bird's nest' of line coils.

↓ Adjusting the drag.

Fitting a reel

Bearing in mind which hand you're going to use to reel in line, slot the front of the reel 'foot' into the recess in the rod handle, then slide the reel seat ring over the rear 'foot' to hold it in place. Now screw up the first locking nut to tighten it into place. Wiggle the reel seat from side to side, then tighten the nut some more. Wiggle and repeat until the reel seating is solid. Then screw up the second nut to lock everything in place.

Flight check: the end of the fly line should issue from the lower front part of the reel and from the bottom of the coils of line on the spool.

↑ Push the reel foot into the recess in the rod handle.

↑ Slip the slide band over the other end of the reel foot and tighten the locking nut. Wiggle the reel, then retighten the nut.

↑ Secure with second locking nut.

↑ The reel in the centre is correctly filled; the reel on the left is over filled, the one on the right is under filled.

Loading the reel correctly

It's important to get enough backing on to the reel without overloading or underloading it, which not only limits the amount of backing available but can also cause excessive coiling of the fly line. Here's how it can be done without trial and error.

3 Temporarily knot the backing to the end of the fly line.

4 Wind on the backing.

5 Continue to wind on backing until the spool is filled but not overfilled.

6 Use a rolled-up newspaper to wind back all the backing.

1 Wind the fly line on to the reel directly off the line holder.

2 Use a pen to allow the holder to rotate.

7 Cut off the backing, then wind the fly line back on to the holder.

8 Use an arbour knot to tie the backing on to the drum of the reel.

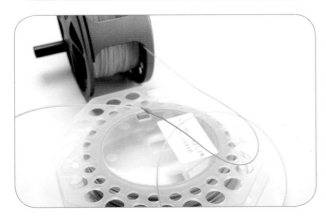

9 Attach the end of the backing to the correct end of the fly line.

10 Wind on the fly line to fill the reel.

Attaching the backing to the reel

The backing needs to be attached to the reel using an arbour knot.

1 Take backing around the spool.

2 Use the tag-end to make a slip knot on the main line.

3 Tighten knot, then make an overhand knot on the tag-end.

4 Trim the tag-end. Tighten on to the drum.

The end of the line

1 Welded loop

Today, many manufactured fly lines have a welded loop at the end.
Advantages: Makes life very easy, as a nylon cast can be attached directly to this through the loop-to-loop system.
Disadvantages: Bulky, can cause disturbance at the surface.

↑ Welded loop on the end of the fly line.

2 Fitting a braided loop

Anglers who find the welded loop a little bulky and dislike the disturbance it causes at the water surface might prefer a more subtle alternative, such as the braided loop:
Advantages: In-line; quick, easy, no glue required; smooth junction.

Disadvantages: Can cause 'hinging' and eventual cracking of line coating at the join; can, on occasion, slip off and fail; requires bulky, loop-to-loop junction, which can cause surface disturbance.

1 Braided loops come with a ready-mounted plastic sleeve.

2 Feed the tip of the fly line into the hollow end of the braid.

3 Use a concertina and pull action to inch the braid up the fly line...

4 ...until a couple of inches (5cm) of braid is on the fly line.

5 Use your thumbnail to push the plastic sleeve up the braid and over the fly line

6 Work it all the way to the end of the braid.

7 Snip away any loose ends poking out of the plastic sleeve.

8 The secure braided loop.

3 Nail-knotted butt leader

A more direct connection from the fly line to leader can be made by knotting 2ft (0.6m) of thick diameter nylon (usually 15–22lb BS) section (butt leader) to the fly-line tip. This acts as a link between the fly line and the leader.

Advantages: In-line; secure; creates almost continuous change from fly line to nylon; simplified version can be tied at the waterside (with practice).
Disadvantages: Tag-end can catch in the tip-ring of rod; knot can be bulky.

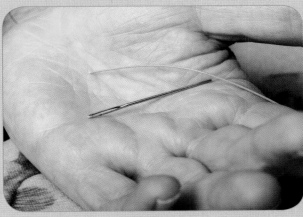

1 Use a darning needle to assist you.

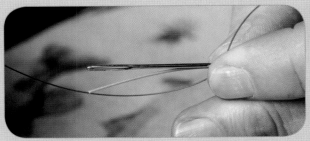

2 Lie the darning needle along the fly-line tip, with its eye at the tip. Pinch the long tag end of the butt leader close to the darning needle point.

3 Spiral the nylon around the needle and fly line, working towards the eye.

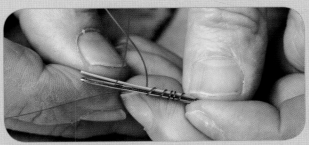

4 Make six turns, then trap these down with your middle finger whilst the other hand pokes the tag-end tip through the eye of the needle.

5 Pull on the needle tip to draw it through the turns you've just made.

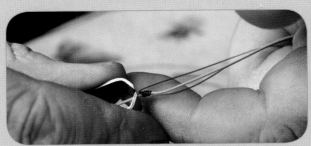

6 Tighten slowly and snug down. Snip the tag-end off short.

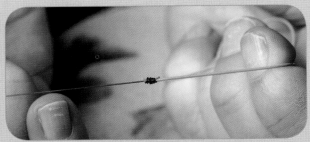

7 The knot should be a series of neat coils gripping the fly line like a fist.

4 Needle knot

A needle knot takes the nail knot one stage further by using a heated needle to create a hollow end on the fly line so that the nylon can emerge directly out of the end of the line.

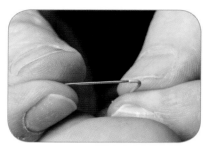

1 Push the tip of a sewing needle into the very tip of the fly line.

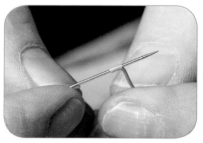

2 After ⅓in (7–8mm) allow the tip of the needle to emerge through the PVC coating.

3 Heat the eye of the needle so that the plastic fly line melts slightly.

4 Allow to cool. Then remove the needle, leaving hollow in the fly line's tip. Feed the end of the butt leader through this hollow.

5 Form a nail knot on the fly line behind the hollow.

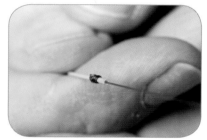

6 Tighten down. The butt leader emerges straight out of the fly-line tip.

Butt-leader loops

The butt leader should be 2–3ft (0.6–1m) long and should terminate in a loop. Loop knots are used a lot in fishing (for loop-to-loop connections). There are two types:

1 Surgeon's loop

Advantages: Simple to tie; quick; secure; double knot.
Disadvantages: Bulky knot; loop kinks to one side.

1 Make a loop at the end of the butt leader.

2 Form an overhand knot with the loop.

3 Tighten to create a loop 1.5in (3.5cm) long.

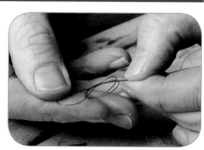

4 The disadvantage of this simple knot is that it kinks to one side of the leader.

2 Perfection loop

A perfection loop creates an in-line loop and is also slimmer than a surgeon's loop.

Advantages: Slimmer knot; loop is in-line.
Disadvantages: More complex to tie.

1 Create a large loop, and pinch it at the crossover point.

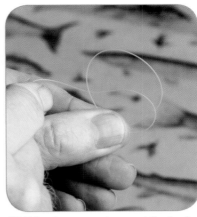

2 Take the tag-end around the back of this loop...

3 ...then come forward and trap this smaller loop too.

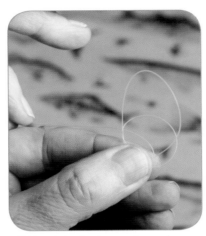

4 Now take the tag-end round again, but this time lay it between the first and second loops.

5 Pinch the tag-end, push your forefinger into the larger loop and hook the smaller loop with your fingertip.

6 Pinching the main line and tag-end, use your fingertip to pull up the small loop...

7 ...to tighten the knot.

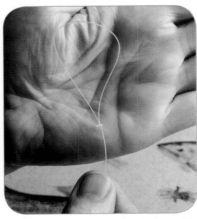

8 The perfection loop lies in-line with the nylon. Note: the tag-end should project at right angles to the main line.

Joining casts

Loop-to-loop

This knot system is used very often in fly fishing. It can be used to join:

- Two different lengths of nylon or backing.
- Two interlocking fly-line sections.
- Nylon to a fly-line loop.

1 Push the fly-line loop through the leader loop.

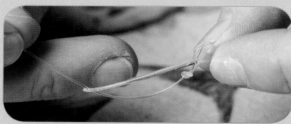

2 Feed the tip of the leader through the fly-line loop.

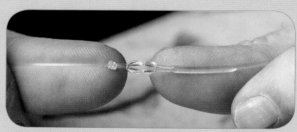

3 Pull through to interlock the two loops.

WRONG WAY

➔ This is a weaker junction, it can catch in the rod rings and is difficult to release.

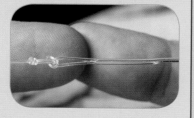

Joining nylon, creating droppers

For joining two lengths of similar diameter nylon, co-polymer or fluorocarbon and/or creating a dropper, there's one universal knot that works well: the three-turn water knot.

1 Three-turn water knot

NOTE: Don't use the three-turn water knot if the diameters of the two lengths of nylon are easily visible as being thicker than each other (ie more than 30% thicker in diameter) OR if the leader material changes from one material to another. In both cases, use either loop-to-loop or silver rings to effect the join, or – where diameter disparity is the only concern – use an intermediate diameter length of nylon as the link between the two.

Note: yellow and brown monofilament used here for demonstration purposes only.

1 Lay the two pieces of nylon to be joined together, one with its tag-end to the left, the other to the right.

2 Grinner knot

This is a very useful knot to have in your armoury for joining two sections of nylon and/or creating a dropper quickly without having to rebuild the leader completely.

1 Lay the two pieces of nylon to be joined together, one with tag-end to the left, the other to the right.

2 Take the tag-end of the lower section of nylon (brown), create a loop and trap this against the upper section (yellow).

3 Use the tag-end to make four turns within the loop.

2 Create a loop and pinch together at the crossover. Note the long, yellow tag-end will become the dropper.

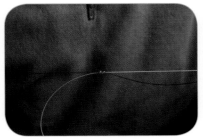

3 Pass both yellow tag-end and additional piece of nylon (brown) through the loop once...

4 ...twice and three times.

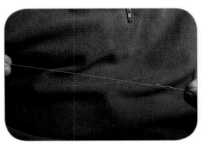

5 Hold all the ends and draw down.

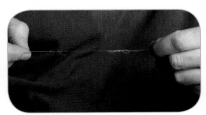

6 The join is complete. Note there are two longish tag-ends.

7 If using the knot to simply join two sections of nylon, snip the tag-ends. For creating a dropper, snip away only the upper tag-end.

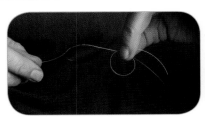

4 Now repeat with the tag-end of the upper section.

5 Make four turns around the loop, then pull on both ends.

6 The two knots close then slide towards each other...

7 ...and meet.

8 One end can be left as a dropper, or both ends can be trimmed to form a neat, reliable junction.

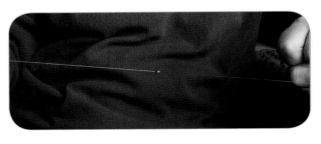

Creating droppers

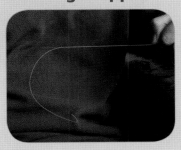

↑ A 4–6in dropper knot created with a three-turn water knot.

The standard dropper is between 4in and 6in long (10–15cm). This would be suitable for wet fly fishing, nymphing, dry fly, salmon and sea trout fishing. However, droppers can vary in length from 3in (7.5cm) to 12in (30cm). Shorter droppers tend to spin and tangle less, while the long droppers are mostly used for stillwater dry fly fishing.

Attaching the fly

Most flies can be attached to the end of the nylon using a half blood knot.

1 Half blood knot

1 Pass tippet end through the hook-eye.

2 Take tag-end around the main line seven or eight times.

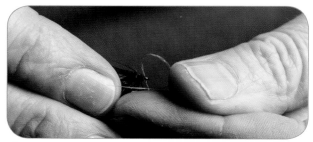

3 Bring tag-end round and feed through the funnel-shaped loop at the hook-eye.

4 Moisten and draw down knot.

5 The completed knot should be neat coils, like a fist. Trim the tag-end close.

2 Tucked half blood knot

For slippery leader material, such as co-polymer, a tucked half blood knot adds extra security.

1 An extra manoeuvre is made before tightening the half blood knot: the tag-end is passed through the large loop created by the half blood knot.

2 This is then moistened, snugged down...

3 ...and trimmed short.

3 Non-slip loop

For complete articulation – for fry patterns and lead-headed patterns, to accentuate and allow extra movement – use a non-slip loop.

1 Before attaching the fly create an overhand knot 2in (5cm) up the main line.

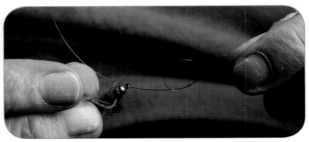

2 Now feed the tip of the line through the hook-eye.

3 Bring the tip up to and through the overhand loop.

4 Wrap the tip twice around the main line.

5 Tuck the tag-end through the overhand loop.

6 Moisten and tighten into a tiny loop connection at the hook-eye. Trim the tag-end.

Tippet diameter in relation to fly size

Flies can be tied on a variety of hook sizes, from 4/0 pike hooks to size 24 dry fly hooks, to imitate aphids. In order to present our artificial fly properly, *ie* naturally, without the nylon breaking, hinging or collapsing, as well as to assist in the energy transfer during casting, turnover and consequently the presentation of the fly, the tippet diameter needs to be chosen in proportion to the artificial fly.

➔ Ally Gowans' two-inch test: Using nylon that's too thick will cause the fly to behave stiffly and fish at an unnatural angle; too thin and it'll tangle easily and kink. To judge, hold the tippet vertically 2in from the end – the leader should curve around with the weight fly, not stick up straight and stiff. Conversely, if the leader is too thin, it'll simply collapse.

4 Turle knot

For up-eyed flies (and even for down-eyed hooks) where the fly has more articulation and has two points of contact with the nylon, use a turle knot, which is a very good knot for salmon and sea-trout up-eyed flies.

1 Push tippet through the hook-eye from the front.

2 Slide the fly down the leader, keeping hold of the tippet tip.

4 Create another, smaller loop and pinch it.

5 Pass the tag-end around and up through the small loop once…

6 …and then a second time.

8 This leaves a large loop with a sliding-knot.

9 Slide back the fly to the knot.

11 Trap the knot on top of the eye, and pull on the main line to tighten the loop.

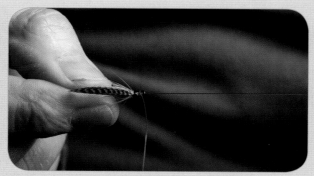

12 The loop closes around the 'neck' of the up-eye.

3 Create a loop with the tip. Pinch at the crossover point.

7 Moisten and pull on the tag-end, still pinching the larger loop.

10 Pass the fly through the loop.

13 Viewed from below, the main line comes directly out of the eye without obstruction.

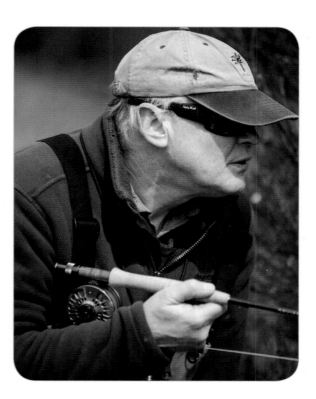

What to wear

The two essential requirements for a fly fisher are a hat and sunglasses. For reasons of safety both should be worn. It's estimated that during casting the fly can travel at 100mph, and the eyes, face and head are vulnerable not only during all stages of the cast but also whenever the line is pulled under tension (by the rod tip or the angler).

Apart from the protection they offer from harmful UV light from the sun's rays, both items can aid the fly fisher too. A hat's brim can cut out extraneous glare and help fishers see into the water by shading their eyes. A dark underside to the peak can enhance this effect further by cutting out extraneous reflected light.

Polarised sunglasses also help fly fishers see through surface glare and into the water. Not only can we see fish more clearly but polarised glasses can also help us see the riverbed or lakebed so that we can wade more safely.

↓ Polarised glasses are available in a variety of tints: brown is good for all-round vision with good contrast, while grey is an excellent choice for general-purpose use and sunlit conditions with high glare.

Waders

Traditionally, waders were either thigh- or chest-high and made of PVC or rubber. Eventually these types gave way to neoprene, which is warmer and enables everyday holes and tears to be mended far more easily. However, neoprene tends to be heavy, cumbersome and hot in warm weather, so today more sophisticated, breathable waders are used. In the main, PVC, rubber and neoprene waders have rubber boots welded to the feet to provide grip, protection and durability.

Modern waders are typically chest high, with waterproof neoprene socks or 'stockings' attached to the legs. This creates an insulated, fully waterproof unit. Over the stockinged foot a wading boot is worn, which provides protection, stability and grip. Such an outfit is usually warm enough for summer conditions in the UK, but in winter, spring and autumn, for extra warmth, fleece long johns and warm socks are worn underneath the waders. Most wading outfits also feature a roll-down tube of material around the ankle, which fits over the top of the wading boot. This is called a gravel guard, and prevents stones, mud and sand from getting between the foot and the boot and making wading uncomfortable and awkward, as well as damaging the waders. It also helps prevent the bootlaces from coming undone.

Boots and grip

Wading boots can be fitted with a variety of soles. The reason for this is that grip on the bank and the riverbed or lakebed is vital for safe fishing. However, different substrates require different soles:

- Soft lakebed – rubber-treaded soles.
- Gravel bed – rubber soles with tungsten studs.
- Stony bed and rocks – composite (felt) and tungsten studs. Composite or felt soles are superb for gripping on slippery rock, their grip being further enhanced by the studs. Studs are also very useful on grassy or muddy banks, where composite on its own can become slippery. The only problem with tungsten studs is that they'll mark a boat floor, indent wood and scratch your car bumper if, like me, you rest your foot there to lace up your boots!

Felt is gradually being phased out of commission today, due to the fact that it can harbour invasive organisms and act as a vector of spread, transferring

← Grip on smooth, weedy rock is enhanced by adding screw-in tungsten studs, at the heel in this photo. Note the location marks for other studs at the front of the boot.

→ Patagonia aluminium crampons have soft, aluminium bars for added grip.

the organism from fishery to fishery. Rubber or plastic soles are replacing it. Patagonia crampons (see photo) are good on some surfaces where rubbery soles slip. The effect is similar to adding studs to the soles of boots. The big advantage of crampons is that, unlike studs, they can be easily removed to protect floors and the decks of boats. The aluminium bars are soft enough to grip on rock.

↓ Life jackets should be worn at all times in water, especially when boat fishing, or where wading is difficult or deep. Life jackets come either as a yoke type, which are very popular, or as a fishing jacket

designed to house the life jacket within. There are two types of life jacket; both inflate due to the release of compressed gas contained in a canister on the jacket. The automatic one inflates if the sensor is activated by water. The manual one involves pulling on a ripcord to inflate the jacket.

THREE FLIGHT CHECKS

Ensure your life jacket is over your coat, not underneath it; ensure the canister attached is 'live'; ensure all clips and straps are done up; if the jacket is to inflate manually, make sure the inflation toggle is easily accessible and that you know exactly where it is, and imprint this on your mind – you'll need to find it fast if you get into trouble in the water.

Essential accessories

'The three wise men'

⬆ The three wise men: floatant gel (eg Gink), amadou pad and sinkant.

Personally, I carry a trio of compounds at all times, and in a place where I have easy, immediate access to each. All are applied by rubbing with finger and thumb:

- Sinkant – when rubbed on to the cast through thumb and forefinger, this dulls any sheen, removes any grease from the tippet's surface and assists the tippet to sink through the film more easily.
- Amadou pad – this is a natural, treated fungus that's highly water-absorbent. It can be purchased in a twin-leafed pad. A waterlogged dry fly is squeezed between the pads to rid it of moisture and prepare it to float once more.
- Gel floatant – a hydrophobic substance applied to a fly to make it float longer or higher in the water. The gel is squirted on to the index finger, rubbed to warm it until it becomes liquid, and then applied sparingly to the fly, or parts of the fly that are required to float proudly. The gel becomes liquid at higher temperatures. A holder that suspends the bottle upside down means that the gel naturally accumulates at the nozzle, ready for application.

Other fly-drying agents

- Dry Shake: a silicone powder into which the fly is shaken to dry it then it's false casted, to rid it of the white powder.
- Tissue paper.
- Fleece (use your sleeve as a standby dry-fly drier).

Other essentials

Mucilin is a silicone grease that when rubbed on to a cast will cause it to float on top of the surface film,

even in rough water. It can also be used to enhance the floatation of the tip of the fly line, or a yarn or wool indicator. With all three applications, the visibility of the line or indicator on the water surface is accentuated, and it's thus a valuable aid in take (bite) detection. To rid the cast of grease, rub it with sinkant (see left).

⬆ Useful tools – left to right, two sets of line-snips, a nail-knotting tool and multi-tool pliers (for wire traces). Snips or scissors are usually held on a retractable cord for cutting line and snipping knots.

➔ Many purpose-designed tools also house a tiny needle spike for clearing hook-eyes of varnish or glue.

⬆ Priest, marrow spoon, hook-hone, de-barbing pliers and artery forceps.

⬆ Forceps are used for removing hooks from a fish's mouth. They can be clamped on to the hook-bend and pressed down (to release the barb, if any) and then backwards to free the hook-point.

➔ A long, rubber-tipped metal or wooden wading staff can be very useful. It can be carried by means of a lanyard.

CASTING

Casting is the action around which the whole sport of fly fishing revolves. The rod, which acts as a flexible lever, and the inherent weight and profile of fly line work together to enable a small, featherweight fly to be delivered at any distance, from a few feet to 40yd or more. The fly is delivered at the line's extremity in a fashion that enables the fisherman to control the distance, track and direction of the fly, and even the way it lands on the water. Casting is a vital fly-fishing skill that varies slightly within the disciplines of fly fishing, but essentially relies on the same principles.

Fly casting is a combination of hand and arm movements, power application and timing. It's a skill that can benefit hugely from sessions with a qualified instructor. Just as with a golf professional, a good casting instructor can make fly casting simpler, easier, less energetic and tiring, and more effective. The modern casting instructor uses proven techniques and teaching aids combined with well-chosen advice to identify and cure the faults of experienced casters, and ease beginners into the sport (see Chapter 23). Money well spent.

However, because it's such a vital skill in fly fishing, we'll look at some basic casting techniques to help you on your way.

Single-handed casting

Getting to grips with casting

For single-handed rods (see 'Choosing the kit to suit' in Chapter 3) the best approach is to imagine one is picking up a small tack hammer; the cork is pinched between thumb (on top) and forefinger (opposite), just as we'd hold a key. The reel hangs down below the wrist, and the four fingers of the casting hand wrap around the scroll of cork, with the heel of the hand on the cork.

Most rods are designed to almost balance in this position, the reel to the rear of the hand counterbalancing the weight of the rod extending 6–10ft beyond the handle.

A second type of grip (for lighter rods) can be employed

↓ Conventional 'key' grip, thumb on top.

↑ 'Finger on top' grip, forefinger on top.

that entails the forefinger running along the top of the handle, essentially pointing to the top of the blank, with the thumb to one side of the cork and the fingers wrapping around the other side. This is often used by mainland Europeans and is popular with Americans, but is generally thought to be not as strong, though some advocate this grip for accuracy.

A third grip often adopted is the 'three-point contact' or screwdriver grip. This is a looser grip with the top of the handle resting between the thumb and forefinger, which lie to the side, and the tip of the forefinger and the other three fingers curling underneath the cork.

↑ 'Screwdriver or 'V' grip, three-point contact.

Pre-casting (getting some line out)

A fly rod needs line outside the tip-ring to work best. If there's no or little fly line outside the tip-ring then making a cast is going to be difficult. Thus, when starting to fish (and,

ROLL CAST

1 To roll cast, start by slowly lifting the rod tip (from 9 o'clock – see description opposite) by bending the elbow and lifting the hand up to the ear, as if answering the telephone. As the rod tip lifts the wrist breaks back slightly so that when the hand is at the caster's ear the rod is at 1 o'clock. If held in this position, the fly line will droop down from the rod tip and then curve back towards the water surface, where the rest of the line is held by the surface tension of the water. This curve of line from rod tip to water surface is called the 'D' loop (think of an italic capital 'D', the rod being the straight part of the letter, the line describing the curved section). This 'D' loop is a vital component part of any water-anchored cast.

2 The rod is accelerated forwards, from 1 o'clock to 11 o'clock, the wrist hinging forwards to a stop at this position.

3 This 'stop' is called the 'tap' and is an important part of any fly cast, as it stops the acceleration of the rod (our lever) while the weighted line continues on its way forward, uncurling over the water.

4 Immediately after making the 'stop' or 'tap' the rod continues to track down to 10 o'clock – as a follow-through – and then drifts down to 9 o'clock, allowing the line to flow above the water and alight gently on to the surface.

importantly, during fishing) it's imperative to keep a length of fly line outside the tip-ring whenever possible. On retrieving line, try to avoid bringing the tip of your fly line into the rod rings.

To get a workable length of fly line outside the rod tip the first thing that can be done is to pull the line out by hand. However, be very careful when pulling line directly from the rod tip if you're also holding the rod, as this direction of pull can cause the rod tip to break. Ideally you should pinch the fly between your fingers, pull a few yards of line directly off the reel, then lay the rod and reel on the ground and, whilst supporting the rod towards the tip, pull the leader and fly line out from the tip-ring.

Then pick up the rod and flick the loose line out on to the water, simultaneously letting go of your fly. Now pull more line off the reel, wiggle the rod tip close to the surface of the water, and the surface tension of the water will pull line through the rings and lay it on the water in front of you. With 4–5yd (4–5m) of line outside the rod tip you're ready to commence casting.

Roll cast

This is the easiest type of cast to begin with, and is also your 'get out of jail free card' should any of your other casts go wrong at any time. A roll cast will straighten line and forms a good starting point for all subsequent casting actions. All casts are ruined by slack line in their make-up – especially at the start – so roll-casting a straight fly line before starting a cast is a good default action.

The casting clock
In order to describe what happens to the rod during casting,

instructors use a clock-face analogy that assumes the caster is facing from right to left and the rod represents the hour hand.

Pick up and lay down cast

Casting overhead uses a linked series of backward and forward casts, but firstly we need to be able to make a basic 'pick up and lay down' cast. This basic casting action consists of four motions: peel, pluck, pause and pat.

Having the line straight out in front of you (from your roll cast) is the optimum starting point, the rod in the 9 o'clock position close to the water surface.

⬇ The starting position for a basic overhead cast. Ensure sufficient fly line (ie 5–6yd or 5–6m) is outside the rod tip. The rod tip is low and the line lies straight out from it.

PICK UP AND LAY DOWN CAST

1 Peel – the rod tip is raised smoothly to the 11 o'clock position, peeling the line off the water surface.

2 Pluck – it's then plucked off the surface as the elbow bends and the wrist breaks fractionally, accelerating the rod tip to just past the vertical (the 1 o'clock position).

3 Pause – with the rod hand now at the caster's ear level there's a pause, to allow the line to straighten on the back-cast.

4 Pat – as the line straightens in the air, the rod is tapped forwards to a stop at 11 o'clock, sending the line forwards.

5 This movement is then followed-through by allowing the tip to drift back down to 9 o'clock as the line unfurls over the water.

NOTE: This technique is well worth practising. Practice with a manageable length of fly line outside the rod tip. You can practise on grass.

Shooting line

Shooting line is using the momentum of the cast line to drag out more line as it flies through the air. Once you've mastered the basic cast this is simply a matter of timing.

Pull off a yard of extra line and trap this line against the cork of the handle with your index finger. Make your basic cast but, after having made your peel, pluck, pause and pat with the line flowing over the water, open your index finger on the cork handle to shoot the line. It should slide out easily under its own momentum.

False casting

Once you can shoot line on the forward cast, your other (non-rod) hand comes into play, allowing you to extend more line on each forward cast. Pull off more loose line. The key is to have the loose line between your reel and butt-ring running through the fingers of your non-rod hand. Having shot the line on the forward cast, and with the rod still at the 10 o'clock position, once the line extends out over the water simply clamp down on the line with your non-rod hand. The line will unfurl and extend under tension above the water's surface. At this point commence another back-cast, still gripping the line with your non-rod hand. Once again, as the forward cast is completed the hand can release the running line to shoot more. Using this false-casting technique, increasing lengths of line can be aerialised until the desired amount of line is outside the tip-ring to produce a maximum shoot without the line touching the water during the casting process. (Note: it's easy to try and false cast more line than you can cope with – at which point the line collapses.)

Double-hauling

Double-hauling is a technique that requires practice but once mastered can become an almost subconscious hand movement that's an invaluable aid to a cast. It's the result of combining a single-haul on the back-cast, and another on the forward cast.

The key two moments occur between the haul on the back-cast and the subsequent haul on the forward cast. In order to make the second haul, the line hand – still gripping the line – feeds line into the back-cast as the line travels back to the rear of the angler, the rod held in the 1 o'clock (pause) position. The line hand reaches the rod hand as the line straightens out above and behind the angler and is thus in position to make a downward haul as the rod is tapped forward (pat) to create the forward cast and the line is uncurling forwards. The three key elements here are:

- The line is fed into the cast under tension (there should be no slack line – the cast should 'pull' the line hand up on the back-cast).
- The haul should be made just as the casting stroke is made, the haul stopping as the rod stops.
- The rod and line hands should start the cast together, pull apart on the back-cast, drift back together during the pause, then move apart again on the forward cast.

DOUBLE-HAULING

1 As the back-cast begins the hands are together, the line hand gripping the line.

2 As the back cast is made the line hand hauls down.

3 As the line straightens behind, the line hand – still gripping the line – rises to feed line into the back-cast.

4 At the full extent of the back-cast the hands are together again.

5 Now the forward cast commences.

6 The line hand hauls down once again.

7 As the line travels forward the line hand releases to shoot the line.

Note: the movement of the casting hand is exactly as with the standard cast – only the line hand makes the hauling action; casting a longer line means making a longer haul.

ADVANTAGES OF THE DOUBLE-HAUL:
- It increases the line-speed with less rod motion, making a neater, more efficient cast.
- It helps aerialise more line.
- It helps to shoot more line on the forward cast.
- It helps to cast into and across the wind.
- It helps in casting large or heavy flies.

Fishing out the cast

A common fault amongst beginners is one of retrieving too much line before the next cast is made. Because the rod requires a reasonable length of line outside the rod tip to get it to work, it's best to still maintain a length of fly line outside the rod tip when making repeated casts. To make your fly work towards the end of the retrieve, use your rod tip to do the retrieving instead. Trap the line at the handle using the index finger (see 'The all-important index finger' in Chapter 14), lift the rod tip gradually to keep the fly moving and keep lifting smoothly until the tip is in the roll-cast position. Your fly will now be just in front of you, fished out. Next simply make a roll cast, and once the line has unfurled over the water grip the line with your line hand and go into a back-cast and your normal casting rhythm.

Parking up your fly

Due to the fact that it can be difficult to pull out the fly-line tip from the rings every time casting commences, this situation can be avoided with a simple fly 'parking procedure' whenever you stop fishing, wind in or move. This keeps about 1½ rod's length of line outside the tip-ring. Instead of hooking the fly into the keeper-ring (just above the handle), hook the fly into the second or third ring up the rod, catch the line and run the long loop of line around the reel foot at the base of the rod handle. Then turn the reel

HIGH AND FAST AND 'FEEL'

When the line travels on the back-cast, although the angler can't see it it's possible for the line and rod to transmit 'signals' to the angler which will help his casting:

- 'Feel' – this is when the line has unfurled on the back-cast and its momentum is still going backwards. At this point the angler will feel the line tension and pull the rod tip back further still. It's the signal to make the forward cast.
- High and fast – a good motto for most overhead casting: if the line travels high and fast behind you, then the odds are the forward cast (and subsequent shoot) will be a decent one.

handle to tighten the line and hold it under light tension, so the hook won't slip off the ring. When fishing recommences, grab the rod handle, reach up and release the fly and you'll instantly have a useful length of fly line outside the rod tip.

Double-handed casting

Casting can be made with two hands, using specially designed rods. These rods are generally longer than standard single-handers. Double-handed rods are usually designed for salmon, sea trout or saltwater fish, and have a distinctive longer upper handle above the reel seat and a smaller grip

↓ The grip on a double-handed rod should be light, using the finger and thumb of the top hand and the ball of the lower hand.

below it. Most anglers will naturally grip the upper part of the handle with their usual casting hand. However, it's a distinct advantage to learn to switch hands, right and left hand up the rod handle, when using a double-hander.

The grip

The hands should be shoulder-width apart on a double-hander, so hold the rod horizontally in front of the body and your hands will automatically assume the best position. The grip on the upper handle should be similar to a single-hander, but not too hard – the grip is concentrated on the thumb and forefinger. The hand on the lower handle should cup its bottom, effectively gripping with thumb, index and third finger at the base (or ball) of the handle.

Spey cast

The safest and most commonly used fly casts with double-handers are Spey casts, which involve positioning the line on the water before redirecting it across the river. The roll cast is a key element of casting with a double-handed rod, because all Spey casts are, in essence, redirected roll casts.

Just as with the single-handed roll cast, the rod tip is lifted from 9 o'clock up into the 1 o'clock position to form a 'D' loop of line. The top hand movement is very similar to the single-handed cast; however, the bottom hand slides across the body during the lifting movement so it comes over to the angler's casting side.

When the forward tap is made (at 11 o'clock) the top hand pushes and stops, whilst the bottom hand pulls into the angler's belly simultaneously. These two opposite forces cause the rod to accelerate forwards – an effect that can be easily practised with an assembled double-handled rod without line. Note the movement isn't an exaggerated one – it's a matter of a 3in or 4in (8–10cm) push-and-pull action.

The head

A double-handed Spey cast requires a length of line outside the rod tip in order to function. This is termed the head, or belly, of the line. When fishing, this head of line is always outside the rod tip, so all double-handed fishing occurs with the fly 'at distance' from the angler. The head of a typical double-handed Spey casting line would be about 65ft long. However, there are short-head Spey lines (around 55ft of head), which are easier to handle when casting, and long-belly Spey lines of up to 75ft, which require more handling skill. A short-belly Spey line is a good line with which to learn and improve Spey-casting skills. Skagit lines (see below) are shorter still in the head, and shooting head lines have the shortest heads of all.

On the dangle

Due to the fact that the fly is, in essence, 'attached' to the rod tip, when a cast is made across a river the current acts on the line between rod tip and fly to draw the fly across the current. When the fly has traversed the width of the river and comes to rest directly downstream of the angler's rod tip, it can travel no further across the river. This point is known as 'the dangle'. All Spey casts start with the line 'on the dangle'.

Why use a Spey cast?

Spey casts are simply redirected roll casts, with the roll cast being the final delivery of the line. The 'Spey' part of the cast is about reorganisation of the line before the roll cast is made. Since the Spey cast uses an 'anchor' on the water in front of the angler, and a 'D' loop of line, much of the cast

occurs over the water surface and therefore is less prone to catch on bankside vegetation than a conventional overhead cast. Thus a cast can be made irrespective of whether there are trees, bushes, a high bank or tall grass behind the angler. It's also a safe cast, which can be conducted safely in any wind, because the line can be placed on the downwind side of the angler at all times. If the angler is unsure as to which way the wind is actually blowing on the river, he/she can quickly check by holding the rod straight out over the river, holding the line tip at the same time, allowing the belly of the line to catch the wind (like a sail) and gauge the wind direction accordingly.

AND WHICH ONE?

In order to determine which Spey cast you should use, the first thing you need to work out is which direction the wind's blowing. This determines the type of Spey cast required in order to make the cast safely (ie with the 'fly and 'D' loop on the downwind side of the angler). The next consideration is what bank of the river you're on. This will determine whether you fish with the right hand at the top of the double-hander or the left (see diagram). The salmon angler who can switch hands on the double-handed rod is at a distinct advantage over one who can't.

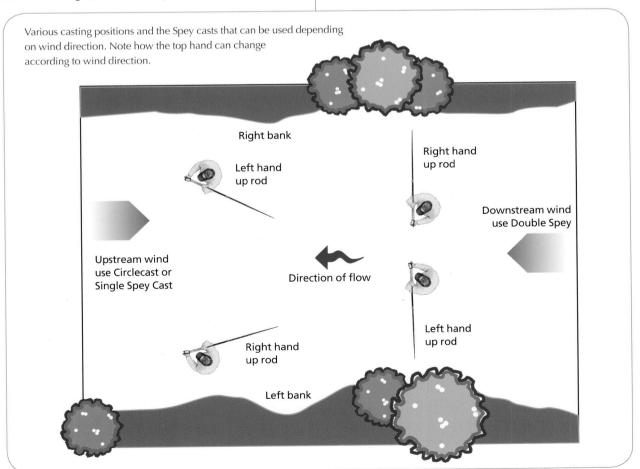

Various casting positions and the Spey casts that can be used depending on wind direction. Note how the top hand can change according to wind direction.

Circle C cast

The Circle C cast is one of easiest – and most useful – Spey casts to master. In an upstream wind, it places the fly upwind of the angler, out of harm's way.

1 To make a Circle C cast, allow the fly to hang downstream, 'on the dangle'. Retrieve line so that only the head is outside the rod tip. Start with the rod tip low and close to the bank.

ADVANTAGES OF THE CIRCLE C CAST
- Very useful in an upstream wind.
- Much easier to time than its cousin, the single Spey cast.
- Can be used with sink-tip lines to create the cast in a single movement.
- Can be used to lift out heavy tube flies to create the cast in a single movement.
- Due to the size of the 'circle', line can be placed accurately ready for the roll -cast delivery, thus the cast can be used to change casting angles and arranged so that the 'D' loop avoids troublesome bankside trees or vegetation (see 'Presentation casts' in Chapter 20).

TIP

In fly-casting, the line always follows the rod tip. In this instance, if the rod top draws a circle the line will simply lift out over the river and flop it upstream of the angler, in preparation for the roll cast.

2 Lift the rod tip to 45°, lifting some of the line between fly and rod tip off the water surface.

3 Begin to swing the tip upstream and, with the rod tip, draw a complete circle over the river and back to the riverbank…

4 …bringing the rod tip back to your starting position.

5 The line will flop up and over the tip, and land with the fly upstream (downwind) of the angler.

6 From here, the angler sweeps the rod tip back over the river, following the line…

7 …and peeling the line off the water…

8 …and then spirals the rod tip up into the roll-cast position.

9 This action forms a 'D' loop on the downwind side of the angler.

10 Once the 'D' loop is fully formed the forward tap is made…

11 …and the retrieved line is shot out across the river…

12 …towards the far bank.

Double Spey cast

This is the cast used to keep both the fly and the 'D' loop on the downstream side of the angler and is thus the safest cast to use in a downstream wind.

ADVANTAGES OF THE DOUBLE SPEY CAST

- Useful and safe in a downstream wind.
- An excellent cast when high banks and trees prevent any other back cast.
- It's relatively easy to time.
- If the anchor of the 'D' loop is positioned fairly close to the angler then this can be a powerful cast, enabling long shoots.

4 …and then down again, as the rod tip reaches upstream.

1 Having allowed the line to swing down on to 'the dangle', the angler retrieves any line to be shot, keeping the head of the line outside the rod tip.

5 For this arc to be described by the rod tip, the top hand crosses over the bottom one, as if both hands were making an exaggerated half-turn of a large ship's wheel.

2 The first part of the double Spey cast is where the rod tip, starting low, lifts out and over the river…

6 This action lays the head of the line out in front of the angler, with the tip of the fly line now positioned 45° downstream of the angler, about a rod's length out, the fly trailing behind it. This is not a cast upstream, it's simply a placement of the line upstream.

3 …describing a rainbow arc upwards, over the river in front of the angler…

7 Part two of the double Spey begins with the rod tip retracing the path of the line, starting from the low point upstream.

8 The hands uncross, causing the rod tip to sweep downstream, over the river, and then the tip spirals up…

9 …and climbs up into the roll-cast delivery position.

10 The momentum of this sweep causes an aggressive 'D' loop to form. The angler pauses, allows the 'D' loop to develop fully…

11 …and then makes the roll-cast delivery with a forward cast.

12 …shooting line as the head travels forward.

13 The head unfurls across the river…

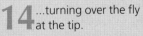

14 …turning over the fly at the tip.

Shooting head

With a double-handed rod a shooting head line is an easy way to achieve distance. The head is typically short (less than 50ft) and the shooting line is comparatively thin (often heavy monofilament). However, because the running line is so thin the friction and drag on shooting is negligible, hence very long shoots can be made. Again the head can be of any type from floater to fast sinker.

ADVANTAGES OF A SHOOTING HEAD
- Shoots for long distances, an asset on large rivers.
- The short head is easily managed.
- Due to the short head casting can be made under steep banks and cramped, tree-lined spaces.
- Easy to change heads.

DISADVANTAGES OF A SHOOTING HEAD
- Presentation of the fly at the end of the cast is secondary to distance.
- Thin running line isn't easy to handle and can tangle.
- The thick, short head tends to land in an ungainly, 'noisy' fashion.
- The running line is difficult to mend once on the water surface making in-stream fly control more difficult.

Casts with a switch rod

A switch rod is basically a mini-Spey casting rod. It's a double-handed rod that varies in length from 10ft to 13ft and can take a range of line weights from #5 to #9 to fish flies of sizes 8–14.

It's a useful rod for Spey casting and overhead casts on small and medium-sized rivers, both for sea trout and salmon and also saltwater. In essence, a switch rod is a mini-Spey caster, a powerful and easier Spey-casting tool than a single-handed rod. However, the line-rating system for switch rods can be confusing: ensure that the line rating given is for either a trout line or a salmon line.

ADVANTAGES OF A SWITCH ROD
- Offers more control and power on a Spey cast than a standard single-handed rod.
- Adaptable to single- or double-handed casting (up to maybe 12ft, but not longer).
- More manageable for tight banks.
- Less cumbersome than a standard 14–15ft rod and thus easier to handle when employing tactics such as backing up, etc.

DISADVANTAGES OF A SWITCH ROD
- Lines aren't heavy enough to handle big flies.
- When wading deep, effective height (ie water surface to rod tip) is greatly reduced.
- Distance casts are less manageable.

Double-handed overhead cast

An overhead cast can be made with a double-hander, but Spey casts are easier, less troublesome and also less dangerous. However, there are times when an overhead cast might be the only option available, in which case casting overhead is a simple matter of keeping a workable length of line outside the rod tip and using exactly the same peel, pluck, pause, pat action as the single-handed cast – only using both hands, with the bottom hand creating the stop to shoot line on the forward cast.

A comfortable fishing position

Many anglers find fishing with a double-handed rod cumbersome. This is usually because they want to hold the bottom handle of the rod whilst fishing. This isn't necessary and causes the angler to lean uncomfortably forward, holding the heavy rod with arms extended. It's only necessary to hold the bottom handle when casting. When fishing, hold the upper handle in the normal fashion, the reel under your arm, and simply tuck the bottom handle under your arm.

Casting a Skagit line

Skagit lines were originally developed by US and Canadian steelhead fishers of the Skagit river, where big, heavy flies are fished with heavy sink-tips. In order to cast such tips, the floating part of the head is short, thick and highly buoyant (see below) and is attached to thin running line. Using either Circle C

or double-Spey-style casts a Skagit head can be shot long distances; consequently the Skagit style has caught on in the UK. The sink-tips are interchangeable (using a loop-to-loop connection), from floating to very fast sinking. In addition, short 'cheater' sections of line (approximately 1–2m) are provided with Skagit systems to lengthen the head, if required, to match a line to a rod (ideally the Skagit head should be 3–4 times the rod's length, depending on what the caster prefers).

Skagit lines and rods are rated differently to other fly gear. Instead of an AFFTA number it will carry a grain or gram weight. As with standard fly gear the line and rod ratings should marry. Note: the Skagit grain or gram weight applies to the thick, floating part of the line only, not the sink-tip. Thus a 550 grain Skagit rod requires a 550 Skagit floating line, to which any of the sinking tips is then attached.

A common cast for maximum distance with a Skagit line is the Perry Poke.

ADVANTAGES OF A SKAGIT LINE

- The Skagit line comes with the same advantages and disadvantages as the shooting head, but in addition:
- The fly can be cast a long distance, but sunk quickly (using very fast sink-tips); thus is a good option for big, cold, fast-flowing spring rivers.
- The short head means heavy flies and deeply sunk tips can be lifted easily in preparation for casting.

Power up the poke

The double-handed Perry Poke is a cast that originated in the western USA and is used for casting short heads carrying heavy sink-tips.

DOUBLE HANDED PERRY POKE

1 Feet set towards your target, the rod is lifted from 'the dangle' and begins to swing upstream.

2 The rod has swung upstream and placed the line, and is now at 45° to the water. Note the tip of the fly line is slightly downstream of the angler.

3 Instead of making a cast, the rod is 'flopped' forward in the direction of desired cast, under very little power, dragging the fly upstream of the angler.

4 Line falls on to the water forming a crumpled V shape. The fly is now upstream of the angler.

5 The rod tip now retraces and uncoils the V shape as the rod is raised into the back-cast position.

6 As the rod swings into the top of its back-cast position, so a 'D' loop forms and a white 'mouse' of water fizzes through the water.

7 As the rod tip is lifted into the casting position a large, powerful 'D' loop forms on the back-cast.

8 The forward cast is made with a high 'stop', and the line flies out over the river…

9 …to land almost on the opposite bank

Notes
- A common mistake is to push the throw down ('poke') too far from the caster. It should be a weak forward placement of the rod tip, a limp, powerless 'cast'.
- This cast can also be used as a simple replacement of the Circle C.

WHICH FLY?

Types of flies

Fly fishing revolves around artificial flies attached to the end of a line; it has always been thus. Way back in Roman times it was documented by Aelianus that the Macedonians used artificial flies to tempt and catch trout. The flies they used, composed of wool wrapped around a hook and then overwound with a 'cock's wattle', were obviously designed to imitate the natural flies flying on and above the water. Today, 1,500 years after this first written description of fly fishing, the concept remains exactly the same, only the 'flies' have developed into many other forms. Instead of representing flies as we know them, a fisherman's 'fly' can also represent an aquatic insect, a fish, a tadpole, a leech or even a frog. Some fishing flies don't actually represent anything natural at all, but have the shape, colour and/or movement to entice (or lure) the fish into taking them, either through instinct, curiosity, hunger or aggression.

As a result there's a vast range of different flies, which can be divided into four main types: lure, attractor, suggestive and imitative. The type of fly can dictate the way the fly is fished.

Lure

The simplest form of fly fishing involves using a lure. This is because a lure is usually (but not always) fished faster than the other three

Viva.

categories of flies. A lure is designed to attract and arouse the curiosity or aggression of the targeted fish – through movement, colour or action – so much so that it chases and 'takes' the fly. The take is often a positive strike by the fish, and thus the angler doesn't have to do much more than continue the retrieve as the fish is already hooked in the process of taking the fly.

Lures can be fished on a variety of lines – from floater to full sinker. They're larger in size than the other types of fly, and are tied in a full spectrum of colours – from brilliant white through to black, including gaudy and fluorescent hues. Lures can be fished singly or as part of a team of flies, with the lure generally taking the point position.

Attractor

The attractor works in a similar fashion to the lure, but attractors are smaller flies and often function as one fly in a team of three. The job of the attractor fly is to entice the fish sufficiently to investigate and thereby 'lead' it towards other flies in the team, which may be more suggestive of food items. However, the fish may take the attractor. Attractors may be small ('mini') lures, or wet flies with brightly coloured appendages – tails, throats, hackles or wings – to catch the

Dunkeld.

fish's eye. In many cases, attractor wet flies may have a passing resemblance to the fish's natural food. For instance, the orange hackle or the gold body of a Dunkeld might attract, but also resemble a small fry. The prime position for an attractor fly is on the top dropper, with more suggestive flies fished below it (see below).

Suggestive

Invicta.

A suggestive fly is one that bears a resemblance to or possesses trigger-points to the food being targeted by the fish. For instance, take the blend of the yellow body, brown body hackle and brown-and-cream hen pheasant wing of an Invicta wet fly. If you squint it looks a bit like some of the attributes of a hatching sedge (caddis). The Hare's Ear Nymph and the Pheasant Tail Nymph are two highly successful suggestive nymphs because, to a trout, they can suggest all manner of different food items, without imitating any organism too specifically. As a result they'll often feature on a cast, particularly when the angler is unsure what the fish are feeding on. Suggestive flies can be fished either singly or as part of a team. They can be fished at all paces from very slow to fast-paced pull-retrieves.

Imitative

Shrimp.

Imitative flies are dressed to represent the items on which the fish are feeding, in terms of size, colour and shape, and they're also designed to be fished in exactly the manner the fish would expect the food item to be moving. For instance, the Olive Buzzer Pupa is fished 'static', drifting on the current as the natural pupa does, whilst an angler's artificial Shrimp is fished close to the bottom in short twitches to imitate the natural movement of this bottom-dwelling, actively swimming crustacean.

Imitative flies can be tied as basic representations of the food item, but they can also be tied to be 'super-realistic' – virtually indistinct from the real insect.

Fly styles

Within the four different fly types come a wide variety of styles that the angler can employ. Fly 'style' relates to how the fly is tied and what it does in the water.

Crane Fly.

Dry fly

The classic trout fishing 'fly'. Designed to look like an adult, flying insect – such as a daddy-long-legs (crane fly) or an adult mayfly – a dry fly is designed to rest on the water surface. This is usually enabled through the use of a wound hackle but can also be achieved by incorporating in the dressing naturally buoyant materials (duck's preen gland feathers or deer hair) or man-made buoyant materials. Otherwise a dry fly can be treated with water repellent silicone gel or one of a few other types of floatant to help the fly float on the water surface.

Wet fly

Whilst the dry fly is perceived as the classic fisherman's fly, the wet fly is probably the most widespread style of fly actually used. Fish feed mostly on things they encounter under the water, rather than on it, and so wet flies – which are fished below the water surface – can mimic anything from hatching flies to drowned flies, spent flies (exhausted egg-laying adults), nymphs, small fish and grubs. Wet flies come in many forms (see below), but traditionally are recognised as creations of fur, feather and tinsel, sporting famous names such as Bloody Butcher and Peter Ross.

Connemara Black.

Emerger

Falling in between wet and dry flies, emergers are designed to float in the surface film. The surface film formed where water meets air is like an elastic skin,

Klinkhamer Special.

which any aquatic insect must penetrate before hatching. It's therefore at this point that a hatching natural fly is most vulnerable to predation. Emergers generally use a buoyant material to keep the upper part of the fly in, on or above the surface film, whilst the rest of the fly sits in or below the surface. The Klinkhamer Special (above) is a classic example.

Pheasant Tail Nymph.

Nymph

Dressed to imitate the immature stages of aquatic nymphs, usually consisting of tails, legs, body and thorax, a typical generic nymph would be represented by the Pheasant Tail Nymph (above). Some nymphs might be less defined, like the bloodworm, which consists of a segmented tube-like body, or the cased caddis, a grub that lives in a protective case constructed of sand, stones or vegetation.

Spiders

A simple, traditionally tied style of wet fly consisting of a thread body and a single, sparse hackle at the front. Classic examples include Waterhen Bloa and Snipe & Purple, names which refer to the colours and feathers used in their construction.

Black Magic.

Tying styles

Fly fishers often group flies by the way they're tied. For example:

Hairwings
Tied with a wing made from a bunch of hair, such as bucktail, squirrel, stoat etc. Most hairwings are lures – the Stoat's Tail, for instance.

Executioner.

Featherwings
Comprising wings composed of either slips or sections of bird feathers. These are generally larger flies, such as Parmachene Belle or Grey

Silver Wilkinson.

Ghost. Featherwings are lures or sometimes baitfish or shrimp suggestions.

Traditional wets
Smaller flies also with a wing of feather, these are tied with fur, feather and tinsel with a wing consisting of slips of a wing feather,

Harelug & Partridge.

such as Hare Lug & Partridge etc. Traditional wets are designed to either attract fish or suggest an insect, such as the Butcher, which could be seen to represent a hatching midge.

Booby flies
Easily identified by their twin, bulbous foam 'eyes' at the front of the hook. Booby flies are extremely buoyant, due to the amount of foam used in their construction and they have thus become integral in

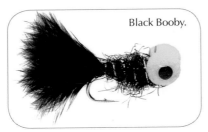
Black Booby.

tactical presentations on stillwaters, as well as convincing lures in their own right. They often possess a highly mobile marabou tail and are generally fished slower than conventional lures due to their enticing, hovering action in the water.

Blobs
Popular on stillwaters, Blobs are simply a small mass of intense colour and flash that's fished quickly through the water, hopefully

Orange Blob.

grabbing the trout's attention, which means it can also be used as an attractor in other tactical approaches.

Bead-heads
Bead-heads can be added to lures or nymphs to add both attraction (they also come in silver and duller

Bead-head Damselfly Nymph.

metals) and weight. They're drilled metal beads, with a plated (or painted) finish, and come in different sizes (mm diameter). The bigger the bead, the heavier the fly. Due to excessive weight at the head of the fly, some mobile-tailed flies will undulate enticingly when fished with a pull-and-pause retrieve.

Bead-chain eyes
Similar to gold-heads, but with two beads of bath-chain tied across the head to provide weight and/or add action. Most commonly used on lures or baitfish, as the beads can look like 'eyes'.

Cat's Whisker.

Tungsten bead-heads

Similar to bead-heads, but heavier due to the dense tungsten metal used in the bead. Can be shiny but tend to be duller colours and used on more imitative flies, particularly in fast-flowing rivers, where a fly needs to get deeper through the current.

Tungsten-bead Hare's Ear.

Leaded flies

In order to get flies to sink more readily, they can be tied with an underbody of either lead wire or flattened lead wraps. This weighting is disguised by the fly dressing and is most commonly used on imitative flies, such as a Shrimp imitation, or Czech Nymph.

Pink Shrimp.

Floating Fry.

Buoyant flies

Tied with either foam or deer-hair (which has air trapped within each individual fibre) to make the fly float on the surface.

Tube flies

The fly is dressed on a narrow tube of nylon, plastic, aluminium, copper or brass, depending on desired sink rate. Tubes can vary from ½in to 3in long, but this style is mainly used for bigger flies and targeting predatory species such as salmon, sea trout and pike.

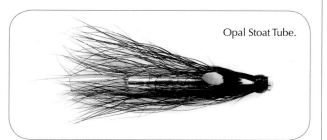

Opal Stoat Tube.

Silver Doctor.

Salmon single

Salmon singles are tied on traditional hooks, usually black. The eye is slightly bent up. As its name suggests, a single has one shank and point – unlike a double or treble hook. Used in low flows.

Doubles

In common usage for salmon and sea trout. The double

Low Water Crathie double.

comprises two singles splayed at an angle of about 60° to produce a single-eyed fly with one shank but two points. Can be up- or down-eyed. If designed for use with tubes, it'll have a straight (in-line) eye.

Wee double

Usually in sizes 10–16, flies tied on 'wee double hooks' are used on the point of a wet-fly cast to help 'anchor' the flies.

CdC Sunset double.

Cascade treble.

Trebles

A double hook with a third bend soldered to it to produce a grapple type of hook. Used mainly for salmon. For flies the eye will be turned up; for attaching to tubes the eye will be straight (or in-line). Trebles are being phased out, and are banned in some waters.

Tandems

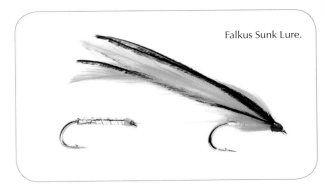

Falkus Sunk Lure.

Two hooks are joined in-line, using nylon or wire to hold them in place one behind the other. Most commonly used for sea-trout flies.

Coneheads

As with bead-heads, these cone-shaped heads are drilled to fit at the front of the fly to provide weight and some flash. More streamlined than Gold-heads, these are often used on salmon and sea-trout flies.

Conehead Cascade.

BARBLESS HOOKS

Some hooks these days are made without any barbs at all, designed to make releasing fish easier. If using barbless hooks, tension must be kept on the fish at all times whilst playing it out; slack line can mean the hook drops out.

⬇ Barbed hooks can easily be de-barbed by simply clamping down on the barb with flat-nosed pliers to crush it down.

Fly colours

Colours form an essential component of flies, and exact colour shades have been sought for centuries. For instance, since the early 20th century the exact colour of the body of a Partridge & Orange was always proclaimed as Pearsall's 6a, dyed by a British silk and thread manufacturer. We're uncertain how fish see colour, but most obsessed, keen fly tyers think that fish see colour as we do, so as a result fly designs often centre around colour shades.

Bearing this in mind, we can consider a rainbow of colours and give an indication of what those colours might represent or trigger:

↑ Black – one of the very best colours for most fish, possibly due to the striking silhouette that any fly tied in this colour produces against the sky above. This is an Ace of Spades.

→ Purple – a good alternative colour for salmon, this can also be attractive to grayling. This is a Snipe & Purple.

← Blue – a good colour for fresh salmon and sea trout, also any predatory sea fish. Blue is the last visible colour in the spectrum, so as the light fades fish can still see blue. This is a Claret Bumble.

← Pink/magenta – very attractive to grayling and also pike. Can make a good hotspot for trout. A good colour in low light, such as at dawn. This is a Pink Czech Nymph.

→ Red – provokes aggression in salmon; a proven attractor colour for brown trout. This is a Soldier Palmer.

↓ Orange – a great attractor colour for salmon and also trout. Thought to represent the colour of insect haemoglobin as it gets ready to emerge, hence it can act as a 'trigger-point' on nymphs. This is a GP Shrimp.

← Yellow – one of the top colours for salmon. This is a Posh Tosh.

← Olive – the dominant colour for natural summer nymphs, so good for trout and grayling. This is an Olive Hatching Caddis.

↑ Golden olive – a favourite colour in Ireland, probably due to its close association to the colour of a mayfly dun. Also a good match for olives and summer duns. This is a Golden Olive Bumble.

↑ Lime green – highly attractive to trout, both browns and rainbows. Also grilse. This is a Green-tailed Kate McLaren.

↑ Grey – a good colour for baitfish imitations (especially saltwater), but also makes a good imitative insect colour, hence the success of this Adams Parachute.

↗ White – an excellent colour for stillwater trout and also good for any predatory fish, as the underbellies of baitfish are usually white. This is an Appetiser.

→ Ultra-violet reflecting material – becoming more popular in flies, but it's doubtful whether freshwater fish older than two years can distinguish the colours, although they might be visible to saltwater fish. This is an Ultra Violet Cormorant.

↑ Brown – see olive (above). This is a Cove Pheasant Tail Nymph..

→ Claret – one of the very best imitative colours for trout, as it suggests the body fluids in a live insect. This is a Mallard & Claret.

← It's unlikely freshwater fish can distinguish uv-reflecting materials, but fluorescence is a very popular incorporation into fly dressings. Fluorescent dyes absorb UV and reflect visible light, so are very bright. This is a CdC Hopper with a fluorescent butt.

IMITATIVE FLY FISHING

A grayling taken on a caddis dry fly in northern Norway.

The case for imitative fishing

We can entice, aggravate, goad and provoke fish to take our gaudy lures. We also know that all fish need to feed, usually on a daily basis. So fly fishers can choose a more practical, logical path to target their quarry by imitating the food that fish eat.

The types of food that fish take are extremely varied, ranging from the full range of aquatic invertebrates to snails, water fleas (daphnia), amphibians like frogs and newts, fish, sand eels and even mice that attempt to swim across the surface. Basically, fish are opportunists and will take whatever's available on the aquatic smorgasbord. All these food species can be imitated by flies tied to look like the prey species moved in a natural way and presented in a position where the fish is expecting to find them. This is called imitative fishing.

The key angling species

For the imitative fly fisher, knowledge of the insects that live in the water is paramount, because they're always present and provide the bulk of the fish's diet, except for those fish that don't feed on aquatic insects, such as predatory sea fish, pike and salmon.

There are four major groups of aquatic insects that are important to trout, grayling and coarse fish: 'flatwings' (such as midges), 'upwings' (such as mayflies), sedges (caddis) and stoneflies. Each group has an aquatic stage, and all have an adult mating stage that occurs out of the water. Thus all have a water-to-air hatching process. All four can be found on both stillwaters and rivers, although stoneflies are the least common on stillwaters.

↓A hatch of upwings. note the broad wings and long tails.

(Aleksandar Kamasi)

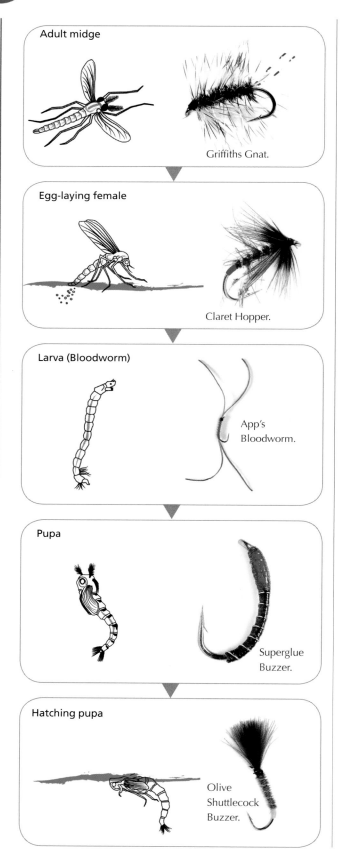

Adult midge

Griffiths Gnat.

Egg-laying female

Claret Hopper.

Larva (Bloodworm)

App's Bloodworm.

Pupa

Superglue Buzzer.

Hatching pupa

Olive Shuttlecock Buzzer.

Midges

The most populous of the four groups, there can be thousands of midge larvae living in each square metre of lakebed. The larvae thrive in silty detritus, so their numbers can be significant in suitable lakes and slow river pools, both of which offer midges the right habitat.

The midge life cycle starts as an egg laid on the surface of the water, which falls to the lakebed. Here, it hatches into a larvae, commonly known as a bloodworm. Bloodworms are commonly blood red, but can be green, brown, or grey. The larva feeds in the decomposing mud of the lake bed and then, when it's ready to hatch, it changes into a pupa. With a noticeably enlarged thorax and a tapered abdomen, it now resembles a comma in shape.

The pupa ascends from the lakebed using tiny, wriggling pulses to rise towards the surface. When it's ready to hatch, the pupa hangs at the water surface and pulls itself through the surface film. Its wing-buds then split and its wings inflate as it pumps blood into them. Now resting on the water surface, once its wings are fully formed it's an adult and can fly away from the water. It flies towards a sheltered area and joins a throng of other recently hatched midges, rising and falling in the air in dense, thin columns of thousands of adult flies that, from a distance, can resemble smoke plumes above hedges or in the shelter of trees. Their thousands of wings can be heard 'buzzing' as they perform their mating dance, hence the angling term for these insects – 'buzzers'.

↑ The comma-shaped Chironomid pupa.

Note that all 'buzzers' are non-biting midges.

Having mated, the female returns to the water surface to lay her eggs, to continue the cycle.

Adult identifying features: Columns of what appears to be high-pitched buzzing 'smoke plumes' above hedges, trees etc. Long abdomen – often held in a curved shape – short thorax. Long-legged, mosquito-like transparent-winged fly. Male has long feathery 'plumes' at the head.

Key angling species: Chironomid species are difficult to distinguish by eye, and anglers tend to segregate them by colour and size only. In general, early season hatchers are black, then as the season progresses grey, green, brown, red, ginger and buff versions hatch, with darker versions again predominating towards the end of the season.

Artificials: App's Bloodworm, Squirmy Worm, Cove Nymph, Pheasant Tail Nymph, Hare's Ear Nymph, Buzzer Pupa (various colours), Epoxy Buzzer Pupa, Suspender Buzzer, Shipman's Buzzer, Hopper, Griffiths Gnat.

Upwings

→ Olive nymph
(Baetis).

↓ Dun (left)
and spinner of
pale watery
(Baetis fuscatus).

Upwings are a more elegant species than midges, and are more commonly associated with weed and shallower water. This broad group includes olives and mayflies, which can be found in stillwaters and rivers. Having hatched from an egg laid on the water surface, the immature upwing spends much of its life as an aquatic nymph, moving around with a short darting action, utilising its three tails to propel itself. Upwing nymphs have more pronounced legs and thorax than the midge, and when it's time to hatch the ripe nymph swims to the water surface, breaks through the film and its wing-buds split and produce a pair of finely veined wings which, once fully formed, allow it to escape from the water surface as a dun. The dun then flies to shelter at the water's edge, where it has one more remarkable step to make before becoming an adult. Having landed, the dun's feet grip into the surface (of a leaf or branch), the dun's thorax splits once again, and a shinier and brighter adult emerges, its tails are longer, and its wings are more transparent. This adult then joins others of the same species in an aerial mating dance, after which the female will return to the water, lay its eggs, and collapse on the water surface, spent.

Adult identifying features: Broad wings, like sailboats on the surface held aloft on hatching. Rise vertically off the water, body and tails hanging down. Two or three tails.

Key river fishing species: Large dark olive (*Baetis rhodani*), iron blue (*Alaintes muticus, Nigrobaetis niger, Nigrobaetis digitatus*), medium olive (*Baetis vernus*), small dark olive (*Baetis scambus*), small spurwing (*Centroptilum luteolum*), Pale watery (*Baetis fuscatus*), Blue-winged olive (*Serratella ignita*) caenis (*Caenis* spp).

Key river and stillwater species: Mayflies (*Ephemera danica, Ephemera vulgata, Ephemera lineata*), caenis.

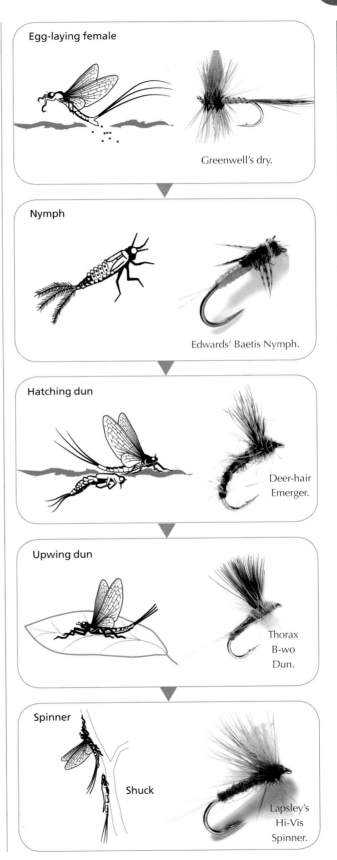

Egg-laying female

Greenwell's dry.

Nymph

Edwards' Baetis Nymph.

Hatching dun

Deer-hair Emerger.

Upwing dun

Thorax B-wo Dun.

Spinner

Shuck

Lapsley's Hi-Vis Spinner.

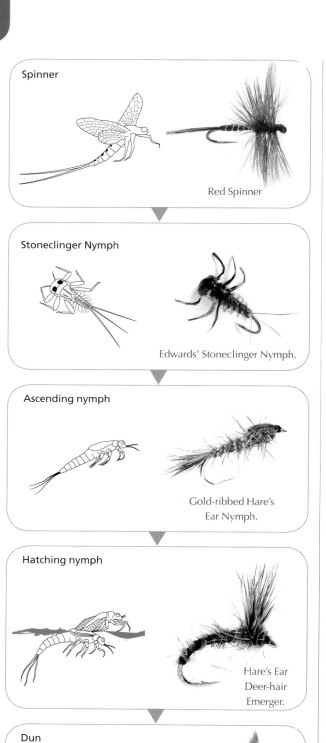

Spinner

Red Spinner

Stoneclinger Nymph

Edwards' Stoneclinger Nymph.

Ascending nymph

Gold-ribbed Hare's Ear Nymph.

Hatching nymph

Hare's Ear Deer-hair Emerger.

Dun

Lunn's Particular.

Key stillwater species: pond olive (*Cloeon dipterum*), lake olive (*Cloeon simile*), claret dun (*Leptophlebia vespertina*), sepia dun (*Leptophlebia marginata*).

Artificials: Pheasant Tail Nymph, Gold-ribbed Hare's Ear Nymph, Baetis Nymph, Walker's Mayfly Nymph, Olive Klinkhamer, CdC Olive, Greenwell's Glory, Olive Thorax Dun, Poly May Dun, Grey Wulff, Deerstalker, Mohican Mayfly, Pheasant Tail Spinner, Adams, Parachute Adams, Sparkle Dun, Olive or Hare's Ear F-fly, Tup's Indispensable, Iron Blue Dun, Snowshoe Hare Spinner, Red Spinner, Sherry Spinner. For Caenis: PVC Nymph, small Olive Nymph, Last Hope.

Stoneclingers (Ecdyonurids)

These are particularly important on rivers, particularly rain-fed freestone and faster rivers with rocky beds. Stoneclingers are so called because of their dorsally flattened body, which offers a streamlined profile to the fast currents while they literally hug or cling to stones in their native streams, and resemble the shape of a modern speed cyclist. When ready to hatch, they rise up through the water column quickly and hatch in an instant as they attempt to escape the surface film. They then moult their skins and the dun

➜ Olive upright nymph (*Rhithrogena semicolorata*).

↑ Olive upright dun.

↓ Olive upright spinner.

become spinners on surrounding vegetation. The resultant spinners dance and mate before the female returns to the water to lay her eggs and die.

Adult identifying features: Larger than most upwings – but not the mayflies – the duns of stoneclingers are instantly noticeable on the water and in the air.

Key angling species: Rivers – march brown (*Rhithrogena germanica*), yellow may dun (*Heptagenia sulphurea*), olive upright (*Rhithrogena semicolorata*).

Artificials: Pheasant Tail Nymph (hare's ear thorax), March Brown Spider, Partridge & Orange, CdC March Brown Emerger, Greenwell's Glory, Olive Thorax Dun, Yellow May Emerger, Yellowhammer, Yellow May Nymph.

Sedges (Caddis)

Caddis (*Trichoptera*) are commonly associated with stony beds of river and lakes, such as upland and Irish lakes, although they're found on reservoirs and small stillwaters too. They provide an important food source for all river and lake fish. The caddis starts life as

➔ Caddis (grannom) larva in its case.

an egg, which hatches into a larva. The larva often – but not always – uses the surrounding materials (sand, gravel, pieces of vegetation on the bed) to create a protective home around itself, which it will either drag around as it predates on smaller insects on the bottom, or uses as a live-in shelter. Other larvae spend their early life as free-living grubs. When ready to hatch,

➔ Adult caddis (*Brachycentrus subnubilus*).

the larva transforms into a pupa that leaves its shelter and uses its strong legs to propel itself to the surface, break through the surface film, and emerge as an adult at the water surface. It then flies off to mate. The mated female will return to the water, dipping its abdomen on the surface to lay eggs for the next generation of caddis.

Adult identifying features: Dusky, 'powdered' roof-shaped wings, often mottled brown. Resemble small moths both in appearance and flight. Often hatch in the late evening.

Key angling species: Rivers – grannom (*Brachycentrus subnubilus*), sandyfly (*Rhyacophila dorsalis*), grey flag and

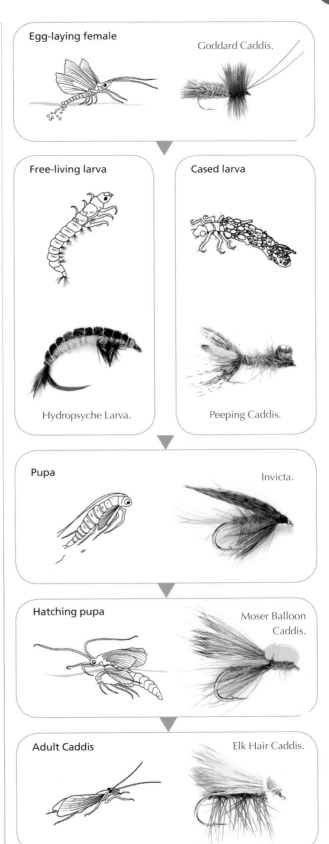

Egg-laying female

Goddard Caddis.

Free-living larva

Cased larva

Hydropsyche Larva.

Peeping Caddis.

Pupa

Invicta.

Hatching pupa

Moser Balloon Caddis.

Adult Caddis

Elk Hair Caddis.

marbled sedge (*Hydropsyche* spp). Rivers and stillwater – cinnamon sedge (*Limnephilus lunatus*), caperer (*Halesus radiatus, Halesus digitatus*), Welshman's button (*Sericostoma personatum*). Stillwater – great red sedge (*Phrygania grandis*), green peter (*Phrygania obsoleta*), longhorn sedge (*Oecetis ochracea*).

Artificials: Teal & Green, Green Sedge Pupa, Parachute Black Gnat, Peeping Caddis, Stickfly, Gold-head Hare's Ear, Hydropsyche Larva, Rhyacophila Larva, Caddis Pupa, Amber Pupa, Invicta, Balloon Caddis, Elk Hair Sedge, Walker's Sedge, Goddard Caddis, Lunn's Caperer, Green Peter, Murrough, Welshman's Button.

Stoneflies

↑ Stonefly adult (willow fly, *Leuctra geniculata*).

The main quality of a stonefly river is its cleanliness. Stoneflies only occur where there is no pollution so are found in upland areas and mountain lakes. The stonefly egg hatches into a predatory nymph. Some stoneflies can grow quite large (the 'gadger' of Scottish rivers can grow to 1½in (33mm), others are more numerous but much smaller, such as the willow fly or needle fly. The nymph, with its two short, stubby tails, thick abdomen, extended thorax and strong legs, is reminiscent of the garden earwig.

Stoneflies crawl to the edges of the water to hatch into adult form. Stoneflies are primitive insects and are laboured, clumsy fliers, thus susceptible to falling into the water. The females also return to the water surface to lay their eggs and, again, their ungainly efforts may attract the attentions of fish.

Adult identifying features: 'Earwigs' with broad, flat wings over their backs, generally crawling or, when they fly, looking like tiny biplanes struggling to stabilise as they rise from the water. At rest, willow and needle flies look like tiny needles, their wings wrapped around their narrow bodies.

Key angling species: River – large stonefly (*Dinocras cephalotes, Perla bipunctata, Perlodes microcephala*), yellow Sally (*Isoperla grammatica*), willow fly (*Leuctra geniculata*) and needle fly (*Leuctra fusca*).

Artificials: Pheasant Tail Nymph, Black Spider, Brown Spider, Dark Needle, Stimulator, Dry Greenwells, Brown Elk Hair Caddis.

Other aquatic insects

Damselflies

A surprisingly aggressive predatory nymph associated with weed beds, where it catches insects and small fish. The nymph is elongated and slender, up to 1½in (3.5cm) long,

↓ The distinctive adult blue damselfly.

(Kletr)

and swims with a sinuous action. Usually olive or brown, it is characterised by three short, feathery tails and a largish head, shaped rather like Ridley Scott's *Alien*. Once ready to emerge (from early summer onwards), the nymph swims towards the shore and uses its long legs to climb up any waterside vegetation. Once out of the water, the nymphal shuck splits and the adult damselfly emerges – usually either bright blue or red. The adult then flies around for a number of days, feeding on other insects, before it mates and the female returns to the water to lay its eggs.

Adult identifying features: Large and distinct, with bright red, green or blue bodies, with two pairs of large wings that are held over the back when at rest (unlike dragonflies, which hold their wings out a right angles to the body when at rest). Flies low, on a direct course.

Artificials: Damselfly Nymph, Gold-head Damsel, Parachute Adult Damselfly.

Corixa (*Corixa* spp)

A member of the bug family, the Corixa (otherwise known as the lesser water boatman) can swim underwater utilising an air-sac held beneath its body (about ⅓in/8mm long), which it has to replenish by visiting the surface at regular intervals. Associated with shallow water, weeds and rotting detritus, on which it feeds, the Corixa uses long, flattened legs to swim in short, erratic, darting movements from the bottom to the surface and into weed. Often present in large colonies, trout will either chase the oxygen-laden insects as they dive, or mop them up off the surface as they rest for air.

⬇ The stickleback is an important source of protein for large, predatory fish in rivers, lakes and brackish water.

(Martin Pelanek)

⬆ Corixa are prominent in weed beds.

Adult identifying features: A tough, brown shellback, broad head, light cream or yellow underbody and two large, oar-like legs for propulsion.

Artificials: Corixa, Chomper, Silver Invicta, Fiery Brown Bob's Bits.

Small fish

Stickleback (*Gasterosteus* sp), minnow (*Phonxius phonxius*), roach (*Rutilus rutilus*), bream (*Abramis brama*), perch (*Perca fluvians*), loaches (*Cobitidae*), bullheads (*Cottus gobio*) and salmon and trout parr (*Salmo salar*, *Salmo trutta*). Small fish are an important source of protein for larger fish that live alongside them. In a river this might come from shoals of minnows or sticklebacks, or it could be solitary, bottom-dwelling loaches, bullheads or (with large trout) salmon parr. In a river, this type of feeding will mostly occur over the gravels at the tails of the pools, often in the evening or early morning.

(Jack Perks)

In addition, the young fry of many coarse fish lake species – roach, bream, perch – are vulnerable immediately after hatching and for many months afterwards. The young fry will seek any shelter offered by weed beds or any other 'structure' – walls, jetties, sunken hedges etc, as they group in tight shoals. Often predators will attack these shoals in aggressive, high-speed lunges, which damage many of the fragile fry in the process. The predators then return to mop up the dying at a more leisurely pace.

The diet of pike and predatory sea fish is almost entirely made up of smaller prey fish.

Artificials: Pheasant Tail Nymph, Silver Invicta, Appetiser, Peter Ross, Dunkeld, Jersey Herd, Polystickle, Sinfoil's Fry, Minkie, Booby Minkie, Floating Fry, Sparkler, Mylar Minnow, Deceiver.

Shrimp (*Gammarus* spp)

Often present in large numbers, these greyish green crustaceans are arched throughout their body length and scuttle around close to the bottom with a side-swimming action. They're most commonly associated with weed, detritus or gravel. Usually the indigenous UK shrimp is a species of Gammarus, ranging from ½in to ¾in (12–18mm) in length. Recently invasive 'killer shrimps' (*Dikerogammarus villosus*) from Eastern Europe have populated some water bodies (including Grafham Water, Cambridgeshire) – these voracious invertebrate predators can grow to 1¼in (30mm) in length.

Often shrimp feeders can be tempted by an orange-coloured fly. A more common component in the diet of river fish, stillwater fish will take shrimp during windy weather (which agitates the lake bed) or early in the season.

Artificials: Hare's Ear Nymph, Shrimp, Red-spot Shrimp, Dunkeld, Kingfisher Butcher.

Hog louse (*Asellus* spp)

These crustaceans (approximately ½in/15mm long) can occur in large numbers, often in shallow, weeded areas but

sometimes at depth in reservoirs. Rare or absent in waters that are nutrient poor. Associated with detritus (on which they feed), they resemble an olive brown garden wood louse.

Artificials: Hare's Ear Nymph, Hare's Ear wet fly, Diawl Bach.

Snails (*Limnea peregra, Planorbis planorbis*)

Numerous in lakes and reservoirs, the commonest species are the wandering snail, which can grow to ⅝in (20mm), and the ramshorn snail. Associated with weedy areas and browsing on algae, snails sometimes rise to the surface en masse in summer, filtering plankton from the surface film. At this time fish can focus on them and feed consistently with

(Eric Isselee)

head-and-tail rises. Migrating snails can be difficult for anglers to see because snails hang under the water surface.

Artificials: Black & Peacock Spider, Orange Nymph, Cove Nymph, Floating Snail.

Alder fly (*Sialis* spp)

A predator of the silt and mud at the bottom of lakes, this insect is most usually encountered by stillwater anglers in its larval form, as the larva offers a good mouthful to early season fish as it crawls around on the lake bottom. It crawls ashore to emerge as an adult, which has hard, strongly

(Bastian Kienitz)

veined wings resembling smoked 'church windows' which rest in a roof-shape above its dark body (the adult is about 1in/25mm long).

Artificials: Alder fly, Alder Nymph, Ombudsman, Ivens' Green & Brown Nymph, Ace of Spades.

Leech (*Hirudidae*)

Easily recognised as long, worm-like swimmers with suckers at either end of the body, leeches move with a looping, sinuous action, are mainly dark coloured, black or brown, and lengths vary (up to 4in/100mm). Due to their free-swimming nature leeches are very often taken by trout.

Artificials: Black Tadpole, Black Marabou lure, Brown or Black Woolly Bugger.

Daphnia (*Daphnia* spp)

Daphnia are tiny crustacea that feed on suspended algae and are found in massive numbers in reservoirs and lakes. The sheer number of daphnia makes them a hugely important part of a fish's diet. However, because each individual is very small (1–5mm/0.04–0.20in) they're consumed by fish as a planktonic food, rather than on an individual basis; trout often cruise through the water, mouth agape, filtering out the tiny morsels from the 'clouds' of individuals (known as daphnia blooms). Daphnia are light-sensitive, so they drop deeper in brighter sunlight and trout often may follow them down. Daphnia-feeding trout are unlikely to fall for a tiny imitation, but during concentrated feeding spells they may take other types of fly, particularly orange ones.

Artificials: Whisky Fly, Orange Nymph, Orange Booby, Coral Booby, Soldier Palmer, Clan Chief, Black & Green lure, Cat's Whiskers.

↓ Daphnia-feeding trout.

Terrestrials (terrestrial insects)

Apart from the water, the other source of fish food comes from the surrounding land. Pasture, crops, forestry, parkland, heather and peat moorland will all have their own associated insect fauna, much of which flies. If these 'terrestrial' insects happen to land in the water, most are ill-equipped to escape the cloying effect of the surface, and are usually drowned.

The contribution of land-born insects to the diet of freshwater fish should never be underestimated, particularly in upland, acidic waters, where the aquatic life is generally poor. In infertile waters, the number of terrestrial insects in a trout's diet is highly significant, and studies show that on other rivers and streams too the amount of terrestrial insects consumed by fish over the summer months is higher than one might expect.

On windy days, the angler should study his surroundings and be aware of any airborne insects that might pitch into the water, because the fish certainly will.

Daddy-long-legs (*Tipula* spp)

One of the most dramatic terrestrials enjoyed by fish and imitated by fly fishers. The gangling crane fly hatches on land, marsh or water from pupae known as 'leatherjackets' that feed on the roots of grasses. In August and September mass hatches can occur for weeks on end, particularly if the summer weather is warm and moist. If a steady stream of these insects is flying on the breeze then a lot will inevitably fall into the water, to represent a sizeable mouthful to a fish. However, at most times of the season a daddy-long-legs can lure a fish to take at the surface. Recently anglers have discovered that sometimes an orange- or red-bodied artificial can attract the attention of cruising fish more than the natural buff or brown.

Artificials: Adult Daddy, Hopper, Foam-bodied Daddy, Orange or Red chenille-bodied Daddy.

(Bildagentur Zoonar GmbH)

↑ Hawthorn fly: the Bibio family of flies are characterised by very long, hairy legs.

Hawthorn fly (*Bibio marci*)

Black, swarming, with long, dangling hind legs, the hawthorn fly is so called because it appears at the same time – but only for a few short weeks – as the white-petalled hawthorn blossom, one of the first bushes to come into flower and a harbinger of spring.

Hawthorn flies are poor fliers (and are even worse swimmers). On windy spring days be alert for slashing rises on rivers and stillwaters, which is a signal hawthorns are being taken by opportunistic fish.

Sometimes, in preference to the dry fly, fishing an all-black wet fly through the waves can be highly profitable.

Artificials: Dry Hawthorn, Black Hopper, Ace of Spades, Black & Peacock Spider.

Heather fly (*Bibio pomonae*)

Similar to the hawthorn fly, the heather fly is associated with summer days and heather moorland. Easily distinguished by its red-orange upper legs, some years yield prolific, prolonged hatches, extending from July through to September.

Artificials: Bibio, Heather Fly, Bibio Hopper.

Black gnats (*Bibio johannis, Dilophus febrilis, Hilara maura*)

Commonly seen swarming close to the river surface during summer, from May onwards. They fly in a shifting, to-and-fro movement. On a windy day these small flies (approx. ¼in/5–7mm) can be forced into the water in large numbers, where they're easily picked off by trout. Sometimes a small wet fly to imitate the drowned insect works better than a more imitative dry fly.

Artificials: Black Gnat, Parachute Black Gnat, Kate McLaren, Black Spider, Black Pennell.

Ants (order *Hymenoptera*)

Artificials: At certain days of high summer when the weather is settled and warm without the threat of rain, swarms of ants appear all over the country. A phenomenon of late July or August, ant hatches are timed to maximise the chance of

(Stephane Bidouze)

↑ Flying ants can signal great dry fly sport.

cross-breeding, so if you see a flying ant you can be sure there are many others about too. Ants aren't good fliers and can become trapped in the surface, and trout in particular have a penchant for eating ants. When this occurs – from lowland reservoir to upland loch – it can signal great dry fly sport.

Artificials: Dry Ant (Black or Brown), Parachute Black Gnat, Black Hopper, Foam-bodied Ant.

Aphids (Aphidoidea spp)

The gardener's greenfly isn't only associated with roses – it's common on many species of plant, including the leaves of trees. As a result these tiny flies are present close to the waterside in their millions. As well as being bright green, aphids can also be black and white. They are very small (0.04–0.4in/1–10mm) and vulnerable to frost and leaf-fall, so settled, clear conditions in autumn with an overnight frost can see thousands fall into the water, where they're taken steadily by feeding trout. Very difficult to see in the water but often the cause of consistent 'metronomic' rising.

Artificials: Tiny, size 18–20 black or green dry flies.

↓ Greenfly: aphids - the curse of the gardener - also live on trees and often fall into the river in their millions after an early frost.

(Henrik Larsson)

Beetles

Beetles are a very common food source, particularly on upland streams, where various *Staphylinidae* species of beetle are predominant. These become active as soon as the soil warms, and are prone to falling into rivers and lakes. Trout see beetles as a regular large mouthful of protein. Peacock herl-bodied flies are useful for imitating beetles, as the feather herl possesses the same natural iridescence as the black beetle's chitin coat.

On upland heather moorland, the coch-y-bonddu beetle (*Phyllopertha horticola*), a small beetle (²⁄₅in/10mm long) it can hatch out in large numbers (generally in June or July). The ¼in (6mm) long heather beetle (*Lochmaea suturalis*) hatches during July or August. Both species are prolific and can pitch into the water en masse, especially on windy days. Beetles aren't easily seen on the surface of the water, as they tend to float in the film rather than on it.

Artificials: Double Badger, Peacock-bodied Klinkhamer, Coachman, Foam Beetle, Bibio, Black & Peacock Spider, Coch-y-Bonddu, June Bug, Wickham's Fancy, Red Tag.

Dungfly (*Scathophaga* spp)

These golden yellow flies are part of the natural breakdown

⬇ Dungfly: worth imitating downwind of pastureland.

of domestic animal dung, as their eggs are laid in the dung and the larvae feed on it before burrowing into the surrounding ground to pupate. The adults are a common, all-season terrestrial 'drop-in', especially on lakes, reservoirs, lochs and loughs that are surrounded by pastureland populated by sheep or cows. This is possibly more so in northern and upland areas. The author has encountered them as reliable fishing imitations on Loch Tay, Orkney and the Outer Hebrides, always whilst fishing downwind of a sheep or cow pasture.

Artificials: Wickham's Fancy, Dry Greenwells, Yellow Hopper, Dungfly, Golden Olive Bumble.

⬇ Droneflies can often fall into reservoirs in high numbers, esopecially after hot, dry spells.

Other terrestrials

There are many other terrestrial flies that may come to the attention of opportunistic trout and are therefore worth considering as options for imitation. Most of them are more likely to be encountered on windy days, when a combination of the insects' vegetation habitat, the proximity of the water and its poor ability to fly mean they end up in the water. This list includes moths, shield bugs (*Pentatomoidea* spp), drone flies (*Syrphidae* spp), caterpillars (all species), slugs (all species), worms (*Annelida* spp), grasshoppers (*Caelifera* spp), wasps and bees (*Hymenoptera*) and green-leaf weevil (*Phyllobius* spp).

Bigger fare

Other non-aquatic animals sometimes end up being the target of the more predatory species. Mice, frogs and newts often appear in autopsies, and pike are well known for taking ducklings.

STILLWATER TROUT FISHING

A rainbow is landed from Tenterden Lakes in Kent.

'Stillwater' refers to man-made reservoirs, pools, gravel pits and man-made lakes that are stocked with trout, rainbows or browns or both. In this context, a 'small stillwater' would be considered to be any water body under 50 acres (20 hectares) or so. Small stillwaters tend to operate more on a 'put-and-take' management whereby regular stockings take place to top up the population of trout removed by anglers. These can be found all over the UK and Ireland, but tend to proliferate where population is densest.

'Larger stillwaters' in essence refers to large water-supply reservoirs, the largest in the UK being Rutland Water at 3,000 acres (1,200 hectares). Such stillwaters hold large stocks of fish, many of which become naturalised and grown-on, feeding on the rich aquatic life supported by the surrounding agricultural land.

Less densely populated areas (south-west England, Wales, northern England and much of Scotland) usually tend to support their own wild lakes, and the fishing there should be treated differently, as the fish stocks are wild and behave in a different manner (see Chapter 10).

Small stillwater trout fishing

Small stillwaters tend to have manicured banks. That's partly because they're managed on a more intensive scale, but also because small stillwater trout fishing doesn't normally involve wading. They too can provide great sport where wild waters are in short supply. A pair of stout boots is all that's required in terms of footwear, as all casting takes place from the bank.

Small stillwaters can be divided into two distinct types: opaque waters and clear – stalking – waters.

Gearing up for small stillwaters

Tackle for small stillwaters includes rods of between #5 and #8 with a floating line, although an intermediate can

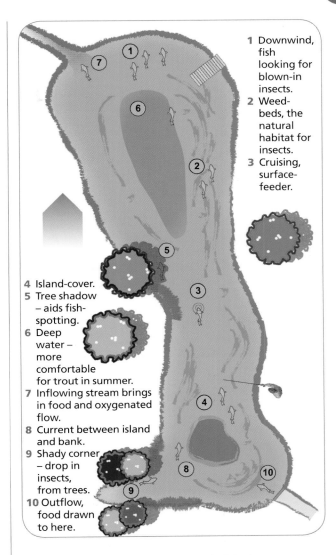

1 Downwind, fish looking for blown-in insects.
2 Weed-beds, the natural habitat for insects.
3 Cruising, surface-feeder.
4 Island-cover.
5 Tree shadow – aids fish-spotting.
6 Deep water – more comfortable for trout in summer.
7 Inflowing stream brings in food and oxygenated flow.
8 Current between island and bank.
9 Shady corner – drop in insects, from trees.
10 Outflow, food drawn to here.

sometimes be an advantage. On heavily fished waters (where fish become 'line shy') a clear or camouflaged intermediate may be a good buy, as would opting for a fly line at the lighter, 5-weight end of the scale. The reason for a heavier, #8 outfit would be if the water was stocked with very large – 10lb plus – rainbows. An #8 rod is stiffer and stronger than a #5, which is useful when landing bigger fish.

A tapered leader with a tippet going down to a minimum of 5lb BS, 12–15ft long with a single fly would be a standard set-up, especially on clear waters. Some small waters let anglers use two flies on a leader. You don't have to fish that way, but it can increase the chance of a fish finding your flies. A two-fly leader would consist of a 9ft tapered leader with a 3ft or 4ft tippet attached, the dropper tied in where the taper meets the tippet. Alternatively, a three-fly cast might comprise a short section of tapered leader (7ft) with two droppers at 3–4ft spacings. (NB: the rules on some fisheries may forbid the use of multiple fly casts, so check before you set up. And some fisheries set minimum leader strengths – again, check the rules).

↑ Fan your casts systematically to search the water.

Where to start?

If the fishery manager or lodge aren't providing any clues, and the fishery itself isn't giving you any direction on what to do or where to fish (see Chapter 15), then you need to think about where to start.

Begin by testing the wind. If it's windy, then you ideally want the wind to come from the opposite side to your casting hand (*ie* from the left if you're a right-handed caster) – this makes casting easier – or at your back. If you're an experienced caster, and enjoy more of a challenge, then fishing into the wind can be rewarding. Fishing with a strong wind blowing on to your casting hand makes casting most difficult of all.

Next, study the fishery itself. Where does it drop away into a good fishing depth (6–12ft)? Is there an inflow? Can you fish close to a weed bed? Is there a quieter corner, overshadowed by trees? If there are fishing platforms, pick one that offers some features to cast at, for instance a weed bed situated in the centre of the lake, or the edge of an island.

General prospecting/searching

Using a floating line is sufficient to explore most small stillwaters, and is the easiest line to handle in terms of fishing and casting.

To start with, it's best to cover the options by using a two- or three-fly leader. However, if you're a novice caster and uncomfortable about using multiple-fly leaders, then keep it simple and stick to a single fly. Untangling a leader of three flies every other cast wastes both time and the opportunity for success.

Make a good start by tying on a general lure/attractor on the point, say a size 10 Black & Green Marabou lure. On the middle dropper try something more suggestive as food, say a Hare's Ear Nymph (size 12). Then, on the top dropper, something the cruising trout might expect to see on any day of the year – a Midge Pupa, size 14.

Cast out, not too far to start with, and search the water close to your feet. By allowing the flies to settle longer after each cast they'll sink, and thus fish deeper. The retrieve (how you move the flies) can vary from a very slow figure-of-eight to a fast, steady pull (see Chapter 14). Fan the casts, working right to left to cover as much water as possible. Count the flies down after each cast (3 seconds, 8 seconds, 20 seconds etc), so if you start to catch the bottom on your retrieve you

can build a mental picture of the contour of the lakebed in front of you. Now cast a bit further if you can, and keep fanning the casts systematically, varying the retrieves and the depth at which you fish the flies.

After a while, if nothing has happened, try changing the flies. If you haven't caught the bottom, fish a slightly heavier fly on the point, and try a different colour scheme. Try a Gold-head Damsel on the point. Change the nymphs: put a Pheasant Tail Nymph on the middle dropper and a Claret Spider on the top.

Start the search process again. Still nothing? It might be time for a move, or a different tactic.

Sink-and-draw

Sink-and-draw is a tactic that suits mobile, marabou-tailed flies well, especially those with weight at their heads, such as the Gold-head Damsel. It's best used on a floating line with a longish leader – 12ft and longer. Having cast out and allowed the fly to sink, the fly is fished with a pull-pause retrieve. Pulls can be anything from 6in (15cm) or 1ft

↑ Gold-head Damsel Nymph – can work all season through, but is best in the summer months when adults are seen flying. Fish it around weed beds with a pull-and-pause retrieve, or 'on the drop'.

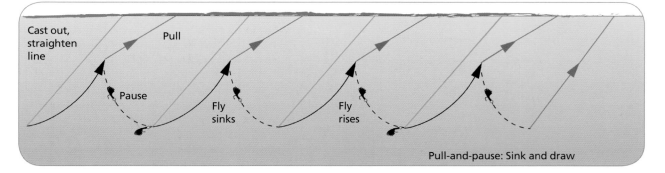

Cast out, straighten line

Pull

Pause

Fly sinks

Fly rises

Pull-and-pause: Sink and draw

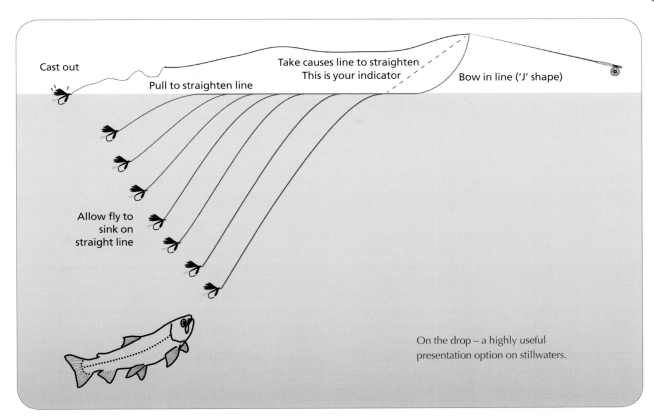

Cast out

Pull to straighten line

Take causes line to straighten
This is your indicator

Bow in line ('J' shape)

Allow fly to sink on straight line

On the drop – a highly useful presentation option on stillwaters.

(30cm) to an arm's length (1m). This lifts the fly in the water, and the pause allows the fly to sink back down towards the bottom, whereupon another pull brings the fly to life. Some fish find this retrieve irresistible. Good flies to fish like this are Shrimps, Chompers, Marabou-tailed baitfish patterns, big Cove Nymphs and Black Tadpole.

Fishing 'on the drop'

Another tactic which some trout find irresistible (probably because it's so natural) is a fly falling through the water 'on the drop'.

↓ Appetiser – another mobile pull-and-pause fly. Designed to mimic a perch fry. Good 'on the drop' presentation for bigger waters, especially when trout are slashing at shoals of fry to maim small fish before returning to mop up the dying.

- ■ Select a fly that will fall slowly through the water column, rather than plummet to the bottom. This might be a nymph dressed on a lightweight hook, or even a heavy hook or a marabou lure (the marabou acts like a parachute, slowing the fall of the fly) – a 'drowned' (sinking) dry fly can be deadly sometimes.
- ■ A vital requirement is for the angler to be in direct contact with the free-falling fly. In order to read a take 'on the drop', the line needs to be straightened after casting out. This means, having made the cast, pulling in line until the angler is certain that the fly line and the leader between himself and the fly are in a dead straight line. This way, as soon as a fish takes the fly the line will tighten and register through the line tightening in the rod-rings.
- ■ In order to further exaggerate the 'on the drop' take, the tip of the fly line, the butt leader and much of the thicker part of the tapered leader can be greased up, using Mucilin. This makes the line much more visible on the surface, and any movement of it is easily seen. If a fish takes 'on the drop' simply lift the rod to tighten into the fish. This is a useful technique to present single nymphs to fish nymphing in lakes.

Dry fly

If fish are rising, then it's simply a matter of working out what insect the fish are taking at the surface (see Chapter 15). Having identified the size, colour and stage of the insect's life cycle that the trout are targeting – let's say a hatching medium-sized olive midge pupa – then we might

→ Claret Hopper – a reliable stillwater dry fly.

select a size 14 Olive Shuttlecock Buzzer. Fluorocarbon tippet sinks, so use a leader of either nylon or co-polymer. Some anglers like to use a short tippet of fine fluorocarbon to disguise (sink) the leader near the fly, but don't use a full-length fluorocarbon leader, as this sinks and will drag the fly underwater with it.

Cast the fly out into the likely area where you've seen fish rising. Gather the bulk of any loose, slack line so you can connect with the fly if required, by simply lifting your rod tip (at the same time clamping the line with your rod-hand forefinger at the handle – see 'The Gather' in Chapter 14). Now wait. A patrolling fish, looking for midge pupae, will find your fly if you've done your detective work and got the colour, size and stage of hatch the fish is taking correct.

When the fish takes, it will confidently push its nose out of the water, engulf your fly, submerge and continue swimming. It's important that you don't strike (lift the rod tip) too quickly. Take your time. Don't panic. Let the fish turn down with the fly. The old adage states that the angler, on seeing the fish take the dry fly, should recite 'God save the Queen' before lifting the rod; alternatively, count to three – slowly. A good guide, and worth remembering. Strike too early and you'll feel nothing, and pull the fly out of the fish's mouth. A golden opportunity missed.

Fishing a dry fly 'blind'

A cruising fish might not be interested in your nymphs and lures, but trout are opportunists and sometimes a dry fly can persuade them to take even when no fish are feeding on dry flies. In fact, this is one of the deadliest and most exciting presentations in the game.

Again, the fly is cast out into a likely patrol area and left to sit. This is a game of patience. Leave the fly sitting stationary as long as you can. If you want to keep busy, then twitch the fly occasionally by lifting the rod tip slightly to tighten the line between rod tip and fly and 'tug' the fly a few millimetres; this will sit it up on its hackles and bring it to life. Sometimes this is enough to attract the attention of a trout cruising way down below. Don't worry if you can't see trout rising in the lake – they can see what's lying on the surface.

Targeting rising fish

In a lake trout cruise upwind. If fish are rising consistently, cast your flies so they come to lie 2yd or 3yd (2–3m) directly upwind in the path of the moving fish. Altering your leader to be shorter – say 12ft (4m) – will make casting accurately quicker and easier.

Stalking (clear) waters

These are mainly located in southern England where chalk-stream aquifers and springs feed the lake and the anglers target fish that they can see. As the term 'stalking' suggests, first the angler needs to spot their fish, so they need to approach the water carefully, keeping a low profile and trying not to appear on the skyline or cast their shadow across the water. The angler also needs polarised sunglasses to cut out any surface glare from the water surface, and a dark-peaked cap to shade any extraneous light from their eyes.

Most stillwater stocked fish will be rainbows, and these tend to patrol on a regular route, so once a fish is spotted you can plan to ambush it next time it comes your way. Remember, though, that if you can see the fish, then in all probability the fish has already seen you, so keep low and move slow; any sudden movement will scare the fish and it won't take, and may disappear.

Having decided on your ambush point you need to decide how deep the fish is patrolling. This is quite difficult to judge, and comes with experience. When you think the fish is coming, or can see it patrolling back into range, cast your fly so that it'll have sunk to the fish's depth by the time it swims on to the ambush point. Now you have a choice – move the fly or leave it still. Either way continue to watch the fish. It's highly likely that you won't be able to see your fly. However, the fish should see it if it's fishing at the correct level. If you see the fish move slightly off-line, rise up or tip down, shudder or flare its fins, or you see the blink of white as it opens its mouth, anywhere near where you think your fly might be then this is the signal to strike. By strike, we mean smoothly lift the rod tip, with the line clamped tightly on to the rod handle by your rod-hand forefinger and your line hand holding the rest of the line tight. This lifting action will drive the hook home.

If the patrolling fish doesn't react to your fly then either it didn't see the fly (it was fishing at the wrong level) or it ignored your fly, in which case switch the fly pattern.

There are legion fly patterns to try on a patrolling fish, from gaudy lures and mobile marabou Damselfly Nymphs to small aquatic nymph imitations and tiny, sparsely dressed leaded bugs. If these don't work, then perhaps the presentation is wrong. The first thing you can do with ease is to alter the retrieve (or don't retrieve at all – just keep in touch with the flies). You could extend the leader by another 3ft to attain more depth, perhaps adding a short tippet section of clear fluorocarbon, or you could switch to an intermediate fly line with a short (9ft) leader, to change the angle of retrieve.

Induced take

This is a tactic that trout (and grayling in particular) often find irresistible. To induce a take we make a fly rise up and

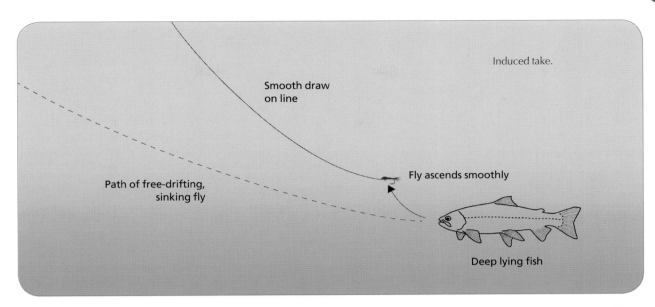

Induced take.

Smooth draw
on line

Fly ascends smoothly

Path of free-drifting,
sinking fly

Deep lying fish

away from directly in front of the fish's eyes. This can provoke an instinctive 'induced' take from the fish – it excites their 'prey drive'.

With a visible stalked fish, pin-point precision is vital for the induced take. The fly needs to be just ahead of the fish's eyes, at the same depth as the fish. Timing is crucial. The fly needs to be drawn smoothly away from the fish – a pull of 6in to 1½ft (0.5m), or a lift in the water, as though the fly is suddenly escaping from the fish. An induced fish doesn't require a strike, as it simply latches on to the fly.

When All Else Fails: leaded with a tuft of white deer hair to aid visibility.

Keys to seeing into water

Fish spotting can be a difficult skill to learn, but it becomes easier the more one practises. However, there are a number of ways to hone your proficiency:

- Try to look into the water, not on to it – *ie* try to focus on the bottom, not the ripples or waves on the surface.
- Use any shadow cast by trees, bushes etc, that cuts out the glare on the surface of the water.
- Look for movement in the water – a fish will either be swimming or, if not, will be using its fins and tail to maintain station, and opening its mouth to breathe.
- Keep scanning the water in all directions, constantly looking for signs of movement. On a small stillwater a fish might appear from any direction.
- Keep an eye on the water surface for boils, sips and rises – giveaway signs of a fish.
- Don't be in a hurry. Study the same stretch of water for a good length of time. As your eyes tune into the light, depth and underwater world you'll find seeing underwater becomes easier.
- If you catch a fish, or land a fish for someone, try to focus

(Timurpix)

on the fish as it's being played. This gets your eyes accustomed to what a fish looks like in the water, its form, how it moves and what shade of colour it is.

■ In sunlight, look for a fish's shadow. Although they're camouflaged, their shadow on the bottom often gives them away.

Reservoir trout fishing

Where to start?

A first visit to a large man-made reservoir or lake for fly fishing can be a forbidding experience. Reservoirs can extend for hundreds, if not thousands of acres, and resemble inland seas. Thus the key to successful reservoir trout fishing lies in the angler's ability to 'read the water'. This means assimilating as much information as possible about what's currently happening on the water and where the fish might be located.

Luckily, most big waters are patrolled by wardens, who are on the water every day and have up-to-the-minute knowledge about which areas are fishing well and what methods are being used to catch fish. As a result, wardens are the best source of information when it comes to where to fish and what to use.

Often a chalkboard in the lodge will give updated details of the best areas to fish, best flies and best methods. (If you're as forgetful as I am, take a photo of the board and a map on your phone/tablet for reference during the day.) Failing this, check the weekly reports in magazines or on websites to try and get a handle on how you should be tackling the water.

Of course, much will depend on whether you're fishing from the bank or a boat. Boats allow a wider range of access and cover more water, but are isolated from information gathering once launched – make sure you and your boat partner have identified the best areas of the reservoir to try before setting out. Take a fishery map if you can get one, so that you're certain you're fishing the right areas. Otherwise, identify the best areas through local landmarks. The phrase 'time spent in reconnaissance is seldom wasted' is very true in all walks of fly fishing.

The visiting bank angler will most likely encounter other, local bank anglers, who are always an important source of information. Asking about flies and tactics is always worth doing should you encounter them when working around the reservoir perimeter. You could follow the locals and fish close to where they're fishing, but bear in mind the rules of etiquette. Don't encroach on their fishing space.

Once out on the reservoir, what other clues can the water, banks and features in the reservoir offer us? The mark of a true angler is finding your 'own' fish. Most anglers like to find their own fish – but where? Although reservoirs offer nothing but a massive grey sheet of water there are plenty of clues within that sheet that can mean 'Fish here!'

Eyebrook Reservoir, Northamptonshire. At 440 acres the wardens or the lodge's chalkboard is the best place for information on the fishing.

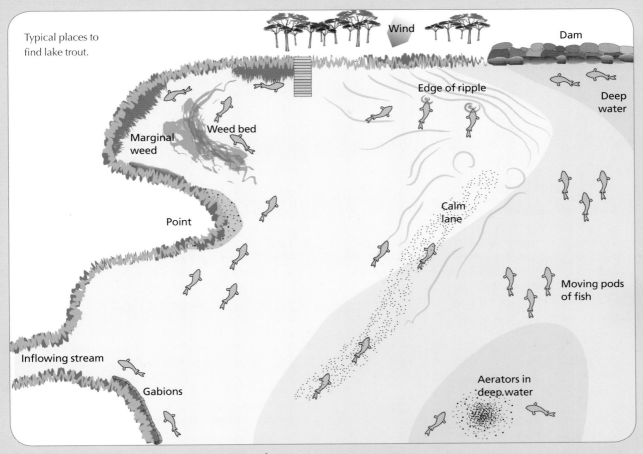

Typical places to find lake trout.

Wind

Dam

Edge of ripple

Deep water

Marginal weed

Weed bed

Point

Calm lane

Moving pods of fish

Inflowing stream

Gabions

Aerators in deep water

Reservoir clues

■ **Points** – if in doubt, head for a point. A point will indicate some accessible deeper water, possibly from three sides. It also offers the best chance of a fish moving past within casting range. Rainbow trout in particular are constantly on the move as soon as the reservoir warms sufficiently.

■ **Weed beds** – most aquatic insects thrive in weed more than anywhere else: olives, damselflies, Corixa, caddis, snails etc and fish fry use weed as shelter. Fly fishers have a tendency to avoid weed, because it catches on their flies. However, those that fish around, on the edges and between weeds are likely to encounter feeding fish.

■ **Streams and dykes** – these cut a deeper channel and bring in silt and nutrients, on which insects and small fish thrive. Streams are also the trout's access to

spawning areas, so are key locations at both ends of the season for gathering trout.

■ **Dams** – offer deep water close in. Usually constructed of stone, a good habitat for aquatic insects. Fish holding off dam walls often move close in, right on the edge. Take care not to over-cast these fish and scare them with the shadow of the line landing above their heads.

■ **Trees and bushes** – provide shelter in wind, and are also an important source of terrestrial insects that blow into the reservoir. Aphids, caterpillars, beetles, hawthorn flies, can all find themselves pitched in, helpless, drowning in the water.

⬇ Weed beds harbour insects and small fish and are obvious places to find trout.

(Kennerth Kullman)

■ **Cows** – what could cows have to do with fishing? Firstly, their dung is the nursery of cow-dung flies; and secondly they browse on pastureland, in which the daddy-long-legs (crane fly) pupates. In addition, a herd of cows can cause a mass mobilisation of these flies, which take off, drift on the wind, and pitch into the water. Fishing downwind of a herd of cows is often a good idea.

⬆ A fish from a calm lane. The smooth water of the lane can be seen stretching downwind of the rowlock.

■ **Calm lanes** – on a windy day the ruffled waves will start to show lanes of flatter, foam-flecked water, which stretch out like Roman roads straight downwind. They're caused by the meeting of two currents, which cancel each other out, and indicate quite clearly where any insects carried on those currents will be accumulated. Trout cruise up these lanes, looking for trapped insects, or daphnia accumulations. Aim to land your flies across or on the edges of these lanes. This is generally only possible from a boat (anchored or drifting), but sometimes the bank angler can reach a calm lane from a point (see above).

■ **Shallows** – wherever light can reach the bottom of a reservoir, the bottom will be more productive in insect life and trout will be present in order to feed. The surrounding topography and slope of the bank will give an idea of how deep the water might be, but the presence of weed beds, islands, rocks and even up-ended swans also suggests shallows.

■ **Muddied edges** – in high winds the water can become agitated to such an extent that a belt of muddied water builds along the windward bank. Although fishing in cloudy water is a difficult proposition for the fly fisher, fishing in the clear water at the edge of coloured water is worth the effort, since the action of the wind kicks up shrimps, caddis and bloodworms in the shallows.

■ **Boils** – during high summer many reservoirs pump air in using diffuser pipes on the bottom of the lake to oxygenate the water. These 'boils' – the lake surface looks like a mass of boiling, bubbling water – not only attract

⬇ Floating net cages are havens for midges and fry.

trout because of enhanced oxygen levels, but also lift and circulate insect-life from the bottom of the lake: hog lice, shrimps and midge larvae/pupae. As a result, these can be focal points for feeding trout in high summer.

■ **Cages** – reservoir trout are often reared in floating net cages anchored over deeper water. The permanent submerged nets, ropes and walk-boards are havens for midge larvae, and shelter for fish fry. This is apart from any fish pellets that might escape through the net. As a result, trout – especially large ones – tend to be found living close to such cages.

■ **Water-towers** – these towers are usually the draw-off point for the reservoir and not only provide structure for midge larvae and caddis larvae to cling to but also structure for fish fry, and sometimes a current, which in turn draws trout food towards the out-take point.

↑ A fish sips on a flat calm surface.

Rising fish

The simplest method of locating fish is seeing them. In calm water, or – to the experienced eye – in a ripple or light wave, surface-feeding trout give themselves away. Rings of the rise in calm water, or noses, pushes, bulges, furrowing, slashes and counter-waves in a ripple all suggest feeding fish…and a feeding fish is a catchable one.

One of the best areas to see fish rising is to stand with your back to the wind and look to the boundary between the calm water and the ripple. It's here that any insects borne on the wind will be deposited. This is also a very good place to fish.

Lie of the land

The surrounding land will give both boat and bank anglers plenty of clues as to the contours of the lake bed close the margins. A gradual, sloping field merging into the water is likely to be quite shallow for some distance into the lake, whereas a high, steep bank dropping into the water from a small hill will probably indicate deeper water close in. Dams are built to be steeply sloping; inflowing streams will cut a deeper channel in the lake bed; a peninsula will drop away into deeper water at its end; a hill on one side of a bay will shelve away steeply into the bay; surface weed will indicate shallows; boat jetties suggest access to deeper water, as do submerged walls or gabions (stone-filled wire baskets placed to protect the bank from erosion); narrow bays are likely to be shallow at the head of the bay but offer deeper water on the points at either side of the inlet; a wide bay with low points either side is likely to be shallow all the way across; steeply shelving rock will usually continue down deep into the lake at the same angle.

↓ A likely corner on Brenig. The steep dam wall offers deep water close in, and the steeply eroded bank and plunging fence-line (right) indicates the water drops away quickly for the bank anglers fishing in the corner. Boat 18 drifts over an ideal fishing depth.

↑ Loch style on Loch Leven, near Edinburgh.

↑ A perfect ripple for a drift means no anchor or drogue was required on this occasion, so the maximum amount of water could be covered.

Boat-fishing tactics

Loch style

Loch-style wet fly fishing involves using a team of wet flies, often with a bushier fly on the top dropper, a smaller, sleeker wet fly or nymph on the middle and a larger wet fly, nymph or lure on the point. A typical leader would be 9, 12 or 15ft (3, 4 or 5m) with two droppers, equally spaced. There are a number of reasons for this arrangement:

- It presents three different sizes, silhouettes and patterns to the fish.
- Tying on the more aerodynamic flies towards the point, with the less aerodynamic fly close to the fly-line tip, means the whole leader of three flies will turn over in the air in sequence, so tangles are reduced.

↓ Short-lining: the rod tip is raised to keep the flies moving at the surface.

- The bushier fly on the top dropper acts as an attractor by disturbing the water surface.
- The team is normally fished on either a floater or intermediate, but can be fished on all fly lines from floaters through to full sinkers.

The team is cast out and allowed to settle for a few seconds before the flies are retrieved at varying speeds.

Setting the boat for loch style

The boat is set broadside on, to drift over or into likely fish-holding areas. The wind will determine the line and speed of drift, and the drift-speed of the boat can be restricted by the use of a drogue (sea anchor).

The speed of the drifting boat determines, to a major extent, the retrieve speed and needs to be taken into account; a boat in a keen breeze will drift quickly, thus a fast retrieve is required to counter this movement towards the flies. Thus, although the loch-style boat fisher may appear to be retrieving his flies with quick, long arm-pulls of line the flies may not be moving as quickly.

1 A short cast is made.

2 The line is retrieved and the rod tip is lifted to keep the flies moving.

3 The flies can be held in the water, twitching at the surface by continuing to raise the rod tip.

4 The flies are still in the water as the rod reaches the 1 o'clock, roll-cast position.

5 The forward tap is made, to roll out the flies...

6 ...shooting out any line retrieved.

7 A fish takes...

8 ...and is landed.

→ Soldier Palmer – a good top dropper fly for traditional loch-styling.

Otherwise called short-lining, traditional loch style involves casting an easily repeatable length of line – a roll-cast and one, perhaps two, back-casts – allowing the flies time to settle, and then using anything from figure-of-eighting to arm-long pulls to retrieve the flies; then, with a decent length of line outside the rod, the tip is lifted vertically until the top dropper fly is bulging and trickling in the surface. This action is called 'dibbling' the top dropper, and a key moment in enticing a following fish to take. This lifting action continues until the rod is vertical, leading automatically to the perfect roll-cast position, which allows the whole process to be repeated.

Long-lining

This involves casting a longer line than is traditional, allowing the flies to settle, then bringing them back using the whole variety of retrieves and finishing with a 'dibble', before

↓ Long-lining involves casting a longer line and retrieving with a variety of speeds.

TIP

It's important not to take in too much line when retrieving – sufficient line for the subsequent roll-cast is required outside the rod tip. Thus the final action of lifting of the rod tip becomes just as important a part of the retrieve as pulling in line.

repeating. This is a good alternative technique for fishing nymphs, wets or lures, and is particularly useful when fishing sinking lines, as more time can be allowed for the line to sink after the flies land. As the flies and line sink, so any slack line produced by the on-drifting boat is gathered by the angler before commencing the retrieve.

A faster fishing style, known by some anglers as 'Loch Leven style' involves casting out a longish

↑ Clan Chief – fish it fast on a long line for daphnia feeders.

length of fly line (15–20yd/15–20m), using a fast retrieve, and then, with a long length of line still outside the rod tip, lifting up smoothly into a back-cast before re-casting the team. This technique relies on luring the fish into making an instant decision on either taking the flies or refusing them.

THE COUNTDOWN

When long-lining, the sink-rate of the line, and the time it's allowed to settle after casting, will determine how deep the flies will fish. For instance, a type 7 sinker (sinking at 7in/18cm per second) allowed to sink for ten seconds before the retrieve, will fish at a depth of approximately 6ft (2m). The angler can count down the flies ('one second, two second…') to calculate the depth at which the line is fishing. Obviously, the longer the line is cast out, the deeper the angler can allow the flies to sink before retrieving. Counting down takes concentration, but it can help build a mental picture of the lake's bed very quickly. It can also identify the exact feeding depth of fish, so it's worth focussing on such a skill.

1 After allowing the flies to settle, they're speedily retrieved with quick strips.

2 The forefinger on the rod is crucial in maintaining tension on the line in case a fish takes.

3 The flies are lifted to the surface...

4 ...and out, into the back-cast.

5 The cast made, the retrieve recommences. This time, a fish takes. The forefinger traps the line against the handle to keep it tight.

The hang

When fishing an intermediate or sunk line, fish may follow the team of flies but not take them. Of course, because this happens underwater the angler may be unaware of this. One technique that can convince any following fish into taking is to 'hang' the flies at the end of the retrieve. This involves lifting the flies up through the water column towards the end of the retrieve and then suspending them or even allowing them to sink slowly (by dropping the rod tip, as if lowering the flies on a crane) before lifting them to the surface and re-casting. In the event of a take, the angler watches the line for sudden tightening, or a sudden change of angle, or looks for an underwater flash of a turning fish as it takes the flies. A brightly coloured top dropper helps both to attract fish and as a 'sighter' to indicate a take to the flies below it. Some anglers whip a short thread 'marker' on to their line so that when they feel it in their retrieve hand they know the exact length of line for a roll-cast and are at the ready following the sub-surface 'hang'.

↑ A fish turns and heads back down into the depths after taking 'on the hang'.

The sweep

The design of fly lines for casting means they sink faster in the belly than at the very tip. Hence the shape of the line as it sinks through the water column describes a 'C' shape or, as it sinks deeper, a sickle.

The sweep of the flies as they're pulled along this curved path can prove attractive to deep-lying fish which might take the flies or follow them (see 'The hang', above).

➔ A Cormorant trailing on the point on a sweep-and-hang cast may entice a following fish to take.

Loch-style dry fly

This is one of the most effective and visual of boat or bank fishing tactics. It can pull fish up from the depths, even if none are showing at the surface, and is well worth mastering. Dry fly can be fished in anything from flat calm to small waves. It involves a longish leader of 12ft (4m) or more, with one or two droppers, depending on whether two or three flies are preferred. A tapered section of leader running between the fly-line tip and the first dropper will aid turnover and presentation.

➔ Claret Emerger – an excellent loch-style dry fly.

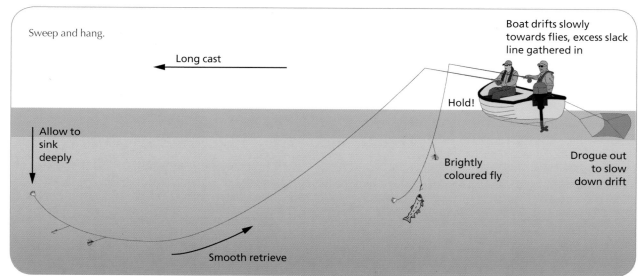

Sweep and hang.

Long cast

Boat drifts slowly towards flies, excess slack line gathered in

Hold!

Allow to sink deeply

Brightly coloured fly

Drogue out to slow down drift

Smooth retrieve

TIP

One of the most difficult things to achieve when dry-fly fishing is being able to see the flies on the water. To help, put a large dry fly – a Sedge, Daddy-long-legs, bushy hackled dry fly, or a white hackle-tufted dry – on the top dropper to act as your 'sighter'. Any surface movement made by a fish in the vicinity of your sighter fly should be considered to be a take to the lower-riding artificial dries, and met with the corresponding timed strike.

Confidence that the flies are indeed floating at the surface is paramount to fishing them successfully. To reassure yourself that the flies are floating, flick them out just in front of the boat before casting to check each one floats, not sinks.

Stillwater dry flies sit fairly low in the surface, relying on oiled seal's fur, CdC, deer-hair, closed cell foam or a hackle for buoyancy.

The flies are cast out, allowed to settle, and then all the angler does is gather line as the boat drift towards them. It demands concentration, as the flies need watching constantly for signs of a take since a take must be met with a tightening of the line, otherwise the fish won't be hooked.

Applying gel to a dry fly

↑ The gel is squirted on to the forefinger and rubbed until it's liquid.

↑ The liquid is then applied sparingly to the fibres of the fly.

Traditionally, a dry fly was heavily hackled to aid floatation. Modern dry flies rely on water-repellent materials and surface tension to sit low in the water. One of the most common applications used to assist floatation is a silicone gel. The gel's consistency is temperature dependent, ranging from liquid when warm to a solid grease when cool. The way to apply it is to squeeze a small blob on to the index finger and rub the gel between forefinger and thumb until it liquefies. Then the fly is rubbed between the fingers to prime each fibre of the body, hackle, legs etc in the hydrophilic oil, but not to 'cake' or soak the fly into a congealed mass.

A cul de canard pattern doesn't require any floatant, as it floats naturally, but it will need drying when saturated (see right).

When a dry fly sinks

If your favourite dry fly sinks then there are various ways to dry it quickly. A few false-casts can help to air-dry the fibres, or a squeeze in an amadou pad can revive it completely, as can a dip-and-shake in silicone powder. Blowing on the fly or – as a last resort – squeezing it in your fleece's sleeve material can rid the fly of water, before you apply more silicone gel.

1 The saturated fly.

2 Squeeze it in the amadou pad.

3 The amadou draws a lot of the excess water off the fly.

4 Put the fly in the Dry Shake container, ensuring the leader is in the slot.

5 Shake the powder.

6 The dried fly is ready for action once again.

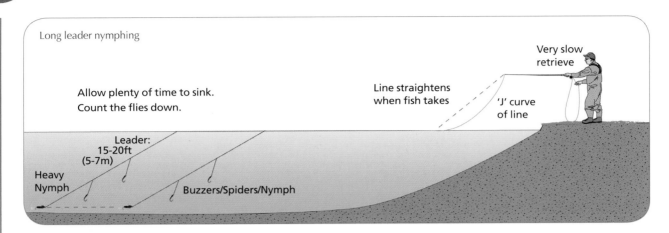

Long leader nymphing

Allow plenty of time to sink.
Count the flies down.

Line straightens
when fish takes

Very slow
retrieve

'J' curve
of line

Leader:
15-20ft
(5-7m)

Heavy
Nymph

Buzzers/Spiders/Nymph

Nymphing

Nymphing is a technique used to imitate the natural aquatic life forms on which stillwater trout feed for the majority of their diet. The skills involved are presenting the flies at the correct depth, making them move in a convincing, natural manner, and detecting the take when a trout takes them.

Long-leader nymphing

Long-leader nymphing requires a floating line with a longish leader and can be practised from both bank and boat. It's easiest with a wind blowing from behind. Three flies are used on a leader ranging from 15ft (5m) up to 20ft (7m) long. The largest nymph, which occupies the point position, acts as a 'controller' – it helps the cast turn over, it sinks, and it 'stretches' the cast between the fly-line tip and the point fly. This could be a large Pheasant Tail Nymph, Stickfly, Shrimp, Cove Nymph, Bloodworm, Damselfly Nymph, large Epoxy Buzzer, or even a Black Lure.

On the droppers are other, smaller nymphs, often a Buzzer Pupa, Hare's Ear Nymph, maybe a Sedge Pupa, or perhaps a small spider pattern might occupy the top-dropper position.

Having made the cast, some line is retrieved so that the angler feels he's 'in touch' with the controller point fly. He then waits for the nymphs to sink to the required fishing level. This can be quite a long time – often a minute, sometimes two minutes if fishing from a boat into deep water – but it's still essential fishing time as the flies sink 'on the drop', and the angler should watch his line carefully in case it tightens due to a fish taking the falling nymphs as it swims by.

➜ Oily Worm: a good point fly for long-leader nymphing.

Then the retrieve starts. Usually this is a very slow figure-of-eight. Most aquatic nymphs don't move quickly – a natural cased caddis crawls slowly across the lakebed, a chironomid pupa drifts and rises on the current – so in order to imitate this as naturally as possible, a fast retrieve isn't required. The great reservoir nymph fisher, the late Arthur Cove, used to say that it should take two minutes to fish out a full, 25yd cast properly.

If your nymphs continually catch the bottom, reduce the sink-time after casting.

Other retrieves to try are 6in (15cm) draws on the line with extended pauses, or a quicker hand-twisting, trickling figure-of-eight. Another is one of yard-long (one-metre) pulls then a long – say ten-second – pause, which can attract fish 'on the drop' and then induce a take to the nymphs.

TIP

If you aren't confident with fishing a team of small nymphs slowly, try fishing two nymphs on the droppers and a leaded Tadpole style of fly on the point. Cast out, let the flies sink deeply and then retrieve them with long pulls and pauses. This sink-and-draw action can often tempt fish into taking any of the flies in the team, and is a good way to introduce the subtleties of the tactic, thereby building confidence to then fish three nymphs on their own.

Reading takes to nymphs

When fishing nymphs the angler needs to concentrate hard on his line, which will transmit any signs of a take. The best indication the nymph angler gets is from the butt of his leader, where it disappears through a 'hole' in the water surface. If the line cuts, accelerates or suddenly disappears through this hole, then the rod is lifted smartly. However, this 'hole' is extremely difficult to see in a ripple, or at distance, in which case the angler should watch along his floating line, looking for any indications of it stretching or drawing away as the fish takes.

↑ When fishing nymphs at distance, the bow in the line between rod tip and the water is your indicator for a take: if it straightens from a 'J' to a '/' then that's the signal a fish has taken the fly.

For the most reliable take indication, hold the rod so that the rod tip is a couple of feet above the water surface and watch the droop of the line between the tip-ring and the water surface. In normal conditions it will hang like a 'J', but the instant a fish takes it will straighten, rather like a coarse-fisher's swing-tip. Lift the rod smartly to connect.

There's one other take that may not manifest itself with any noticeable physical indication. Brian Clarke, one of the main protagonists of modern stillwater nymph fishing, calls it a 'sixth sense' take, which happens when the angler is so in tune with their nymph fishing that a strike is made just because they believe a fish has taken their fly. I believe this may well be due to a tiny, subliminal indication on the line or in the water that results in a reflex lift of the rod resulting in a fish hooked. Another explanation might be that the flies and fly line don't do what our experienced angler is expecting them to do in the normal passage of events, the only possible reason being that a fish has taken the flies. Whatever the magic, it does exist, and is a wonderful feeling when it works!

FLUOROCARBORN OR NYLON?

The presentation of nymphs can be varied by simply changing the leader material. This is because fluorocarbon leader material is dense and sinks far faster than nylon or co-polymer, and has a tendency to pull the flies down in the water. This is ideal if the angler wants his flies to hold deep (particularly if the flies are being dragged around in a strong cross-breeze). However, to fish the nymphs higher in the water, or drift suspended in the surface layers, a better option is to use nylon or co-polymer as a leader material.

On the swing

1 The cast with a floating line is made up and across the wind.

2 As the flies settle, the breeze starts to bow the line in the middle.

3 The wind 'bellies' the floating line, and the angler follows the belly with his rod tip.

4 The angler continues to follow the line round with his rod tip on the wind, retrieving just enough to stay in touch with the flies.

→ The Flexi-Buzzer is sufficiently realistic for cruising fish to take as it swings around inertly in the water.

This is a similar procedure and set-up to long-leader nymphing but is employed in a crosswind. It's a superb tactic to use when trout are moving upwind and past the angler's position taking buzzer (chironomid) pupae as they drift on the current. It can be employed from both bank and boat. Typically, a team of three Buzzer Pupae – the largest on the point (this can be any large nymph pattern) – is cast out across the breeze. No retrieve is required; the angler simply retrieves sufficient line to stay just in touch with his flies as they drift around on the breeze – the fly line should have a slight tautness to it. However, if the wind is too strong it may pull the flies around too quickly. In which case:

■ Make an upwind mend of the line between rod tip and flies to slow down the drift-speed of the flies.
■ Walk along the bank, working downwind, keeping pace – and always staying in touch – with the drifting flies.

DEAD DRIFTING

Actions (1) and (2) ensure that the nymphs drift more naturally, inert and at the whims of the current, rather than being pulled round by the line. This is called 'dead drifting' the team of flies, and creates a natural nymph presentation. In the above scenario, if the angler walked along the bank at the same pace as the drifting flies then this would be true dead-drifting – an excellent presentation technique.

■ Switch the leader to fluorocarbon, which sinks faster and 'bites' deeper into the water.

The take to a nymph 'on the swing' is a positive draw on the line as the fish takes the nymph and continues swimming upwind. This should be met by a smooth, sideways sweep of the rod to tighten the line and set the hook.

Straight-line nymphing

Straight-line nymphing allows for a natural presentation of nymphs, from a boat, at depth. A floating or midge-tip line is used, with a 15–20ft (5–7m) fluorocarbon leader, with equally spaced nymphs (usually Buzzer Nymphs) and a heavy,

↓ For presenting static Buzzer Nymphs at depth.

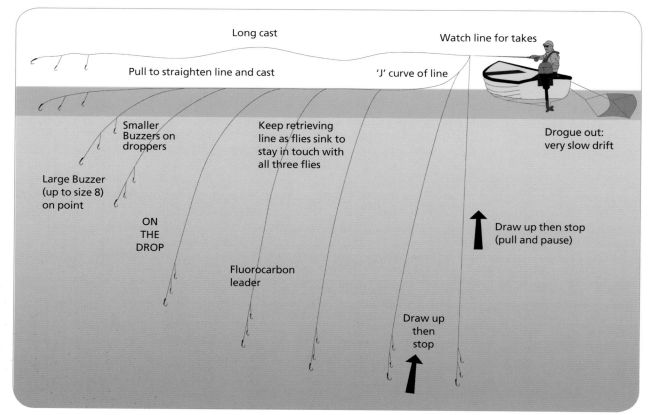

Long cast

Pull to straighten line and cast

'J' curve of line

Watch line for takes

Smaller Buzzers on droppers

Keep retrieving line as flies sink to stay in touch with all three flies

Drogue out: very slow drift

Large Buzzer (up to size 8) on point

ON THE DROP

Draw up then stop (pull and pause)

Fluorocarbon leader

Draw up then stop

→ A large (size 8 or 10) Superglue Buzzer on the point stretches down the cast of a straight-line nymph set-up and also helps it sink.

→ The FAB Blob has foam tied in as a tail, and when fished on the point sinks slowly under the weight of the line and nymphs.

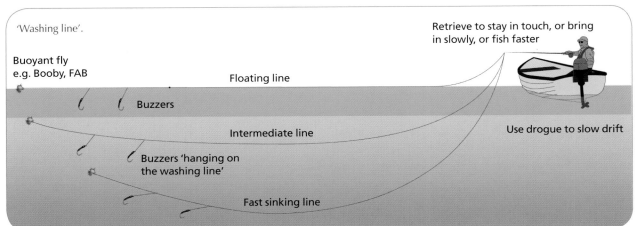

large Epoxy Buzzer Nymph (or Gold-head Bloodworm) on the point.

Ideal conditions for this method are fish feeding at depth and a very slowly drifting boat (or the boat can be at anchor). A drogue can be employed to slow the boat's drift to a minimum.

The cast is made straight downwind, then sufficient line is retrieved to straighten it and create a direct connection between retrieve hand, rod tip and point fly. The angler needs to be convinced any slack has been removed completely.

The team of flies are then allowed to sink deeply whilst the angler takes up only the slack line created by the onward-drifting boat. The flies can be allowed to sink for a minute, sometimes two, the angler studying the 'J' curve of his line between rod tip and water surface for any indication of interception of the flies by a cruising trout 'on the drop'.

Once the flies are fishing at the required depth they can be lifted through the water column with long pulls. This action causes the flies to rise naturally, and will possibly also attract any deep-lying fish's attention. It also ensures the angler is in total connection with his team of flies. After pulling, the flies are, once again, allowed to sink down in free fall, before another pull causes them to rise again. Providing the boat doesn't overrun the line, this procedure can continue until the full line has been retrieved and the leader and flies hang directly below the rod tip. They're then lifted to the surface prior to re-casting. Takes are normally solid draws on the line as the cruising fish intercepts the nymph and swims on.

The 'washing line'

The washing-line tactic is effective for suspending nymphs and fishing them slowly just under the surface. It relies on the high buoyancy of a foam-based point fly – usually a Booby, possibly a Floating Fry or Suspender Buzzer – or a Muddler (which has natural buoyancy).

It can be fished from both bank and boat, and can be fished on any line from a full floater through to a fast sinker, depending on the depth at which the angler suspects the fish are feeding. It is, however, at its most potent on a floater or an intermediate.

The leader is 12–15ft with two droppers. A long cast is made – downwind, or across the wind – and any slack line is immediately gathered to ensure the angler is in touch with all three flies. The key to this tactic is the highly buoyant point fly, which arrests the sink-rate of the team. If fished on a floating line, then the point fly doesn't sink – it stays on the surface and the nymphs sink a few inches down, suspended from the droppers between the floating line and the buoyant point fly, as if they were socks hanging from a washing line. At the same time, the point fly stretches the leader as the nymphs on the droppers continue to sink. If fished on an intermediate line the point fly will be dragged under eventually, due to the weight of the sunken line, flies and leader, but its inherent buoyancy holds the cast up on a suspended, slowly sinking curve.

Retrieves vary from static or slow figure-of-eight – which allows the nymphs to be fished in realistic, suspended fashion – through to a fast pull, which generally brings the point fly into contention as an out-and-out surface lure.

'Washing line'.

Buoyant fly e.g. Booby, FAB

Floating line

Buzzers

Intermediate line

Buzzers 'hanging on the washing line'

Fast sinking line

Retrieve to stay in touch, or bring in slowly, or fish faster

Use drogue to slow drift

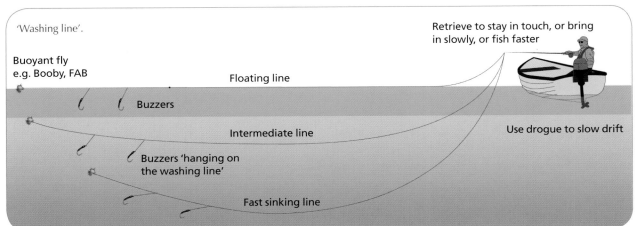

↑ A bung can be simply a buoyant indicator.

↓ A bung can be a buoyant fly – trout often take the bung!.

Coral Bung.

The bung

Another method of fishing a team of static nymphs at depth is to use a 'bung'. This is a large, buoyant, coloured polystyrene ball or foam cylinder, lashed to a hook and disguised as a 'fly' before being attached to the cast as if it was the top dropper. Its high buoyancy means it can be used to suspend a team of nymphs below it, and hold them at pre-set depths without sinking further, the bung being the all-important indicator. Some fly fishers think the method is too close to using a coarse-fisher's float, so the method has its detractors, but there's no doubt as to the efficacy of the method. The bung can also be used to allow the flies to drift around on the breeze, again maintaining the depth and acting as indicator.

For purists wishing to experiment in this 'darker' side of fly fishing, an Ethafoam Floating Fry or an Orange foam-bodied Daddy can cover both jobs of 'bung' indicator and imitative fly, suspending a team of buzzers on the droppers at 6ft (2m) and 12ft (4m) below.

Booby fishing

The inherent high buoyancy of the foam-based Booby fly lends itself to another effective tactic, this time for fishing deep, close to the lake bottom. It can be employed from the bank or from an anchored boat, and is a good method to turn to if you suspect fish are lying deep and being uncooperative, such as on a very cold day or a very bright, hot one. It's a tactic to break an otherwise 'blank' day.

The simplest set-up is to use a single Booby on a short (4–5ft/1.3–1.7m) leader attached to a fast-sinking line (type 7).

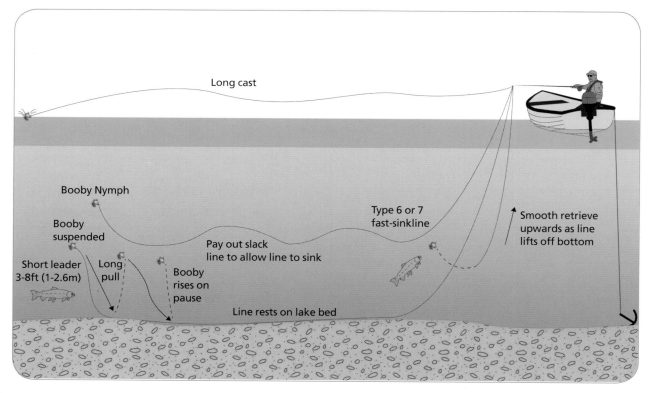

Long cast

Booby Nymph

Booby suspended

Short leader 3-8ft (1-2.6m)

Long pull

Booby rises on pause

Pay out slack line to allow line to sink

Line rests on lake bed

Type 6 or 7 fast-sinkline

Smooth retrieve upwards as line lifts off bottom

↑ The foam 'eyes' of the Booby Minkie make it highly buoyant.

Some authors advocate a very short leader of 2–3ft (0.6–1.0m), but this can tether and restrict the Booby's action.

A long cast is made, and the line is allowed sufficient time to sink to the bottom of the lake. From a boat this may require stripping off extra line from the reel and paying out this slack line into the water – by moving the rod tip from side to side to allow loose line to be pulled through the tip-ring – to allow the cast line to sink 'untethered' to the rod tip.

Once the line is on the lakebed the buoyant Booby remains suspended above it, tethered by the leader. One tactic is to simply leave the fly static and await a passing fish to pick it up. (Check the fishery rules – at certain venues this 'static Booby' tactic is banned.)

Otherwise, a figure-of-eight or pull-and-pause retrieve commences to animate the Booby as it twitches, swims, falls and rises just above the lake bottom.

Takes are often solid draws on the line, but sometimes fish can be felt 'pecking' and tugging at the fly as it's retrieved, yet a strike results in no hook-up. The solution to this problem is to either:

- Change the Booby colour or size.
- Continue to retrieve without being tempted to strike, until the pecks eventually result in a solid take.
- Add a dropper between the Booby and the tip of the fly line. To this can be tied a nymph, such as a Buzzer Pupa or a Bloodworm, which fishes deep, below the Booby and close to the lakebed. This gives the deeply lying fish a natural feeding option, other than the Booby lure.

TIP

Towards the end of the retrieve when fishing from a boat, allow the fly to rise up from the bottom, all the way to the surface as you slowly retrieve the rest of the line prior to re-casting. Often fish take the ascending Booby, so be alert for any signs of a take during the latter stages of the retrieve.

Rainbow trout and the importance of depth

Due to the fact that rainbows cruise as they feed, it's vital that the angler – particularly a boat angler – discovers the depth at which they're cruising in order to catch them. For instance, let's take a sunny summer's day with the fish moving at a depth of 8ft, feeding on the daphnia (water fleas) which are concentrated at this level. The angler who can present his flies at a depth of 8ft consistently is more likely to encounter and attract one of these trout. However, let's say some heavy cloud obscures the sun, and the daphnia concentration – being photosensitive – rises in the water column to, say, 2ft below the surface. The trout may react in the same fashion, following the food source, and begin cruising at a depth of 2ft. Suddenly, the angler fishing his flies at 8ft finds he's no longer attracting trout (his flies are being fished underneath the trout), but the angler fishing just under the surface begins to get more action.

This is just one scenario. The depth at which rainbows feed varies, and needs to be discovered on every fishing session in order for the angler to be consistently successful. For instance, in very cold water rainbows will feed hard on the bottom.

This behaviour helps to explain why fly fishers have developed such finely tuned sinking lines of specific, varying rates, and why it's important to consistently search the depths until you can contact fish consistently, and also why 'counting down' flies and lines is a particularly important route to success.

↓ Finding the depth at which rainbow trout are feeding is crucial to success.

RIVER FISHING

Casting a dry fly under the far bank in Umbria, Italy.

Types of river

Rivers vary not only in size but also in their surroundings and – more importantly – the underlying substrate (rock) that reflects their character. We can see in the accompanying boxout how pH (acidity) can affect a water's productive nature, and this is reflected in the types of river that anglers fish.

Spate stream

↑ A spate river in the French Alps.

Bouldery, running off steep, high ground, often flowing through peat moorland on an acidic, granite base. Spate streams tend to have dark, peat-stained water, support little weed-growth and hold small, dark trout. They can become mere trickles in a dry period, but also can support migratory fish populations of salmon and sea trout. They tend to fish best after rain, when the water level is high (ie in flood or in 'spate'), but dropping.

Larger spate rivers

As spate streams flow further downstream and the gradient becomes less steep, they open up into a repeating series of necks, runs, glides, dubs, tails and riffles with boulders, cobbles, ledges, gravel and sand, and some in-stream weed growth. The Americans call such rivers 'freestone rivers'. Some spate rivers flow over underlying limestone and have a higher pH, producing more weed beds and fat trout. Their height and water colour is affected by recent rain

↓ The spring-fed Nera, in Italy.

HOW ACIDITY AFFECTS WATER TYPE

The acidity of water varies throughout the country, and affects the type and productivity of the fishery. A water's acidity is is mainly due to the surrounding land of the river's or lake's catchment area and measured as a pH value – the lower the pH number, the more acidic the water. UK waters range between pH5 (acidic) and pH8 (alkali).

The most suitable pH for fish is between pH7 and 8 and those streams emanating from an underlying chalk or limestone bedrock have a pH 7.4-8.0. They run clear and mineral-rich, supporting a rich variety of plant-life and therefore a corresponding variety of aquatic insects. In contrast, the rivers and lakes of northern England and Scotland run off the peat moorland and ancient rocks and are typically of pH 5-7. Low pH water is nutrient poor, dark-tinted and supports far fewer weeds and less insect life. Fish in such waters depend to a certain extent on wind-borne terrestrial insects to supplement their diet. Any river running over a bed of chalk or limestone will see its pH elevate and its productivity rises correspondingly.

draining off the surrounding hills. They usually carry a tinge of colour – resembling a bitter beer – but become clearer the longer the rain holds off. These rivers also support grayling, pike and chub and other coarse fish.

Spring-fed stream

Springs originate from water held in 'sponge-like', porous rock. They run clear, consistently and are often of a high pH, as both limestone and chalk are the most common porous rocks. These 'silver spoon' streams are rich, productive, heavy in weed growth and gravel and support butter-coloured fat trout, pike, grayling, chub and other coarse fish. The traditional 'home' of English fly fishing is based on the clear, chalk-fed rivers of Hampshire, Wiltshire, Dorset, Sussex, Berkshire and Hertfordshire and the fly-fishing section of

↓ The peat-stained Tees, in Northumberland.

← Pike fishing on the slow-flowing Nene, Northamptonshire.

→ Searching for mullet and mackerel in St Just Creek, Cornwall.

Izaak Walton's famous book, *The Compleat Angler,* was based on the limestone streams of Derbyshire and Staffordshire. Other chalkstreams exist in Lincolnshire and Yorkshire, northern France and Belgium.

Lowland river

As a river's gradient flattens the current slows, and any sediment carried from the upland stretches is deposited as silt. Such rivers produce wide flood plains through which they meander and on to which they spill during wet spells. The lowland river temperature is warmer than further up the river, and thus carries less oxygen. Deep bends with lily pads and rushes growing at the riverside are typical, and here the river supports mainly coarse fish, along with some trout and travelling migrating salmon and sea trout.

Estuary

Where the river meets the sea, it's linked by a mud-lined or sandy boundary. Twice a day this brackish water zone extends far up the river during high tide, only for the freshwater to reclaim this zone as the tide recedes. Rich in lug and ragworm, estuaries attract a number of transient fish species. In large estuaries the freshwater may flow over the saltwater in the upper to middle reaches, meaning chub and dace can be caught at the surface, and bass on the bottom.

River tactics

The main difference between fly fishing in a river and tackling a lake is that the angler needs to use, manipulate or combat the flow that every river possesses. However, although the techniques are sufficiently different to be covered here, stillwaters are, in fact, rarely completely 'still', and any techniques learned on rivers will place the angler in good stead for fishing on lakes.

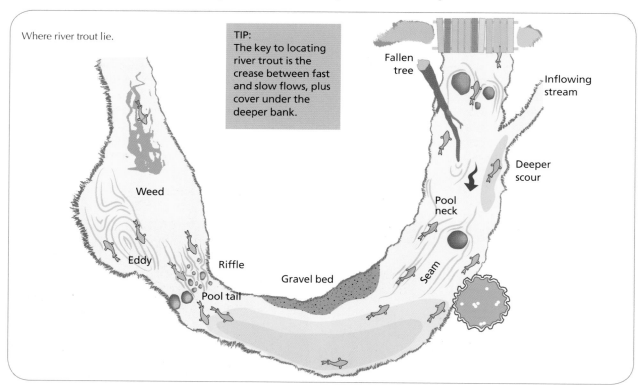

Where river trout lie.

TIP:
The key to locating river trout is the crease between fast and slow flows, plus cover under the deeper bank.

Fallen tree

Inflowing stream

Deeper scour

Pool neck

Weed

Eddy

Riffle

Gravel bed

Seam

Pool tail

Upstream dry fly

1 The fish is spotted lying between the two weed beds.

2 The cast is made just upstream of the fish.

3 The fish is hooked and turns downstream.

4 Well worth the effort!

Upstream dry fly is the purest and simplest form of fly fishing. Using a single dry fly on a tapered leader, the angler makes a cast upstream, allows the fly to land and then lets the river flow bring the fly back towards him. The line between the rod tip and fly should always be slack; if the line tightens, it'll pull the fly off of the natural line of the current. This is known as 'drag' and is to be avoided in all but the most exceptional tactical circumstances, because it is unnatural, and puts the fish off taking.

Typically, a 9ft (3m) tapered leader is used, with an extra 1–2ft (0.3–0.6m) of lighter tippet attached to the end. In a tightly overgrown stream this could be reduced to 6ft or 7ft (2–2.3m). It's a busy technique: as the fly begins to drift back on the current, so the angler needs to pull in (or gather) line in order to make a direct connection with a fish (by lifting the rod tip) should one take the offering. Pull in too much line too fast and the fly will drag, so it's important to watch both fly and line as it drifts.

River fish 'lie' in certain positions in the river's flow, so in order to get one to rise to your artificial you need to ensure the fly drifts right over its lie.

To tackle a rising fish, cover the water with different casting angles and lengths, always extending line to ensure casts are made only over water already covered. Gradually extend line to cover the full section of river without 'lining' (casting over) a lying fish.

When fishing a dry fly, you want the fly to float back at the mercy of the currents, just as an insect would sitting on the water surface. The easiest way to present a dry fly naturally is by casting directly upstream, but the more the fly is cast across (and up) the stream, the more the angler needs to be aware of the tethering effect of the fly line on the fly, which causes unnatural (and generally unsuccessful) drag. Avoiding this entails casting or working slack line in between the rod tip and the fly to negate the pull of the current.

↓ It's important to watch the fly and gather in the drifting slack line as the fly drifts towards you.

1 A fish rises downstream in this narrow tree-lined side-stream.

2 The cast is aimed in line, but short of the rising fish. The rod stops high to create lots of slack.

3 The rod is lowered slowly to form more slack between fly and rod tip.

4 The rod tip is lowered completely to allow the fly to drift downstream on the slack.

5  It's a grayling. Grayling are highly susceptible to downstream dry fly.

Downstream dry fly

This can often be the only way to get your fly to a fish. A single fly is used on a long (12ft/4m) tapered leader. The cast is made directly downstream, with a high stop of the rod tip to land the fly upstream of the targeted fish, building plenty of slack in the line and the leader. The current bears the fly down to the fish as the angler extends and lowers his casting arm to allow even more slack line into the drift. Grayling respond really well to a downstream dry fly. A very useful presentation on slow-flowing rivers.

Rising fish

Fishing an upstream dry fly to consistently rising fish is one of the most exciting and visual aspects of fly fishing. If a river fish rises then you know its exact position, and an accurate, suitable cast a few feet upstream and drag-free drift over the same spot should encourage another rise if your fly pattern and size are sufficiently convincing.

However, the attitude of the targeted insect at the surface can also be crucial to success. Fish quickly lock on to a stage of the insect's hatch, usually the stage of hatch where it's most vulnerable, and it's less likely to escape from their attempt to eat it. As we've seen, many insects have to break through the surface film in order to hatch, and this occurs in stages:

holding under the surface layer as a pupa; pushing through into the air (half-in, half out); breaking through the surface, shedding the pupal shuck; at the surface, fully hatched, and drying its wings ready to fly off. All are vulnerable stages that fish target, and all can take place very quickly, or very slowly. For instance, dull, drizzly weather means that newly hatched duns can take much longer to fly than on a breezy, dry day. As a result they're vulnerable to predation for a much longer time – 'sitting ducks' is an apt expression here. Also, in any hatch there are also a number of insect casualties that fail to break through the surface and lie trapped in the film, half in and half out of their translucent shucks. These unfortunate individuals are easy prey for fish, and are a common target during a hatch.

Be aware, though, that rising fish may actually be taking terrestrial insects that have become trapped in the surface film, or they may be taking adult aquatic insect females (spinners) that have returned to the water to egg-lay and, during the process, become trapped in the film and ultimately die on the surface, spent.

The key to successful dry fly fishing is to identify the insect targeted by the fish, and then to fish a floating fly that matches that insect's size and colour, and – just as importantly – the exact stage of its life cycle (*ie* the targeted insect's orientation at, in or on the water surface).

Having pinpointed the rise, target your fly to land a yard or two (1–2m) upstream of the rise – the faster the water, the closer your can cast – allowing for the current to float the fly over the exact same spot on a dead drift. If the fish doesn't oblige, keep working your dry fly over that spot, changing fly pattern or size if necessary. If the fish doesn't take, remember the spot, and come back to it.

Non-risers

Even when fish aren't rising, an upstream dry-fly technique can still be employed effectively. This is called 'search fishing', the angler casting a large, enticing single dry fly on a shortish (7–9ft/2.5–3m) leader upstream and allowing it to dead drift back over likely lies. The key to this tactic is to keep moving, and to cover different lies with each cast. As you walk or wade upstream, keep changing the angle of cast to bring the flies back on a different current path. What you're trying to do is to force the fish to make an instant decision – take it or leave it. If a fish is interested it'll take on first viewing. Fan your casts, cast

shorter then longer to avoid 'lining' close-lying fish. With each cast try to imagine where a fish could be lying – in the flow at the pool-neck, behind, to the side or in front of a boulder, under an overhanging bush, in a 'crease' or current seam, or in the run-in to the tail of the pool – and float your fly over that imaginary lie.

Keep moving.

Proven 'search' dry flies are: Klinkhamer Special, Elk Hair Sedge, Adult Caddis, Daddy-long-legs, Humpy, Double Badger, Foam Beetle, Sun Fly.

SOUND THINKING

➜ This dusk Mayfly feeder on Tuscany's River Tiber took an artificial with a slurp that was the giveaway signal to lift.

To an experienced angler in tune with the surroundings, and concentrating with all their senses on any signs of a take, sometimes the sound – rather than the sight – of a fish taking a fly at the surface is sufficient to trigger an instinctive lift of the rod into a fish.

Another common scenario of sensing a take through the sound of a rise occurs at night, and usually involves caddis. After a dusk hatch, which is common for caddis, there's a post-hatch lull after the frenzy of hatch activity. On both river and lake, the slashes and slurps of fish making the most of a mass emergence die away and with the darkness comes quiet. However, there are always casualties of a hatch that don't make the transition from water to air. Stuck-in-the-shuck, drowned and abortive hatchers drift aimlessly on the surface, and the occasional hungry fish will still be on the lookout for them.

In the quiet of the summer darkness, it's possible to hear a fish slurping down these unfortunate failed hatchers. If a Balloon Caddis, or Elk Hair Sedge, is cast somewhere in the vicinity of the audible rise, it's almost a certainty the fish will find it, and take it with the same noisy slurp. This is your signal to lift the rod and hook it: a fish on the dry fly in complete darkness. A good trick to round off a beautiful summer's night.

↓ ↘ Klinkhamer and Humpy: both good 'search' dry flies.

↑Sometimes changing position can make dry-fly fishing easier and more effective. Here, wading closer to the bush means it's easier to get a cast underneath to where a fish might be lying.

Dry-fly tips

The longer the cast, the more fly line there is for the current to act on, thus the more difficult it is for the angler to control his dry fly to produce a drift that's convincingly 'drag free'. So a shorter cast makes good, convincing presentation much more simple. Consequently careful wading into the river (should fishery rules allow), to shorten the distance between rod tip and fly, can work to the angler's advantage. The same applies to accuracy – a regularly rising fish may be difficult to tempt off its lie, even by just a few inches – so an accurate cast is essential for the fish to investigate your dry fly.

In most river situations, slack line between rod tip and fly helps eliminate drag. 'Mending' the line – throwing a bow of line upstream with an upstream sweep of the rod – or adopting various slack-line or mended casts, will all assist the dry fly angler achieve this (see Chapter 20).

What is drag?

Drag is what most anglers try to avoid whilst fishing rivers, with either dry fly or nymphs. If dead-drift is the most natural way to present a nymph or dry fly, drag is its antithesis.

River fish spend their lives in flowing water, and most of the food they take, day in day out, comes to them either on the current or on the surface of the water above them. These food items arrive on the same line of current, drifting inertly (ie dead-drifting), and the fish simply tilts its fins up or down to line up with the item, opens its mouth and sucks it in.

Unless the insect or food item is highly active and powerful, it's rare for it to move across or off this line of flow. However, this is exactly what happens the instant our fly starts to drag, caused by the onset of tension in the line between the rod tip and the fly becoming too great and pulling the fly unnaturally across the stream towards the angler.

When drag works

Drag is generally to be avoided, but there are certain situations where it might provoke a fish to take. These are:

↑A dragging dry fly. Usually drag is avoided, unless circumstances mean a dragging fly can work.

- Caddis/sedge – adult caddis 'run' across the water, both on hatching and when egg-laying, thus a Caddis allowed to drag can sometimes convince a fish to take.
- Upwings in a wind – when upwings hatch they drift inertly on the surface, at the whim of the current. However, in a strong wind their wings can act like sails that can cause them to skate across, upstream or downstream, in which case drag can simulate this action and provoke a take.
- Midges – discussing with the late John Goddard, we both realised that a Midge Emerger allowed to drag could sometimes elicit a take from hitherto uncooperative trout. He thought that the action might be due to the midge writhing in its attempt to escape through the surface film on hatching.

Drag test

Reproducing such drag presentations is best done at the end of a drag-free drift. Simply delay re-casting and allow the fly to swing on the tethered line for just a few feet (one metre) or so before re-casting. Only do this if you suspect fish might want a dragging fly, as this is a quick way to drown your dry fly.

Wet flies on the river

Upstream wet fly

Upstream wet fly is a traditional method for fishing flies just sub-surface, and is used when fish are rising to ascending or hatching nymphs, or taking drowned spinners or terrestrials. The leader is kept short (7–10ft/2.3–3.1m – shortist for tiny streams) with either two or three flies – spiders or traditional wets. Casts are kept short (3–4yd/3–4m), made directly upstream or slightly across the flow and the line retrieved quickly to stay just in contact with the fly on the top dropper. Lifting the rod tip forms the final part of the retrieve, after which the flies are flicked out upstream once again. This is a busy method, involving constant casting and retrieving, and

← Upstream nymphing on a French mountain river.

the angler should also move with each cast to cover a new area. It's often best fished by the angler wading upstream. To fish the flies just under the surface film the whole cast can be 'greased', which also helps with seeing a take. Otherwise the angler looks for signs of any sip, boil, flash, slash or splash where he expects his flies to be, or a tightening of the line or a downward stab of the line's tip as a fish takes. All are met with a smart lift of the rod tip.

Upstream nymph

Upstream nymph is similar to 'upstream wet' but uses more realistic nymph imitations, and also can be adapted to be fished singly, as on a chalk stream (where rules sometimes state 'upstream nymph only'). If the fish can't be seen, then greasing the leader from the butt to within inches of the fly will help with take detection, the floating nylon drawing, sliding or stretching across the surface. Otherwise, a sight indicator – of either wool, yarn or foam – can be attached to the butt leader, just below the fly-line tip. If the indicator stalls, slides, dips or shoots away then it can indicate a fish has taken the fly/flies underneath.

TIP

In fast water, don't make the distance between indicator and flies too long. Any leader longer than 9ft (3m) between indicator and point nymph is difficult to control. Even in smooth flows – where control is easier – the leader length should only be about 50% more than the required fishing depth (ie to fish a heavy nymph 5ft/1.7m down, a leader of 7.5ft/2.3m – minimum – is required).

(Fabien Monteil)

Up-and-across

1 The cast is made angling upstream.

2 The rod is lifted to ensure there's no slack between the point fly and rod tip. The rod tip is held high.

3 The line is tracked by the rod tip as the current takes the line and flies downstream. More line can be paid out as the flies sweep across the stream.

4 The angler extends his rod tip and arm downstream to slow the flies as they sweep on to the 'dangle'.

5 A nice fish has taken the up-and-across wet fly.

This is a common method used for 'searching' a river, in anticipation of taking trout from anywhere in the stream. It can be used with a team of wet flies, spiders or nymphs or a combination of all three (the heaviest on the point), and is an excellent method for smooth, even flows and glides. Again, a leader of 9ft (3m) would be the maximum used.

The aim is to deliver the flies upstream and across the river, then dead-drift the three flies on the current for as long as possible, maintaining contact with them at all times, any takes being registered through the fly line.

1 Cast the team of flies at an angle upstream and across the river.
2 Stopping the rod high on the delivery cast 'pitches' the flies into the water, point fly first, one on top of the other, which allows them sufficient slack line to sink freely.
3 Sweeping the rod tip upstream and mending upstream can buy more time to let the flies continue to sink.
4 As the flies drift to a point just upstream and across from your position, you need to be in touch with all the flies, from rod tip to point fly, so they can be fished effectively. This is achieved by keeping the rod tip as far upstream as possible, and retrieving line, even pulling on the flies initially to straighten the cast to ensure you're in contact with the sunken fly in the point position.
5 With the point fly, droppers, fly line and rod tip all in a straight line, as the flies and line drift downstream, track round with the rod tip to maintain a direct line of contact between point fly and rod tip.

6 As the flies drift past your position, slowly arc the rod tip round, sometimes even making small mends downstream, continuing to track the flies and maintain the straight line.
7 As the flies and line sweep downstream, continue to track them, extending the arm and rod tip downstream in the final throes of the drift.
8 The line now tightens and lifts the flies in the water, and they then swing into the angler's bank. Apart from the dead-drift both the lift and the subsequent swing can provoke a take.

TIPS

- The key to this tactic is for the angler to be certain that the slightest take to the point fly will register through the line.
- Casting further upstream will allow the flies more time to sink deeper.
- The angler should fish new water with each cast.
- You can work either upstream or downstream, although it's less frenetic and more leisurely working downstream.
- Taking a pace or two downstream, in line with the flies as they drift, can buy an extra yard or two of dead drift.

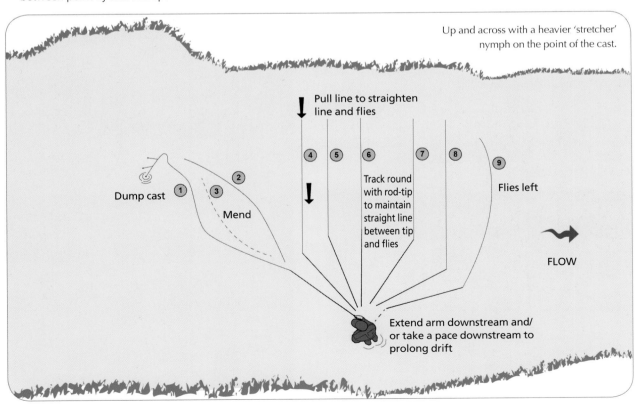

Up and across with a heavier 'stretcher' nymph on the point of the cast.

Pull line to straighten line and flies

Dump cast   ① ③ ②   Mend

④ ⑤ ⑥ ⑦ ⑧ ⑨

Track round with rod-tip to maintain straight line between tip and flies

Flies left

FLOW

Extend arm downstream and/ or take a pace downstream to prolong drift

As the flies are being fished and the rod tip tracks their movement, the 'J' shape of line hanging between rod tip and river surface is your take indicator. It's important to maintain this 'J' shape as the rod tracks round by neither pulling on the flies nor allowing any slack. If the 'J' straightens (ie the 'J' tightens into a '/'), this is caused by a pull on the flies, and the rod should be lifted to connect with the fish. Sometimes a fish will boil as it takes the flies, so keep an eye open for this as a signal too.

Duo system

↑ Duo: the nymph is attached to the bend of the dry fly by a short section of tippet.

Also called 'klink and dink', 'hopper dropper' and 'New Zealand style', the advantage of the duo system is that it allows you to present dry fly and nymph simultaneously should you be in any doubt as to what the fish might be taking. Again, this is a good method for 'searching'. The duo system requires a buoyant dry fly with a short section (1–2ft/0.3–0.6m) of fine tippet attached to the bend of the hook using a blood knot. To the end of this tippet a small nymph (often with a tiny bead-head) is attached. The idea here is for the dry fly to act just as a coarse fisher's 'float', to both suspend the nymph just under the surface and also to act as a bite indicator. The method is fished in exactly the same manner as upstream dry fly, covering as much water as possible, drag-free, the angler controlling slack, gathering excess slack line and keeping a studious eye on the dry fly's progress at all times. If the fly dips under, then it could indicate that either a fish has taken the nymph or it has caught on the bottom or some weed – a lift of the rod will confirm which. Of course, the fish could ignore the Nymph and take the dry fly instead.

TIP

This is a very good method for fast water, such as pool-necks and riffly flows. It's also one of the best methods when search fishing.

Disadvantages

The duo method is best suited to faster water, as on smoother water drag between dry and nymph can come into play, in which case a single dry fly or a sub-surface team of nymphs might be a better option.

Down-and across

1 The cast is made across and down the river.

2 The flies are lead across the flow and into the angler's bank.

3 Often, the fish hook themselves.

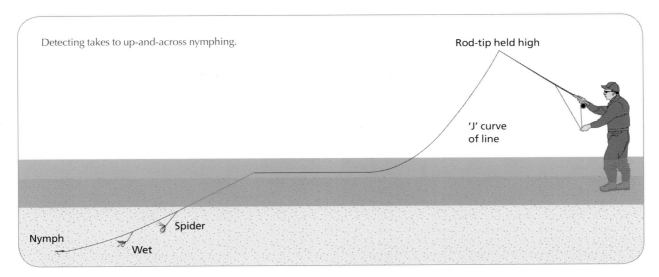

Detecting takes to up-and-across nymphing.

Rod-tip held high

'J' curve
of line

Nymph

Spider

Wet

Down-and-across wet fly is the most commonly observed method of river fishing, and is the preferred presentation employed for bulk sea trout and salmon fishing. The cast is made at an angle across the stream and the current causes the fly line to belly and swing the flies back into the angler's bank on a tight line. Takes can come at any time, and due to the tightness of the line a take is normally felt.

The pace of the flies as they track across the stream can be altered by changing the angle of the cast. A cast made straight across the flow will swing round far faster than one made acutely (ie more downstream than across). 'Mending' – throwing a curve of line upstream – can also slow down the track of the flies across the stream.

Disadvantages

This is one of the easiest methods to fish a river, and is commonly adopted, but it's also one of the least effective for trout due to the fact that the flies are 'tethered' to the rod tip at all times and swim across the flow in a fast, unnatural way, and taking fish tend to drop the fly. However, there are occasions when this method can be useful for imitating any food that 'swims' in or on the current, such as hatching and egg-laying sedges (caddis), hatching Yellow May duns or fishing streamers like fry and baitfish. It's also a pleasurable, easy way to fish, but it can still cover a lot of water quickly.

TIP

In order to hook more trout takes on downstream wet fly, lift the rod tip high to introduce more slack line into the system, which may give the fish a chance to turn with the fly and hook itself.

Indicator fishing
FITTING A FOAM BOBBER INDICATOR

1 This type of foam bobber is fed on to the line and up to the desired position...

2 ...where it's trapped by inserting the plastic peg into the hole.

FITTING A YARN INDICATOR

1 Yarn sight indicators in a variety of sizes and colours.

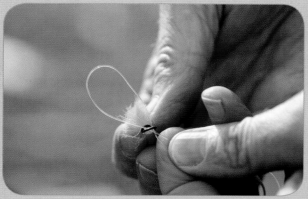

2 To fit, push a loop of butt nylon (close to the fly-line tip) through the rubber loop...

3 ...push the yarn tuft through the loop...

4 ...and pull on the yarn to lock down on to the nylon.

Using an indicator allows nymphs to be fished deeply, on a natural 'dead drift', allowing the angler to register takes at the same time. The indicator is small, visible, streamlined and buoyant and acts just as a coarse-fisher's float. Indicators can be yarn, wool, foam, plastic etc and are attached to a butt leader, close to the fly-line tip. Maximum leader depth below the indicator would be 9ft (3m), unless a very slow-moving river was being fished that might advocate a slightly longer leader.

1 Work upstream or downstream to cover a pool.
2 The key to indicator fishing is to cast upstream to allow the fly/flies to sink – the further upstream the cast, the deeper they can be allowed to sink.
3 Loose line is gathered as the flies drift down, and as much fly line as possible is kept off the river surface to avoid any drag occurring between rod tip and indicator.
4 The rod tip tracks around as the indicator drifts downstream. At this point you can move downstream, level with the indicator, to extend the natural drift of the nymphs.
5 Your arm can reach out downstream to extend the drag-free drift.
6 The take is registered by the indicator stopping, sliding or dipping underwater.

High-sticking

'High-sticking' is a term used for fishing nymphs deeply with an indicator, and describes the rod-action – arm and rod tip extended high in the air in an effort to keep as much fly line as possible off the water, thereby reducing the drag that destroys the dead-drift presentation of the nymphs under the indicator. The angler can work upstream or downstream. It's a good system for faster pools and runs.

TIP

When working downstream, a pace downstream can be taken as the indicator draws level with the angler to extend the effective drift.

High-sticking is often associated with wading, as it's difficult to fish this system effectively if any distance exists between indicator and angler. To cover water, the angler can work at one depth, say knee-depth, then rework the pool, wading this time down a line at thigh-depth.

↑ Keeping the rod tip high keeps line off the water and prevents drag.

1 Cast upstream.
2 Once the flies have sunk, gradually lift your rod tip higher and higher as the indicator floats downstream to level with you.
3 As the indicator floats past, the angler and rod tip pivot to follow the drift and maintain the high rod tip.
4 Extend the arm high and reach downstream to complete the drag-free drift.

Czech nymphing

Czech nymphing is a technique popularised in Eastern Europe that's useful for fishing fast pools and 'pocket' water (broken, rocky fast water), with a team of heavy, dense nymphs, and is a good technique for grayling. The heaviest nymph is usually on the point, but some anglers like to fish the

→ Typical Czech Nymph – streamlined, heavy and dense.

heaviest nymph on the middle dropper, to take the point and middle dropper flies right down. Due to the fact that this is short-distance nymphing, a floating indicator isn't required (although some anglers prefer to use one). The usual form of indication is through a highly visible fly-line/butt-leader connection (a 'mini-con') on which the angler focuses closely for takes as it tracks under his rod tip.

A typical set-up is a 9–10ft (3–3.1m) of 6lb BS fluorocarbon leader with two droppers attached to a floating line via a highly visible 'mini-con' connector. To the 6lb length are attached two successive lengths of 4lb BS fluorocarbon, at a spacing of just 24in (60cm), each with a 4–6in (10–15cm) dropper at each junction. To both droppers and the point dense, streamlined nymphs are tied.

Overleaf we see Czech international angler Jiri Klima using the technique on the Derbyshire Derwent. Like high-sticking, this technique revolves around fishing a short line, casting maybe just a yard or so of line, so wading skills are essential to get the flies into the fish's position. The angler can move – cast and pace, cast and pace – upstream or downstream, drifting the nymphs on the fast flow. At the very end of the drift the line tightens and the flies lift in the water. This lift can often induce a fish to take, particularly grayling.

Czech nymphing

1 Jiri 'lobs' the heavy flies upstream, just over a rod length out from his position.

2 The flies sink quickly after the cast. As they sink they sweep downstream, and Jiri raises his rod tip to tension the line.

3 Jiri then swings round, following the path of the 'mini-con' downstream, rather like a crane's jib with a heavy load attached on a long line.

4 As the flies are swept downstream, so the angler can extend and reach downstream to lengthen the drift. A fish takes just as the flies start to lift.

5 The result: a brown trout took the dropper.

Leader-to-hand

This is also called French Nymphing or Euro nymphing and is a controversial method, in so much as a conventional fly line is largely redundant. Instead, a long (30ft/10m) co-polymer tapered leader is used to 'cast' the flies. The technique relies on a leader of about 5–6ft (1.7–2m) with two flies – one of them at least being a weighted fly – the team of nymphs being fished below an indicator section of brightly coloured Stren nylon or a specialised coloured bead indicator.

Due to the fact that no fly line rests on the water between rod tip and indicator, any drag imposed by the current is minimised, thus the presentation of the nymphs, even at a distance from the angler, is almost natural. This is not possible to do with conventional fly line due to its inherent weight causing a 'sagging' effect, which drags the flies with it, rather like a heavy anchor rope pulls a ship into a quayside. In addition there's no thick fly line landing on the water to scare the fish.

1 Welsh internationalist Sean Jones uses the weight of the flies to shoot out the monofilament 'line' upstream and across, into the flow.

2 He carefully watches his indicator as it drifts down.

3 He lifts his rod tip high to keep any line off the water, to reduce drag.

4 The indicator dips, Sean lifts, and a grayling comes to the net.

5 A nice grayling on the Euro-nymph style.

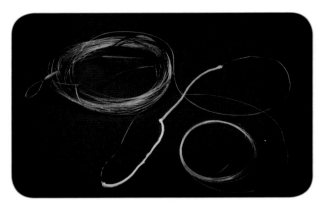

↑ French leader showing the monofilament casting line, the dual-colour braid indicator and the leader.

The difficulty in this technique lies in casting the nymphs, which is done outside the conventional fly-casting style. Firstly, the rod tends to be longer and have a soft-actioned tip (the AFFTA number on a typical Euro-nymphing rod might be marked as #2, #3 or even #2–5, but this is academic, as fly line rarely passes through its rings). Secondly, the level (20lb BS) monofilament, which is used for 'shooting' the cast across the river, is held in loose coils in the line hand.

With a few yards of the tapered leader plus the flies outside the rod tip, the power of the downstream current and the combined weight of the flies pulls on the line to load (bend) the rod tip. This potential energy is released with a forward tap of the wrist and a short haul by the line hand, causing the rod tip to spring forward and launch the heavy nymphs, catapult-style, upstream. The shooting line is thin nylon, so once the flies are launched they have sufficient momentum – and the line has so little friction – that the flies can travel a good distance (20–25ft/6–8m).

Having landed, the nymphs are allowed to sink as the angler regains any slack line then immediately raises the long

rod upwards with an extended arm to keep as much nylon off the water surface as possible and stay in contact with the indicator. The rod tip then tracks round with the indicator as it drifts downstream. If the indicator hesitates, stops or dips then the rod is lifted to tighten into the fish.

For short casts the length of nylon outside the rod tip is kept constant, and is flicked upstream, the nymphs being allowed to straighten and load the rod on the back-cast.

Streamer fishing

This technique centres on the predatory, fish-eating habits c some species of river fish, which can include large trout, chub, perch and, of course, pike.

Tan Minkie.

It uses a baitfish dressing (anything from a minnow to a bullhead or a small roach), and usually involves using a sink-tip (or intermediate) line and short leader (4–5ft/1.3–1.6m) to get the fly fishing deep and hold it there. Alternatively, a bead-

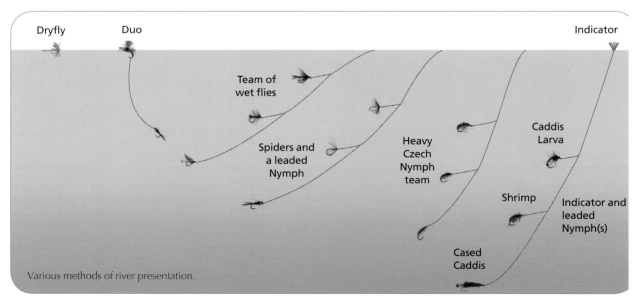

Dryfly   Duo   Indicator

Team of wet flies

Spiders and a leaded Nymph

Heavy Czech Nymph team

Caddis Larva

Shrimp

Indicator and leaded Nymph(s)

Cased Caddis

Various methods of river presentation.

chain-eyed or lead-headed fly can be used on a floater on a longer leader (12ft/4m) of fluorocarbon. Generally streamers are fished by casting across-and-down. Mending or stepping downstream after casting will help introduce slack line to allow the baitfish pattern to sink deeper before it starts to swing.

During the swing the angler can use short (2–3in/5–8cm) strips of the line to imitate the movement of a small fish. A take will register as a solid pull on the line.

TIP

Presenting the fly upstream will cause the baitfish fly to 'flee' on a downstream arc, which may be a more realistic presentation and provoke a take. Fishing the streamer in 'pocket water', or at the tails of pools, is likely territory for a big, predatory trout.

Clear river tactics

In some rivers, when the water is low, and typically on chalk streams where the water has been effectively filtered underground, the fishing can be focussed on sighted fish, using either a dry fly or nymph. In either case, the fly is chosen to match the trout's anticipated food, and cast upstream or up-and-across in order to dead-drift over the fish's head. However, in order to accomplish this you need to locate a fish.

First see your fish

One of the primary chalk-stream fly-fishing skills is learning how to spot fish in the water. All fish are designed to be camouflaged from above (from bird predators) and from the

⬇First, see your fish.

TIP

Most people find it difficult to spot a fish in a river initially. However, there are ways to train your eyes to become more accustomed to finding fish.

If you or your fishing partner are playing a fish, try to locate it underwater before you land it. Follow the angle of the tight line. Once you've located it, study how its coloration appears in the water, study the shape of its body, the set of the fins. Watch it all the way into the net to see how it moves. Then the next time you're looking for fish in a river remember how that fish appeared in the water.

↓ The principle of mending line. A straight cast across (1) results in an immediate bow in the line (2). If the line is mended (3) then the slack belly of line will allow the fly/flies to drift freely (or sink) for longer (4).

side (from predatory fish species, such as pike), so how can we humans possibly see one?

First, you'll need polarised sunglasses, and a peaked cap to cut out any extraneous light entering your glasses. It's why people shade their eyes when looking into the distance, and is enhanced if the underside of the peak is black or dark, again to avoid reflecting light into your eyes.

A crucial part of the fish-spotting art is patience. Rarely will you see a fish instantly. Study the water hard. Let your eyes grow accustomed to what the bottom and the weed looks like. Try to study the gravel on the bottom. Now look for something that might resemble a fish – a gently fanning tail, the white blink of an open mouth as a fish breathes, the tilt of a pectoral fin. Look for lighter areas of gravel – it's easier to spot fish over these. Remember to look closely down your own bank as well as the far bank, study the weed edges hard. One of the major giveaways of prey to a predator is movement. Movement catches a predator's eye instantly. And you're the predator. So look for movement.

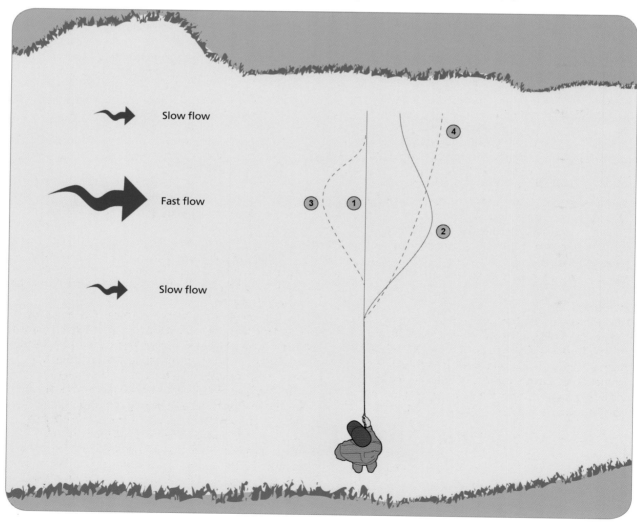

Slow flow

Fast flow

Slow flow

The other sign to look for is the best and the most enervating. This is the fish giving away its presence by the disturbance it makes at the surface when it takes an insect trapped on, in or just under the surface film – the 'rise'. The ebbing rings of a rise indicate not only the presence of a fish, but one that's actively feeding, and a likely candidate to be caught on fly.

Casting a nymph to a fish lying deep

Having spotted a fish that's lying on the riverbed you want your fly to be presented so that the fish will see it. There are three things to think about regarding the fish's position before making your cast:

1 The line of current on which the fish is lying.
2 The depth the fish is lying.
3 The speed of the current.

Presenting your fly is a three-dimensional problem. The line of the fish is the easiest to judge, although this comes with its own problems. Due to refraction, the apparent position of the fish appears higher in the water (and closer) than it actually is (and thus bigger than you think too!). As a result you may cast your fly too short. The good thing is that casting short of the fish is likely to cause no harm; over-casting can cause the fish to be 'lined' (the line lands over its 'window') and it's likely to be scared and bolt. Thus you should begin by casting short and gradually lengthen your cast until you're certain your fly is in the vicinity of the fish.

The third component of this three-dimensional equation comes when the flow is taken into account. A nymph will be swept downstream as it sinks. Thus, you need to give your targeted fish on the riverbed some 'lead', casting upstream of it so that the fly has time to sink to the fish's depth before the current carries it past.

There's also a fourth variable, but it's one you can control: the weight of your fly. The heavier the fly, the swifter it'll sink to the bottom, therefore the less 'lead' it requires to get to the fish's depth.

Cut some slack

When allowing a nymph to sink, it mustn't be tensioned or pulled by the fly line, otherwise it won't be able to sink physically. Thus, managing to put some slack line in the system – between rod tip and fly – is essential. To accomplish this, slack-line casts and upstream mends are used by the angler to allow the fly to sink freely on the leader before it reaches its fishing depth.

The dead-drift and induced take

The aim of getting your nymph to the fish's depth is to then dead-drift it close to its head so it believes it's a natural insect drifting past its lie, just like dozens of natural nymphs do every day. If the fish decides to take your nymph it will either:

1 Open its mouth to suck it in, and you'll see a white 'blink' of its mouth as it opens.
2 Tilt on the current, open its mouth and turn down.
3 Swing off to one side, and return to its lie.
4 Shudder its pectoral fins and twitch its body.
5 Tilt, drift downstream then turn to take the fly.
6 Turn aggressively on the fly and snatch it.

If it makes any of these movements when your nymph is close to it, assume it's your nymph that's caused this reaction and lift the rod to set the hook.

If you can't physically see your nymph, you must judge its approximate whereabouts (taking into account the flow, the depth and the weight of the nymph) by estimating its track and watching the fish.

The Leisenring lift – a basic instinct

If the fish ignores your nymph, you can turn to a more basic instinct to get it to take. This works with most fish species, but particularly grayling and trout (see 'Induced take', Chapter 8). Getting a fly close to a fish's head (let's call it its

↑ The Killer Bug is one of the best flies to use for this technique when targeting grayling.

'personal space'), and then drawing the fly up and away from it in a smooth, positive movement, can trigger an almost involuntary reaction from the fish, which is to turn on the fly and take it.

On a river the fly can be made to rise in this fashion by dead-drifting a nymph down towards a fish and then, when it's estimated to be just in front of the fish, checking the line so the pressure of the current acts to accelerate the fly so that it lifts in the water. This is called the Leisenring lift.

The fact that this technique works was demonstrated famously by Oliver Kite, a TV angling personality of the 1960s, who would locate a shoal of grayling on a chalk stream, put a blindfold on his head and then cast and present the fly so it sank to their level. On lifting the rod tip to tension his line, a grayling would hang on to the rising fly to the bemusement of the audience. Kite would unhook the fish and then astonish his audience by repeating this trick time after time.

WILD TROUT FROM LAKE, LOUGH AND LOCH

Alone in the Assynt hills: fishing one of the thousands of wild brown trout lochs in Scotland.

Throughout Scotland, Wales, Ireland and England there are thousands of natural waters that support wild populations of trout. From the huge lochs of the Great Glen to the tarns of the Lake District, and from the natural llyns of North Wales to the Greatest Western lakes in Ireland there are waters that hold stocks of natural brown trout. All can be fished with fly, from both bank and boat, and all have contributed to the traditions and culture of fly fishing.

Loch style

As seen previously in Chapter 8, loch style is a technique that can be used from both bank and boat and is probably the most traditional and still the most common method employed on wild trout lochs.

The classic approach is to use a two-dropper leader of 4–8lb BS nylon or co-polymer with three flies, spaced 3–4ft apart (1.0–1.3m) on a long rod 10–11ft (3.3–3.6m) coupled with floating line (or sometimes an intermediate). The team of flies is a bushy 'bob' fly on the top dropper, a smaller streamlined wet fly on the middle dropper and a larger attractor, or Nymph, on the point. All these flies can be chosen to suggest whatever insects might be attracting the fish's attention. For instance, in a caddis hatch the top

⬇ Loch-style fishing can be carried out from bank or boat.

dropper might be a Claret Bumble, on the middle an Invicta, and the point fly a Fiery Brown or a Caddis Pupa. A midge hatch might see a Bibio on the top, a Mallard & Claret on the middle, with a Connemara Black or a Pheasant Tail Nymph with a coloured thorax on the point.

➜ Golden olive – a favourite colour in Ireland, probably due to its close association to the colour of a mayfly dun. Also a good match for olives and summer duns.

The loch-style technique centres around casting out the flies, letting them settle, then pull-retrieving them, at any pace from a trickle to a fast strip. The final part of the retrieve is the most crucial, where the bob fly is drawn to the surface, just prior to being roll-cast in preparation of the next cast. At this crucial point, the rod tip in conjunction with the retrieve hand is used to control the track of the bob fly so it just furrows at the surface and then breaks through, as if it were about to hatch and escape from the water. This is called 'dibbling' the fly, and often persuades a take from an unseen following, interested fish.

Avoiding tangles: a balanced cast

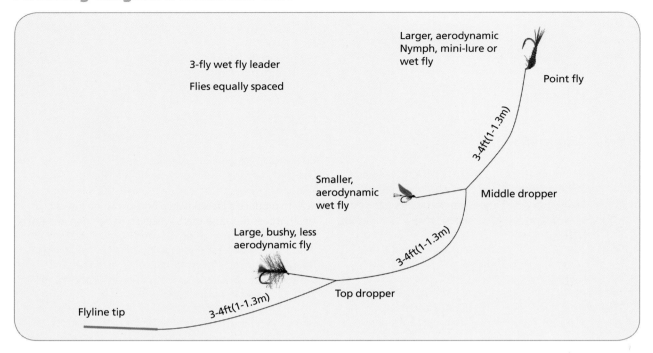

Larger, aerodynamic
Nymph, mini-lure or
wet fly

Point fly

3-fly wet fly leader

Flies equally spaced

3-4ft (1-1.3m)

Smaller,
aerodynamic
wet fly

Middle dropper

Large, bushy, less
aerodynamic fly

3-4ft (1-1.3m)

Flyline tip

3-4ft (1-1.3m)

Top dropper

↑ A balanced three-fly cast.

TIP

In windy conditions the size of the flies increases:

- Calm: sizes 14–16
- Gentle ripple: size 14
- Steady wave: size 10–12
- Big wave: up to size 8

To help anchor the flies in a big wind, a 'wee double' on the point can help, or a switch to an intermediate will keep the flies down in the waves.

INTERMEDIATE ADVANTAGE

An advantage of using an intermediate is the amount of time the line is allowed to sink. A type 1 will sink at one inch per second, so letting it settle for ten seconds will allow the flies to fish about 10in (22cm) under the surface, 30 seconds would be 30in (75cm) etc. By counting the line down you can explore the upper layers of a lake to ascertain the exact feeding depth of the fish. Having established the feeding depth, the intermediate can fish the flies at the crucial depth with consistency.

Dry fly on lochs

An alternative method to fishing wet flies is to employ a team of dry flies. Usually two are fished on a tapered leader of 9ft (3m), tapering down to 5lb or 6lb BS, with a dropper and 4–5ft (1.3–1.6m) of matching tippet.

The key here is presentation, from the moment the cast alights on the water until lift-off. Do nothing but retrieve any slack line, constantly alert to lift into a take. On a drifting boat, the angler simply waits until the boat catches up with the resting flies, lifts off when they're close to the boat, re-casts and repeats the process.

From the bank, the angler can adopt one of three styles:

- Cast out and let the flies sit static for a minute or two.

TIP

If the wind drops to a flat calm, remove the fly on the dropper and simply fish a single fly on the point of the tapered cast of 13ft (4m). If this doesn't work, switch the dry fly to a small wet fly and retrieve this with a steady figure-of-eight retrieve just under the surface.

can act as the trigger for a fish lying on the lake bottom. An almost instantaneous, instinctive rise can occur.

Twitching a static dry fly can often elicit a take. An easy way to produce a lifelike twitch of a drowning insect in its death throes (because that's what you're trying to imitate) is to be in touch with your dry fly, then simply lift the rod tip with your rod hand as if you were gesticulating or trying to interject in a conversation. This short raise of the hand, which is allowed to drop slowly, pulses the fly/flies to life, and skate maybe an inch (2.5cm). Deadly.

Locating loch trout

Wild lakes can vary in depth markedly, and understanding the depth over which you're fishing is vital to success. This is a far more important factor to consider than when fishing a stocked, lowland reservoir, where rainbow trout will roam over all depths of water.

The food production of any lake – plankton, algae, weed and insects – depends on light. Depths at which light can't

⬇ A point is a likely place to find loch trout, as are the skerries on the bank opposite the angler.

- Fan-cast around the clock to land the flies in different areas. Leave the flies to settle for a few seconds (as if they were unfortunate insects being 'blown in') then lift them off and pitch them into another area of 'unfished' water.
- Cast out, let the flies settle then draw on the line to twitch or skate them before allowing them to settle again. Twitch/skate and settle the flies all the way into the shallows.

Bring your flies to life

The moment your dry fly lands is a key part of this presentation. It should alight on the surface just as if the wind has deposited a natural fly on the water. This action

penetrate are, therefore, less likely to hold fish, due to a lack of food. Water depths down to 30ft (10m) have 100 times more trout food than water deeper than 30ft.

In any wild lake the clarity of the water will determine the depth at which light can penetrate to the lakebed. In a clear, limestone Irish lake this might be down to a depth of 18–24 feet (6–8m), but in a peat-stained Scottish loch this might be only 6–7ft (2–2.3m). It means the angler should concentrate his fishing on the shallower water at the margins of the lake – where light can reach the lakebed – rather than the middle. The bank angler can achieve this easily, by working his way around the edge of the lake, but if fishing from a drifting boat this might entail making short drifts into the bank from, say, 30–40 yards out (30–40m), or drifting parallel to the bank, close in.

Brown trout, being territorial, also like to lie close to features and, as we've just seen, relatively shallow water, where their food lives. Fish such features with confidence!

Places to aim for

- Shallow areas (bottom just visible)
- Rocky points
- Skerries
- Bays
- Islands
- Inflowing and outflowing streams
- Sandbanks
- Weed beds
- Reeds
- Lily pads
- Fence lines, walls etc

The lie of the land

As well as visible features in the water, you can use the surrounding topography to help draw a mental picture of what the lakebed might look like under the water. For instance, a rapidly shelving rock bank is likely to continue

↓ Fishing an inflowing stream at Scourie, north-west Scotland.

OLD AND NEW WAYS OF DISCOVERING DEPTH

When it comes to finding out about deeps and shallows, anglers in Scotland have a unique resource at their fingertips. It's called the *Bathymetrical Survey of the Fresh-Water Lochs of Scotland, 1897-1909* and was compiled by Sir John Murray and Laurence Pullar. It features soundings taken on 562 of Scotland's major lochs. Many of these soundings, taken over 100 years ago, are still accurate today.

Another way to investigate waters is to study their form through Google Earth. The satellite images show inflowing rivers, shallows, skerries and islands, weed beds also show up, and Panoramio photos can help confirm the waterscape.

↑ Massive natural waters like Loch Tay should not be inhibiting, as most trout will lie at the edges, in the shallower water.

under the surface in the same plane, plunging down into the depths and offering limited opportunity for holding fish. However, a gently sloping grassland bank which eases into the water's edge is likely to continue at this gradient for a long distance out into the lake, offering much shallow water, and potential for fishing.

Cast-and-step: a key tactic

Due to the brown trout's territorial behaviour, it's vital the wild-trout angler keeps on the move, constantly covering new water. Remaining static, fishing in the same place – as a reservoir rainbow trout angler can easily do very successfully – is destined to end in wild-trout-fishing failure.

The key tactic in the wild-trout angler's approach is to cover as much water with their flies as is possible. To accomplish this, a 'cast-and-step' technique is used. Most anglers will take a pace of at least a yard or so (1m) along the bank after each cast, whilst others will cast and fish whilst moving at a slow walking pace. Either way, the aim is to cover a 'fresh' piece of water with every cast.

⬆ Working the edge involves constant moving: cast and step.

TIPS

■ Keep on the move to cover as much water as possible.

■ Wading is not usually necessary.

■ Shallows are important food sources – fish will be found here.

■ Wind and waves disguise your approach, but you'll need larger flies.

■ Identifying the current hatch of the day (or insect 'fall') can be the key to success.

■ Moving along the bank as you retrieve brings back the flies on a curved path – this brings many more offers.

RIVER SEA TROUT FISHING

A 9.5lb sea trout taken on a Surface Lure in the dead of night. The fish was returned.

Sea trout fishing at night is one of the most exciting of all aspects of fly fishing, involving our most explosive, powerful and beautiful fish, and relying on just the angler's senses of timing, touch and hearing. It's skilful, suspense filled and entails the angler sharing the quietest and most magical part of the day with only the owls, the bats and the moon for company, while the rest of the world is asleep.

Many British rivers support a run of sea trout, particularly those in south-west England, Wales, northern England, southern, eastern and northern Scotland and parts of Norfolk. Twenty-five years ago north-west Scotland supported big runs of sea trout, but these have dwindled due to overwhelming parasitism from sea lice emanating from the salmon-farming industry.

Mostly sea trout fishing on rivers centres around fishing at night during the summer months, although it can be successful in daylight if the river is running high after rain. Sea trout are extremely shy fish, and tend to move – both from pool to pool, and around their 'home' pool – at night, and hide up during the day.

On a low, clear river, however, sea trout can be caught from dusk until dawn. They're most easily caught when they've just run into the river, which might occur on a falling spate, or following a high tide (during a full or new moon) when they can access and negotiate the mouth of the river from the sea and make their journey upstream. Once they enter a river, like the salmon the sea trout loses its urge to feed, although there are exceptions to this rule, as we shall see later.

When to start fishing…and where

There are many arguments throughout history and literature about when to commence sea trout fishing at night in order to avoid scaring the fish and ruining the pool. I've heard 'wait until you can see seven stars in the sky', but I work on the following mantra: the slower the pool, the later you fish it. By reserving the big, deep slow pools for the middle of the night you can start fishing in confidence at dusk in the faster runs and necks, where the water is broken and disguises casting and wading. The biggest sea trout are usually caught in the deep, slow pools that require a quiet and unclumsy approach – so you need all the help you can get. The darker the night, the better the disguise.

How do I cast in the dark?

Most fly fishers find casting in the dark far more difficult than during the day. Thus it's important for the fly fisher to concentrate on his casting as darkness falls. If you 'feel' for the line straightening behind you during the back-cast, then you should be able to make a decent forward cast. The more one casts in the dark, the easier casting gets (provided you don't get tired, which is another cause of bad casting).

↓ Fast water at the neck of a pool is a good place to start in the evening.

↑ Casting at night is all about consistency and ease. A Spey cast is easy to time and is less likely to catch on the bank.

At first, it's best to shorten up your casting aspirations and just be comfortable with the amount of line you're handling. A simple, easy, repeatable shorter cast – involving the minimum of false casts – is better than striving to cast long. There's nothing more frustrating than having to constantly untangle your line, or wade out of the river to free the line from bankside vegetation in complete darkness. By casting well within your limits you'll be able to cover the water consistently and efficiently…and catch more fish.

Another way to efficient casting in the dark is to learn to Spey cast. Many Spey casts involve a waterborne anchor, and timing of the cast isn't so crucial. Also, the angler can listen to the peel of the line on the water surface and time his cast accordingly (with practice!). Again, an easily managed, constant line length assists consistent casting.

↓ Cast well within your limits to cover water consistently and efficiently.

During the summer there's often little wind at night, so the Double Spey and Circle C cast can be used with confidence with a single-hander or a switch rod, and are the two casts I generally employ during sea trout fishing at night.

It's never dark in the sea trout's world

It's amazing how a sea trout can take a black fly, just ½in long, from just under the surface in what humans would call 'pitch dark'. How different our vision must be from a fish's! When a sea trout is resting on the riverbed the sky must always appear far lighter in its window of vision. Thus a careful approach to the pool you intend to fish for sea trout is an important step to success. If approaching from downstream, walk round the pool's edge to avoid appearing in the fish's 'skyline'. I'll always enter a sea trout pool from slightly upstream rather than walking straight down the bank into it.

Time spent on reconnaissance is never wasted

Never attempt to fish at night without having first studied the pool(s) you intend to fish. It's dangerous not to do so, and it also eliminates much frustration and time-wasting.

If you can, fish quickly down the pool during the day – get a feel for the wading and casting distances, the obstructions, and the flow pattern of the pool.

Here's a list of things to note:

- Entry and exit points of the pool (mark these by noting gaps in the trees, gravel beds, a rock or any other landmark that may still be visible in the dark).
- Wading path and wading depth, taking note of any holes (not only for safety – these may contain resting sea trout at night).
- Overhanging trees and other obstructions that may snag your casts and back-casts.
- Likely sea trout lies (see diagram opposite).
- Weed beds.

On a very dark night it may be necessary to resort to more mechanical methods of fishing. To do this, you must have already run through and noted (either mentally or on paper) the exact fishing tactic you plan to employ, and the sea trout lies, during daylight.

- If it's difficult to find in the dark, tie a white handkerchief to a bush to mark your pool entry point.
- Count the paces up or downstream to your fishing position.
- Strip off a predetermined amount of fly line (measured by arm lengths) to reach the lie exactly (under a tree, for instance, rather than casting into it).
- Be aware of the angle you need to cast.

This exacting approach will not only save you a huge amount of time but is also very exciting, and may just catch you a fish.

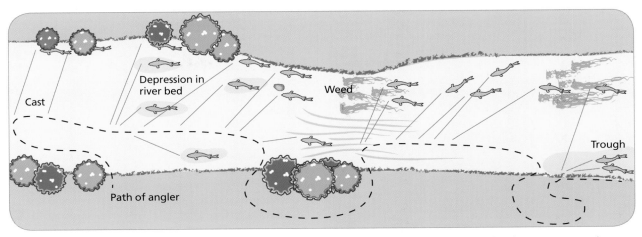

Cast

Depression in river bed

Weed

Trough

Path of angler

↑ Two actual sea trout pools and lies fished by the author, indicating the path he walks and wades and the casts he makes.

Wet flies – the standard tactic

The simplest and often the best approach for sea trout is to use a cast of about 9–10ft (3–3.3m) of 8lb BS with one dropper 3ft from the point. In clear, calmer water (and perhaps at dawn and dusk) this can be increased to 12ft (4m) using a tapered leader of 9ft tapering down to 6lb BS, with a 3ft (1m) section of added 6lb BS. This set-up can be fished on either a floating line, a midge-tip, a sink-tip or an intermediate. The floater is the easiest by far to handle at night, and should always be used by the newcomer.

↓ The basic cast for sea trout is one made down and across the river.

The cast is made across the flow; fairly square in slower glides.

Two wet flies are tied on, and it's best to use two sizes, the larger one on the dropper. For instance, a size 12 Connemara Black with a size 10 Teal, Blue & Silver on the point is a good choice.

As with brown trout, the sea trout angler always keeps on the move, taking a step downstream after each cast, covering new water with every swing of the fly.

← The line tightens and the flies are led across the flow whilst figure-of-eighting.

← The rod tip leads the flies across the flow.

↓ The flies continue to swing in towards the angler's bank until they are 'on the dangle'.

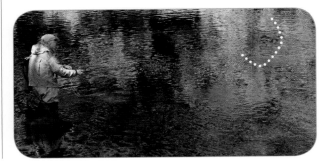

The flies are cast across the river and allowed to swing round to 'the dangle', the angler 'leading' the flies by tracking his rod into his/her bank as the flies fish round in the current. To speed up the track of the flies, a cast squarer to the bank can be made; to slow up the pace of the swing, cast at a more acute angle to the bank, or use an upstream 'mend' after casting across the river.

Ready for a take

There's no need for the line hand to do anything more than a very slow figure-of-eight retrieve, simply to stay in touch with the flies as they swing on a slightly tensioned line, the rod tip held horizontally or slightly higher. (Remember, the sense of touch is one of the few senses available to you in the dark, and your fingertips are highly sensitive, so often the first indication of a take is felt in the fingers of your line hand).

Darkness falls

As it gets darker, the angler may want to change his approach, especially if he's no longer getting takes or, indeed, hasn't had any takes. This is most easily and quickly done by:

- Switching the top dropper to a waking pattern – a heavily palmered, greased-up wet fly, a big deer-hair Sedge or – best – a Muddler. In the dark, sea trout see and react to surface activity well, even in smooth, quiet water. A wake pattern draws extra attention to the flies.
- Changing the flies to fish deeper. This is most easily effected by changing the point fly to a low-water double hook, which is heavier than a single. Increasing the size will also fish it deeper, as will increasing the top dropper by a size.

- Changing the line to fish deeper. By switching from a floater to a sink-tip the flies will automatically fish deeper. A quick and simple way to switch a fly line to a sink-tip is to add a 5ft (1.6m) sinking poly leader to the tip of the fly line. In order for the sink-tip to have full effect on the sunken flies, shorten the leader to 5ft or 6ft (1.6–2m), keeping the dropper 2–2.5ft (60–75cm) from the point.

A take!

Sea trout are usually positive takers of a fly, and as they take and turn down with the fly the fly line tightens and the angler feels this through his line hand and the rod. All that's required now to complete the hook-up is to gently lift the rod tip whilst maintaining a tight line, in order to tighten into the fish.

Short takes and 'tail nipping'

Sometimes sea trout have an uncanny ability to snatch at the fly – quite a hard, sharp pull – without a hook-up resulting. On some nights they appear to be able to do this consistently, apparently 'nipping' the tail of the fly. In such circumstances a 'secret weapon' can be used, which is a similar fly, fished in the same way, but with a tiny treble hook trailing out the back.

Secret Weapon.

Into the dead of night

If the above techniques are working, then there's no need to change. However, often at the dead of night the air temperature can drop, and the splashing of active sea trout ceases. It's likely they're sitting deeper, but possibly still running.

The following three methods are all worth considering if the night goes 'quiet'.

1 Tube flies

For sea trout this nearly always means aluminium, nylon or plastic tubes, from ½in (12mm) to 3in (75mm), although a new, thinner 'needle' tube is becoming very popular. Plastic, nylon and aluminium are three of the

➔ Alexandra tube fly.

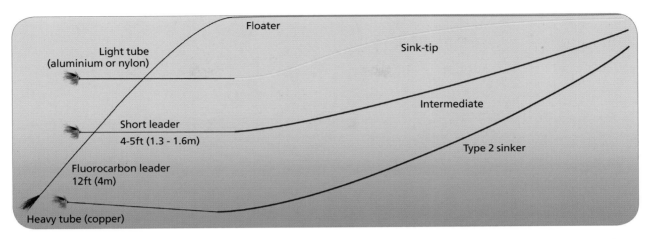

Floater

Light tube
(aluminium or nylon)

Sink-tip

Short leader
4-5ft (1.3 - 1.6m)

Intermediate

Fluorocarbon leader
12ft (4m)

Type 2 sinker

Heavy tube (copper)

↑ Various approaches to fishing deep on a sea-trout river. A floater with a long fluorocarbon leader and heavier tube-fly can be used on slower currents.

lightest tube materials and are chosen for sea trout due to their ability to 'swim' in the light currents that pervade in summer flows. A brass or copper tube would simply sink towards the bottom and 'die' as it swings off the current, which causes an interested following fish to turn away. The fly has to look lively throughout its fishing arc, especially as it swings off the main flow of current – a lightweight tube can do this. However, your fly will still need to fish deeper, so a sinking line is chosen to take the fly down. On the other hand a floater is a much easier line to handle at night than a sinker, so would be the best option for a novice, coupled with a heavier, short copper or aluminium tube on a long, 12ft (4m) leader.

If you're using a lightweight tube fly, then these can be fished on all manner of sinking lines – sink-tip and intermediate lines being favourites, but type 2 and 3 can also be used in the dead of night – depending on the flow and

the depth of the water being fished. The higher and/or faster the water, the quicker the sink-rate of the line.

When fishing with a sunk line, use a single tube and keep the leader short enough to allow the sunken line to govern the fishing depth of the fly, yet long enough to allow for the fly to 'swim': 6–7ft (2–2.3m) is ideal.

2 Snake flies

Snake flies are long-winged flies that are tied on very light, slinky, slim, pliable mounts – such as nylon braid or wire – and are thus highly mobile in the flow, dancing and shimmering in the current. These flies are fished singly on leaders of 8lb BS upwards, with the leader tied to a loop fashioned from the mount material at the front. They can be fished on all manner of lines, from floaters (9ft/3m leader) through sink-tips and intermediates (6–7ft/2–2.1m leader) and through a range of full sinkers, and will tempt fish into taking from just under the surface to just off the bottom, at all speeds of retrieve.

3 Surface lures

Sea trout, especially big ones, can sometimes be tempted to the surface to take a floating lure on nights when they won't look at anything else. It's fly fishing at its most exciting – the silence and stillness of a warm summer's night shattered by an explosive surface take of a monster sea trout isn't for the faint-hearted.

The tactic works best during the darkest part of the night and works very well on quiet, slow pools and smooth glides. It usually involves a heavier outfit, due to the bulky flies used – Jambo, Surface Lure, Night Muddler – being awkward to cast. So an eight-weight rod and line is employed.

It's best to wade quite deep when fishing the Surface Lure. A long leader of 10ft (3.1m) of 10lb plus BS is

TIP

If you aren't sure how your fly is working in the current off the main flow, and you're wading, simply hold the leader 2–3 ft (0.6–1m) above the fly and drop the fly into the water. Shine your torch directly down into the water* to watch how it moves on the tethered leader. If it looks lively, dancing in the current like a fish, then fish it with confidence. If it sinks inertly, then you might want to think about changing it for something lighter in weight.

*Normally, I wouldn't advocate shining a torch on to the water at night – I believe it can put fish on the 'alert' – but with night fishing confidence is paramount, and if this helps you fish more confidently in the dark then it'll be worth it.

Fishing the Surface Lure

1 Cast long across and down.

2 Take a pace or two downstream.

3 The line tightens, then the retrieve starts.

4 Lead the fly round into your bank as you retrieve slowly. Note how the surface lure wakes in the water.

attached to a floating line and cast across the stream. Due to the fact that the line and fly float, you can pay out line to allow the lure to float, inert, over a 'lie'. As soon as the line tightens, the Surface Lure will lurch into action, ploughing its way across the calm surface, creating a distinctive V-shaped wake, which sea trout find hard to resist. Lead the waking fly across the river by swinging your rod tip into your bank, gently figure-of-eighting to keep the fly on the move. The fly swinging to fish on 'the dangle', directly downstream, is a crucial time, as a fish may have followed the lure. At this point, draw in the line using a couple of long pulls to incite a following fish to take, believing that the creature it's been following is trying to escape.

Another night-fishing tactic sometimes employed is to cast the surface lure upstream and strip it back downstream. Again, varying the approach is worth trying.

USING THE SURFACE LURE AS A FISH-LOCATER

The take may be instant and vicious, but at other times sea trout may tap, knock, splash, slash and slurp at the surface fly, seemingly doing everything bar take it as it furrows across the flow. All is not lost, however, as a Surface Lure fished in this fashion can be used to locate exactly where fish are lying. Once a fish has been located using this method, the angler can then return to target the same fish with a big sunk fly, using one of the above methods. Fishing a sunk line over a known, targeted lie in the dark is also a very exciting, exacting, nerve-jangling aspect of fly fishing…but not quite as suspense filled as fishing a surface lure.

Sea trout on a dry fly

1 Anthony uses the light of the setting sun to help him see his fly.

2 He allows it to drift right over the sea trout's lie, lifting his rod tip to keep the line off the fast flow at the pool tail.

3 A dry-fly-caught sea trout.

4 This is the pool tail in daylight.

Contrary to popular belief, on many rivers sea trout do feed, and can often be drawn to the surface to take a dry fly. There are two different aspects of this behaviour that the angler can exploit during daylight hours.

The first is to fish a large dry fly, such as a Daddy-long-legs, or a Sedge. Even if a hatch is occurring, it's best to ignore this and not try to 'match the hatch', but persevere with the big dry fly. The dry fly is cast up and across and allowed to drift over any likely lies, drag-free, before being lifted off and cast towards another likely lie. Even fresh-run sea trout will rise to take the fly.

The other tactic was shown to me by Anthony Steel at Kirkwood, on the Annan, where he's perfected the art of taking rising sea trout on a size 14 Pheasant Tail dry fly during an evening rise, or again at dawn. He finds the very tails of the pools are the best places for this, with the sea trout making slightly clumsy, bulging rises, very close to the rocks that mark the tail of the pool. Using the setting sun in the bright western skyline to see the outline of his fly on the flat water, he wades in the shallow pool outflow so he can cast up above the fish and allow his Pheasant Tail to dead-drift over the rising fish. Unusually, this type of rising sea trout is generally not easily put down. Such a fish can be 'worked on' until it eventually takes the dry.

↑ Pheasant Tail: Anthony's preferred dry fly for this approach.

A single tapered leader of 9ft of 4x (5lb BS) is the best option here – although slightly heavy in the tippet this is necessary, as these fish tend to turn and head downstream, out of the pool and into the weeds of the next pool's inflow when hooked. The most difficult challenge of this approach is avoiding drag from the speeding water at the outflow acting on the fly line. The best way to avoid this is to wade as close to the tail as possible and raise the rod tip to keep the line off the overspill.

The best conditions for this tactic are with the pool at summer low level, and a late-evening sedge hatch or spinner fall drawing the fish to the surface. The heaviest fish Anthony has taken with this method is 5lb.

TIPS FOR NIGHT-TIME SEA TROUTING

Sea trout can be fickle and suddenly switch on to taking. They also move at night both around the pool and from pool to pool, and they run the river at night too. So a pool can change like the flick of a switch. However, constantly flogging through a pool at night, in pitch dark, with a tactic that isn't producing can be soul-destroying. It's better to stop, take a rest, and switch tactics completely to see if you can change your luck and fish with renewed confidence.

It's easy, also, to get too 'mechanical' in your approach in the dark. Remember to alter the speed of the fly by occasionally casting directly across, or even up and across, to allow the fly to accelerate across the current.

Here's an example of a typical night, and accompanying tactics:

- **9.45pm**: Dry fly at the tail of the pools.

- **10.15pm:** Wet flies fished through the streamy runs.

- **12 midnight:** Turn attention to slower-flowing runs. Switch top dropper for Muddler. If this works, continue until well into dark, but change point fly for something much bigger – size 6 or 4. Otherwise try a size 10 double on a floating line with a sinking poly-tip.

- **1.00am:** Switch to bigger flies and start fishing deeper. If really dark, switch to surface lure.

- **2.30am:** Switch to big flies and start fishing deeper, especially over identified lies where fish swirled at the surface lure.

- **3–4am:** Fish big flies deep, but be prepared to change line and fly type. For instance, switch from fishing a tube on floater and a long fluorocarbon leader to a sunk line coupled with a lightweight, long, lithe Snake Fly, perhaps fished faster. Fish the pool tails.

- **4.00am onwards:** Switch back to the floater and wets, changing to smaller flies as the sky lightens.

- **5.30am:** Home, a whisky with the dawn chorus, and bed. There's always tonight!

EYE LEVEL

Ensure you keep an eye on what the river's doing during the night. A summer thunderstorm many miles upstream can cause the river to colour and rise without you noticing, unless you keep a check on the water level. A rising river isn't only dangerous, it also makes night fishing with fly extremely challenging, and it's best to fish these conditions by day (see right).

⬆ A gauge enables you to keep a constant check on the river's height.

Sea trout by day

Rain and high river levels mean night fishing's going to be more challenging. However, a rise in water level will mean sea trout might be running, and they can be caught during the day in these conditions. Standard wet fly tactics will take them, so switching your tactics from night fishing to fishing during the daylight hours can be a good strategy until the river falls and clears. Good daytime wet flies are Connemara Black, Teal, Blue & Silver, Silver Invicta and Mallard & Claret.

Avoiding weed

Sea trout often like the cover of weed fronds and lie up in these shallow, streamy pools at dusk and also at dawn. Fishing a wet fly such as a Teal, Blue & Silver in and amongst the weed fronds can be exceptionally productive, but it's important not to be too ambitious. Fishing anything more than one fly on the cast will invariably mean the cast hooks up with weed. However, a single fly (size 12 or 14) on a longish 10–12ft (3.3–4m) light tapered leader (5lb BS) doesn't seem to hook-up, the fly simply twitches over and around the weed fronds to dance in the spaces between, where the sea trout lie. A rewarding way to start – or finish – a night.

⬇ Fishing a single wet fly on a long, tapered leader in amongst the weed beds at dusk or dawn can be productive.

RIVER SALMON FISHING

A fresh-run Tay salmon is returned to the river.

It's a common misconception that salmon fishing in Britain is expensive. It isn't. It can be – if you want to fish the best, most productive of beats at the best time of the season – but salmon run many British, Irish, French and Spanish rivers from January through to December, and they spawn high in the headwaters of those rivers, so if you fish the right part (and this can be any part) of the river at the right time you have a chance of catching one. It's a never-to-be-forgotten experience.

Starting out: across-and-down

Casting wet-fly style across the river and letting the fly/flies swing into your own bank is the simplest and most common approach used for salmon. Most salmon anglers start fishing with a floating line (highly recommended, as it's far easier to learn to cast with this type of line) with a 9ft or 10ft (3–3.1m) leader of 15lb BS or more. However, on many rivers a more effective fishing (as opposed to casting) line is a sink-tip or an intermediate, which holds the fly/flies slightly deeper and prevents them skating on the surface, which isn't desirable. Unless the water's very cold a salmon will rise to take a fly that's presented just a few (4–12in/10–30cm) under the surface, so fishing any deeper than this is really only essential during the opening months of the season – January, February, March and into April.

When using an intermediate or sink-tip, don't be tempted to fish too long a leader – 6ft (2m) is plenty, some anglers only use 4ft (1.3m); by keeping the leader relatively short you don't negate the sunken effect of the fly line.

The size of the fly is generally dictated by the water temperature – the colder the water, the bigger the fly.

Varying the presentation

The down-and-across presentation using the same line and fly can be varied in a number of ways:

1 The angle of cast

Casting across the flow at right angles means the current will act on the line, form a big belly of line downstream, and the fly will accelerate on a high-speed curve across the river. The opposite effect is achieved by making a long cast downstream at an acute angle to the bank. This will cause the fly to track across the river far slower. Generally, the colder the water, the slower the fly needs to be fished.

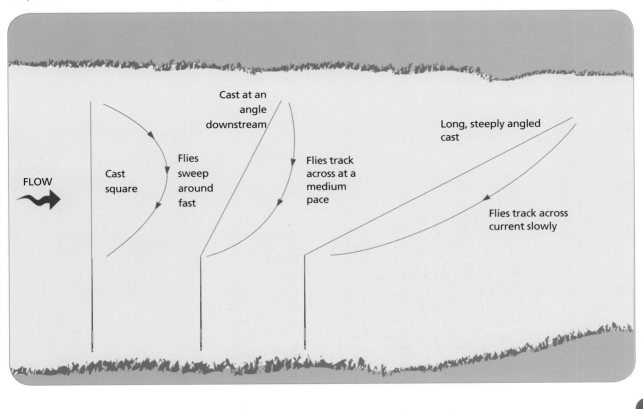

FLOW

Cast square

Cast at an angle downstream

Flies sweep around fast

Flies track across at a medium pace

Long, steeply angled cast

Flies track across current slowly

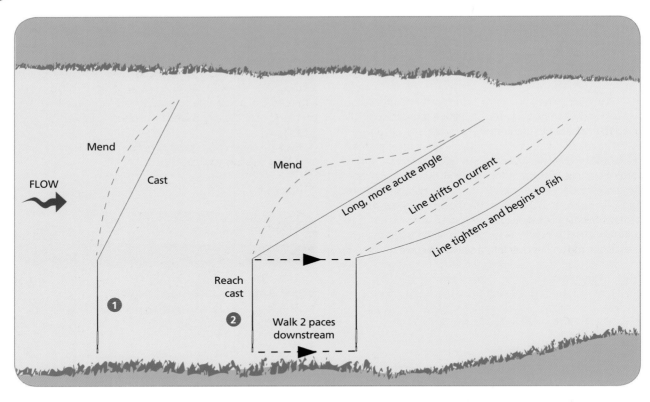

Mend

Cast

FLOW

❶

Mend

Long, more acute angle

Line drifts on current

Line tightens and begins to fish

Reach cast

❷

Walk 2 paces downstream

2 Mending

An upstream mend, put into the fly line by lifting up and reaching upstream with the rod tip just before the current forms a 'belly' in the line, will slow the track of the fly. It also allows the fly and line slightly more time to sink, by delaying the tightening effect of the current on the line, leader and fly.

3 Use of the rod tip

The rod tip can be used as a 'reach mend', by holding the rod tip out at right angles over the river as the line shoots. Again, this reduces the angle between rod tip and fly, thus slowing down the tracking speed. This also allows the fly and line more time to sink, by delaying the action of the current.

4 Stepping downstream

Another way to allow the fly more time to sink is to take a pace downstream immediately after the cast has landed. This adds an extra yard (1m) of slack into the system, allowing the fly extra time to sink. Of course, taking two paces (2m) downstream doubles the effect. Note this tactic should only be employed when the angler is totally confident in wading that particular pool.

5 The sum of all these parts

When trying to get a fly to sink deep and fish slow, a long, acute-angled cast, made with a 'reach cast' followed by a mend and two paces downstream, will allow the fly to attain far greater depth.

Don't strike!

One of the biggest challenges for anglers new to salmon fishing is that of resisting the urge to strike. If you strike too soon you'll feel nothing...apart from stomach-churning deflation at missing the angling equivalent of an open goal.

You need to ensure that the salmon, having taken the fly, has turned and is on its way down to the bottom of the river before the rod is lifted. Lifting too early simply pulls the fly out of the fish's mouth.

There are two ways to prepare for this vital delay:

1 Holding a loop

Learn to pull off a yard of line (1m) from the reel after each cast, and hold that in a loop drooping down from the reel with the index finger of the top hand trapping the line against the upper part of the cork handle. If a salmon takes, do nothing, but let that loop of line

↓Holding a loop.

slip through your tensioned forefinger until it's tight to the reel drum (the reel-drag needs to be set reasonably tight so it won't overrun). Only then should you lift the rod to tighten into the fish.

2 Off the reel

Actually easier for the beginner to prepare for, as it's one less thing to think about after casting. However, it does require much more self-control when a take occurs. It relies on the reel's drag being set to allow the fish to draw off line, against some resistance of the reel's drag, but not set so lightly that the reel overruns. When a yard (1m) of line has been pulled off the whirring reel, the rod is lifted to set the hook. Again, it's essential the reel's drag isn't set so light as to cause overrun when the dead weight of the salmon is brought to bear as the rod arches over into a satisfying curve.

Right time, right place, right fly

'Right time, right place, right fly' is a saying often used by successful salmon fishers, otherwise construed as 'sheer luck'.

But is it all luck? Hugh Falkus, one of the most influential salmon fishermen of the post-war years, once explained it to my friend Rick Turnock, who'd ventured out at dawn – in vain – to see if he could catch a salmon we'd seen jumping in the Spey the previous evening. 'My dear sir', said Hugh at breakfast time, when Rick arrived back from the river tired, fishless and exasperated, 'when you consider that a salmon on entering a river ceases to feed, why on earth would it rise from the bottom of the river to take your half-inch long fly? When that happens, it's a miracle.' He then went on to add, 'All that happened today was...a miracle didn't happen!'

Yes, successful salmon fishing can be put down to pure

↓When the miracle happens.

luck, or even a 'miracle', but there are ways of tilting those odds in your favour, to make that magical, miracle of a salmon taking your fly more likely. In salmon fishing, 'miracles' do happen. Quite why a salmon should rise to take our fly is unknown: it may be an instinct, an act of aggression, or a territorial response – but it's one of the best feelings in the world when it happens on the end of your line!

Here are some ways that may help you improve your luck, or at least improve your chances:

1 Right time

↑Low light levels are good 'taking times'.

Overall, this has much to do with water level. The best salmon fishing comes after a 'spate', which is a rise in water level following rain. As the flood recedes and the coloured water clears, so the salmon uses the improved flow to enter the river from the sea, or head up the river from its lie.

If the fish are newly arrived in the river – fresh from their feeding grounds in the sea – then they're more likely to take a fly than those fish which have been in the river for weeks (otherwise known as 'stale' fish).

Other taking factors may be due to the fish's environment: a slight lift in water temperature, a stabling of high pressure or a change in the light. Low light levels as dusk falls or dawn approaches seem to bring salmon 'on the take'. Some older gillies swear that snow or a hailstorm will bring fish 'on', but I believe that it's probably the darkening of the sky (and possibly a slight warming of the air) before the impending snow or hail arrives that actually switches on the fish.

2 Right place

It's when the fish actually stops moving on its journey up the river, and comes to rest in a new 'lie', that it's extremely vulnerable to a fly.

Perhaps due to enhanced territorial awareness in its new surroundings, it'll readily take a fly that swims over its head at this time. Salmon 'lies' are well known in a river (and explain why a gillie should be listened to very carefully), and are where the fish will take up residence behind a rock, in a gravel dip, in the neck of a pool, at a deflection in the current, under a bush etc – anywhere where they can rest in comfort and safety. However, most lies only fish well when

↑ Right place.

the river is at a certain height. This is because salmon lies will change as the river rises and falls. For instance, the lie at a stone in the mid-current may hold fish directly in front of it in low water, but in high water the lie may be 20yd below the same stone.

3 Right fly

A crucial part of salmon fishing is picking the right fly. Whilst colour may have a bearing on the outcome, the size is often crucial. Generally, the colder the water, the larger the fly. But how large do we mean?

The water temperature governs fly size, as can be seen in the photograph below. In very cold water, at the very beginning of the season, a long tube fly is called for. Salmon are cold-

↓ There's a massive range in salmon fly sizes, but a basic maxim is 'the colder the water, the bigger the fly'.

blooded and are more torpid in cold water. They want to conserve their energy and will only move if coaxed into doing so. A small fly is less likely to provoke them into moving. As the water warms in the spring, say 6–8°C, so salmon will move a longer distance to take a smaller fly, so shorter tube flies of ½–1in (12–25mm) come into play, and with the arrival of spring and a temperature of 10°C plus the angler can start to fish doubles (size 8s and 10s) rather than tubes. As we move into summer and the river warms, the angler progresses through hook sizes of 12 into 14, and as summer reaches its height he may consider going down to tiny ¼in (6mm) lightweight tube flies. Then, as autumn sets in and cooler weather and frosts arrive, so the water temperature begins to fall, and bigger flies can be tied on again.

Whilst water temperature is a good guide for fly size, the fly must show plenty of animation in the water. A very warm river is most likely to be a river at a low, summer level, and the key to salmon fishing is to present a mobile, lifelike, shimmering life form to the fish. A large metal hook will look lifeless and inanimate in low flows, whereas a small fly dressed on a dainty, light hook will swim realistically.

It is a good idea to test the river's temperature to help you make your fly and line choice. The warmer it gets, the smaller the fly should be.

4 Consistency in casting

Another way to improve the odds in salmon fishing is to fish consistently, to a rhythm. Casting well within your maximum distance means you can attain a consistent distance easily, and the line won't collapse, fall short, land at a different angle, land with the fly not turning over or require re-casting. It's not only the cast that catches the fish – control of the line that fishes the fly can make a difference, and is far

↑ Keep moving. Move down a pace or two between each cast.

easier to accomplish if the same amount of line is outside the rod tip after each cast and the fly is presented well at the end of the leader, with good turnover. Striving for distance can lead to inconsistency in presentation.

5 Keep moving

If you have the chance to watch a salmon being fished for in clear water (say from a bridge or high bank), watch how it reacts to the fly. The first time it sees the fly is its biggest reaction. It may move a couple of feet, take a good look at the fly, turn and return to its lie. The second pass of the fly may see it half turn as the fly swings over its head, and the third pass of the fly may only be registered as a quiver of the fins.

The salmon angler should strive to make the next cast the first time a salmon will see the fly, in order to evoke its biggest reaction – which is to physically take it. This is why some salmon fishers move a yard or two, or even three, before making their next cast. The appearance of the fly in the salmon's window of vision has to be a surprise, rather than a thing that's been gradually encroaching its space over the past few minutes. For a beginner, keeping on the move and fishing 'fresh' water with every cast is probably the best lesson of all to take on board.

Lines for salmon

Sink-tips

The most versatile lines for the salmon angler are sink-tips, which keep the fly just under the surface, or they can be used to get the fly really deep if the tip is long and dense. The simplest approach for the beginner is to learn and use a floating line and then, to create a highly effective sink-tip,

add a 5ft (1.6m) sinking poly-tip to the braided/welded loop at the tip of the floater, using the loop-to-loop system.

Multi-tip lines

A more sophisticated sink-tip system consists of a long floating section of line that culminates in a welded loop. This line comes with a wallet containing a variety of tips, usually in two lengths – 10ft and 15ft (3.1m and 5m) – of floating, intermediate, type 2, 4, 6 and 7 sinkers, which also have welded loops. You can switch the tip of your line simply by

↓ Multi-tip fly lines mean the angler can construct the line he requires according to water temperature and flow on the river being fished.

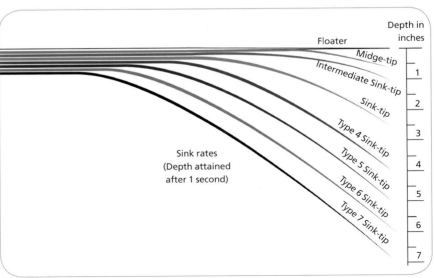

Floater

Depth in inches

Midge-tip

Intermediate Sink-tip

Sink-tip

Type 4 Sink-tip

Type 5 Sink-tip

Type 6 Sink-tip

Type 7 Sink-tip

Sink rates (Depth attained after 1 second)

1
2
3
4
5
6
7

removing one tip from the floating section and attaching another of your choice. This versatility of sink-tip options gives the angler enough line variations to suit all but the most extreme conditions throughout the season. It also provides a chance to vary the presentation as the fly is fished during the day, and from pool to pool. For instance, in the spring in cool water, the 15ft (5m) type 4 section might be used to present the fly deep in the neck of the pool. However, downstream in the belly of the pool a fly fished this way might fish too deeply, and constantly catch on the bottom. A switch to a 10ft (3.1m) type 2 tip to work the fly across the pool might be better. A few days later, on the same pool, as the river level lowers and the flow eases, this approach might change to a 10ft (3.1m) type 2 tip at the neck, switching to an intermediate tip for the slower main body of the pool. If the river continues to fall and slow, a floating tip might be required.

Floating line

↑ A floating line on the Annan, Dumfries-shire.

As the water warms, so salmon will rise towards the surface to take a fly. A full floating line is an option as soon as summer weather arrives, especially on smaller spate rivers, but a short sink-tip shouldn't be discounted. If using a floating line on a big river, consider using a long leader (15ft/5m). This helps disguise the landing of the cast and fly in clear low water. However, on a small spate river 9–10ft (3–3.1m) is as long as you can go realistically.

Nylon, co-polymer or fluorocarbon? Nylon is useful (it rarely tangles), but fluorocarbon fishes the fly just that fraction deeper, and is less visible.

The dropper option

Adding a dropper to the leader is always tempting. I find it gives the option of presenting a small fly on the top dropper and something larger on the point. A typical cast of mine would be a size 12 Stoat's Tail or Executioner on the top dropper and a size 10 Allys Shrimp or Cascade on the point. However, fishing a dropper is fraught with disaster. Once a

→ Executioner.

fish is hooked the trailing hook can catch on rocks, weed or an obstruction. I distinctly recall losing a big summer Tay fish hooked at dawn that ran straight out of the neck of the pool: the dropper caught on a rock and my cast was smashed like cotton. If you're insistent on using a dropper, then the maxim is to have the point fly no more than one salmon's body length behind the dropper fly, so the fly doesn't trail uncontrollably behind a hooked fish but swims alongside it. Being ambitious, I make this distance 3ft (1m).

Sinking lines

Full sinking lines for salmon are gradually being replaced by shooting-head profiles and skagit lines, which are easier to shoot to greater distance and offer denser tips to fish deep. However, because they bite deep into the river flow, a full sinker can fish a fly slower across a river, so remain a presentation option. They're available in intermediate, Type 2 and Type 4 sink rates. The problem with full sinkers is that the shooting line also sinks, so should be held in coils before shooting; otherwise the resistance of the sunken line in the river reduces the efficiency and length of the shoot. Also, a sunk line should always be rolled to the surface, using a roll-cast straight downstream, after the line has swung 'on the dangle'. If you don't make this pre-cast preparation the sunken line will never respond properly to your casting movements.

Shooting heads

Shooting-head lines have enabled the salmon angler to Spey-cast long distances consistently. A shooting head is a length of fly line that, when outside the rod tip, loads the

↓ Slick, thin running line allows the head (orange) to fly a long way.

rod fully on the back-cast. This length of line is attached to thin, slick 'running line', which is the key component of a shooting head in that it offers very little friction or resistance to the shoot. As a result, when a shooting head is cast it can fly a long way.

Manufactured shooting heads are also categorised with the AFTTA number so that the line can be matched to the rod and vice versa.

Casting a salmon shooting head is done in exactly the same way as normal – whether overhead or Spey cast – apart from two prerequisites:

- The whole of the head is outside the rod tip when the cast is to be made, with just a foot or two of 'overhang' of running line.
- The running line is held in long coils in the line hand to prevent it washing around in the river current, or catching in the bankside vegetation. Due to the fact that the running line is so thin it can twist and tangle very easily, so unless the angler is standing on smooth grass or a platform the running line needs to be handled sympathetically, in long coils.

Although shooting heads are good for distance casting they tend not to present a fly well, the line and fly often landing heavily; certainly not as well as a full Spey line.

Scandinavian (Scandi) heads

Originating from Scandinavia, these are generally quite short shooting heads – and thus easy to manage and cast – with long front tapers that make them also good for presenting the fly at distance, as the line turns over better than a standard shooting head. However, these lines aren't so good for delivering large, heavy flies.

Skagit lines for spring

The skagit line originates from the western seaboard of the USA, and was first used by steelhead fishermen using single-handed rods and fishing big flies on fast-sinking lines. Now the lines have been adapted for salmon fishing with Spey casts. Skagits are made up of thin running line, a very short head of thick floating line (about 27ft/9m long) that terminates with a welded loop. To this loop a sinking section of line can be added. This floating/sinking line section forms the 'head' of a shooting head system, which can Spey cast far across the river. Skagit rods aren't calibrated by an AFTTA number but are marked for a certain weight, which is usually measured in grains. This is the optimum weight for casting with the rod. For instance, a skagit rod calibrated 200–400 grains takes a similarly rated skagit line.

Due to the fact that the head is short, a dense, weighty line can be cast and large flies can be launched. Distance, dense lines and big flies means that the angler can today come close to the same presentation as the spin-fisher, who casts a heavy spinning lure across the river for salmon in the spring.

Using tube flies

↑ A Willie Gunn copper tube in fishing mode with the hook eye and knot clearly visible seated securely inside the plastic extension tubing.

Tube flies are popular flies for salmon. All tube flies – aluminium, copper, brass – are attached in the same fashion. The selected tube has a short section of plastic extension-tubing fitted over the rear of the tube. The tube fly is attached to the leader by feeding the end of the leader through the front of the tube and out of the back. The hook – straight-eye single, double or treble – is tied to the leader using a blood knot or tucked blood knot. Once the knot is clipped, the leader is pulled to feed the eye of the hook into the plastic tubing so that it snugs inside and is held there during casting and fishing.

Once a fish takes, this flexible tubing can articulate in any direction without any rigidity or leverage.

If the tube is flexible and narrow, such as a nylon or plastic tube, the barrel knot of the blood knot can be pulled inside the rear of the tube, thereby eliminating the need for any plastic extension tubing.

↑ The end of the tippet passes through the tube and the hook – either a single, double or treble – is tied on the end and then drawn up into the end of the tube, where the hook eye is held by a piece of soft plastic tubing. Tube-fly hooks have straight eyes for this purpose.

Mini-tubes

This is a technique using small – ½in and ¼in (12mm and 6mm) – plastic hairwing tubes to

➔ A mini-tube Willie Gunn.

Alternative approaches

If salmon don't respond to conventional tactics, it's often a good idea to vary your approach. Here are a few of the best ones to try, starting with the mini-tube:

1 The flies are cast across the flow. Allow a belly to form in the line.

2 As the line tightens a steady retrieve is maintained whilst the rod tip lifts to keep the flies moving at a steady pace.

3 The aim is for the tubes to 'furrow' across the water surface.

bring up salmon from smoother water, demonstrated here by Robert Gillespie, expert Irish salmon angler. The leader is 10ft (3.1m) of monofilament 12–15lb BS with one dropper, 4ft from the point. Two mini-tubes are mounted, one on the dropper, one on the point.

Working the fly
A popular technique in Ireland for slower flows, using standard salmon flies – and in particular Irish Shrimp flies – cast across the flow and retrieved with figure-of-eight or short pulls. Can be used on a long (15ft), or shorter (10ft) rod.

Riffle-hitching
Popular in Russia and Iceland, but less so in the UK, riffle-hitching is another method to draw up salmon, especially over smoother, quieter water such as glides and pool tails. A floating line is used, along with a 9ft (3m) nylon leader of 12–15lb BS. Nylon helps keep the fly right in the surface. The fly is a tube fly tied on a plastic tube and can be anything from ½in (12mm) to 3in (75mm). The Sunray Shadow is a popular fly for riffle-hitching.

The easiest way to create the riffle-hitch effect is to make a tiny hole at the side of the tube fly, just in front of the

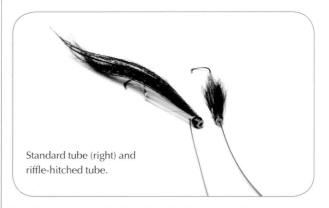

Standard tube (right) and riffle-hitched tube.

head. Rather than feed in the tube fly straight through the opening at the front end, the nylon is fed through the hole at the side before passing through the opening at the rear. The effect of this offset opening causes the tube to 'riffle' just under the surface, as it fights to swim straight. A long-winged fly accentuates this movement, and this lively actioned fly can bring up a salmon to investigate when other, less animated flies don't arouse the same interest.

Backing up
Another tactic change is to 'back up' the pool. Having fished down the pool in the conventional down-and-across manner, this tactic is used to present the fly at a different angle and speed to the fish.

For backing up, a sink-tip or intermediate line is useful, coupled with a biggish fly. A typical candidate for a backing-up fly might be a 4in (10cm) Collie Dog, but a size 8 Ally's Shrimp can also work.

Using this tactic the angler can work up the pool quickly.

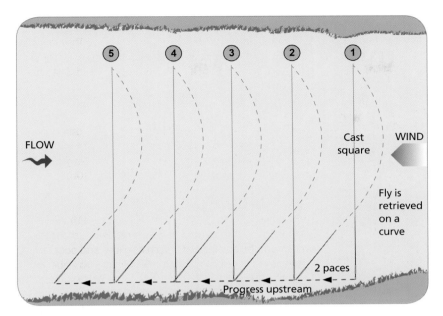

FLOW

WIND

Cast square

Fly is retrieved on a curve

2 paces

Progress upstream

⬆ Backing up a salmon pool.

Starting at the tail of the pool, the fly is cast out at right angles to the flow and as far across the stream as possible. As it settles the angler takes two paces upstream and then starts to draw on the line, pulling to create a fast, smooth retrieve. The fly will accelerate round the curve that the

⬇ Sunray Shadow – an ideal fly for backing up.

BEST FOR BACKING UP

The optimum conditions for backing up are a strong upstream wind that blows to create waves against the current. In addition, because nearly all the line is retrieved after each cast a shorter rod – say 10ft 6in (3.5m) – makes the process of re-casting easier, and is also less clumsy than a long doubler-hander when retrieving.

On club and association waters, backing up is made difficult simply due to a regular procession of fishers moving downstream. However, if you have the pool to yourself and the rules allow, backing up is worth a try.

angler and current have put into the line, and pass quickly over the fishes' heads. The fish has to make up its mind quickly whether to take fly or not. If it decides to take, this will be a positive, heavy pull on the line and the fish will hook itself. Having retrieved the fly into the angler's bank, it is re-cast at right angles across the stream and the process is repeated.

How salmon lies change

Where salmon lie in a river depends on the flow, and lies will change constantly as the river falls or rises. A salmon needs to lie in a position where it won't consume too much energy fighting excessive flow but will feel safe, and get sufficient flow in order to breathe easily and maintain its position in the river.

In normal river flows a typical lie might be behind a rock, mid-current. However, in a flood the salmon is forced to vacate this lie and move to where the current is less boisterous and forceful. This might mean migrating to a gravel bank on the inside of the bend in the pool. Then, as the spate eases and the river level falls, so the fish will slide across the pool to resume its lie behind the stone in the middle of the river once again. So, apart from migrating up the river to spawn, salmon are also on the move when the river levels change, and are also more likely to take a fly.

⬇ In low water the inside bend of this pool is a gravel bank and fish lie under the far bank. In higher water the gravel bank becomes a salmon lie.

SALMON AND SEA TROUT FROM LOCHS AND LOUGHS

Salmon and sea trout migrate up to the Dubh Loch in remote Knoydart, western Scotland.

There are a number of migratory fish systems in both Scotland and Ireland that offer the chance to fish for salmon or sea trout that have migrated into large bodies of stillwater (lochs and loughs respectively). These water bodies often act as extensive holding pools for the fish, which, having run up the river, will gather and wait in the lakes until the autumn, when they'll continue their run up into the streams and rivers that feed such waters to spawn.

These lakes can be fished from the day the fish arrive in the lake until the end of the season.

Increasing your chances

The optimum time for fishing any salmon or sea trout lake is after a spate, following heavy rain. When I fished on the Berriedale in north-east Scotland, my host, Johnnie Paul, would watch the farm track like a hawk whenever it rained. If the rain fell hard enough to cause water to start to flow down the farm track, then he would get excited about fishing the next day, because the resultant spate would be big enough to draw fish up into the river.

With fish having run the river and entered a connecting lake, these new fish eagerly take up and protect new territories or lies in the lake, and are highly susceptible to taking a fly. The arrival of fresh fish in the lake puts the older,

↑ A sea trout is hooked on Lough Currane, south-west Ireland.

staler residents 'on edge', and they too become more aggressive to a fly's presence.

In addition, if it's windy then this stirs the surface, which oxygenates the water and encourages the fish to become more active. Consequently a windy day after heavy rain can amount to an exciting day ahead!

Basic set-up

A long rod (10.5–11ft/3.5–3.7m) is used to fish the flies loch-style, through the waves, creating a wake if possible. A usual cast would be just two flies, 3ft (1m) apart on a 9ft (3m) leader of between 10 and 15lb BS for salmon, and 6–8lb BS for sea trout.

The top dropper position is taken by a bushy 'bob' fly,

→ A heavy hackled Bibio – designed to create disturbance through the waves.

such as a Claret Bumble, Bibio, Green Peter, Daddy-long-legs or even a Muddler, and the point fly would be bigger and sleeker, like a Silver Stoat, Teal, Blue & Silver, Dunkeld, Blue Charm or Ally's Shrimp. A floating line, midge-tip or an intermediate fly line is used.

The whole set-up is cast out and retrieved at varying paces whilst the boat is set to drift over known areas where fish lie. The movement of the top dropper 'bob' fly is often crucial to success, as its push-and-bulge-at-the-surface action attracts both salmon and sea trout. As with all loch-style fishing, the bob fly is left to 'dibble' in the waves for a few seconds just before it's lifted off into the next cast. If a salmon rolls over the fly with a slow head-and-shoulders porpoise movement, try not to lift into the fish too quickly; let it turn before lifting the rod...although this is easier said than done! Sea trout tend to take with gusto, although they can sometimes follow and 'nip' at the flies.

The importance of a gillie

A gillie that can handle a boat, and has fished a migratory fish lake for a number of years, is a valuable commodity! The areas in which fish are caught tend to be the same year after year, so a gillie of many years' experience will know exactly where the fish in the lake lie. A good gillie will also be able to drift or hold the boat right over the lies. Find a good boatman and you have the best chance of finding a fish.

DIY migratory lakes

If you don't have access to a gillie you'll have to work out the lies for yourself. There's a lot of satisfaction in doing this successfully, but you'll need all the help you can get:

Find a good boatman and you have the best chance of finding a fish.

- Glean any information on lies that might be available from locals or that a gillie might volunteer. Write this down before you forget each lie's specific location in the lake.
- Use any visual features of the lake that might suggest migratory fish lies – skerries, prominent rocks, steep drop-offs, inflowing streams, outflowing streams and weed-bed edges.
- Project the surrounding topography to draw an imaginary depth chart of the lake to estimate where the drop-offs, ledges and rocks might be. Aim to fish over water that doesn't plunge down to unfathomable depths; instead try to fish on the ledges where the water plunges away. Sea trout tend to hold in slightly shallower water than salmon. If in doubt, work along the edges of the lake, rather than the middle.
- Fish from a boat that offers some control, either with your boat-partner working the oars or by commandeering a non-fishing friend to guide or hold the boat over likely water by careful use of the oars.
- If you can't control the boat it can sometimes pay to fish from the bank instead – some salmon and (especially) sea trout should lie within casting distance. Select likely areas and lies and keep moving.
- Cast and move along the bank to retieve the flies on an irresistible curved path.

A salmon on a wild and windy day. It took a Muddler.

TWO SECRETS

An intermediate secret

There's a subtle – but often significant – difference between retrieving lines 'loch style' with a floating line and using an intermediate. Whilst a floater tends to skip and skate the flies across the surface (especially the top-dropper fly), an intermediate line will hold the flies a fraction deeper, which causes them to 'furrow' through the surface rather than be pulled across it. The style of fishing them is exactly the same, but the intermediate line cuts through the surface film whilst the floater remains buoyant. We can often use the intermediate to our advantage, and I find this is particularly so when I'm after sea trout. Even if fishing a Muddler on the top dropper, drawing it just sub-surface rather than through it can entice a sea trout into taking, rather than ignoring the fly.

A double secret

In windy weather, fishing through the waves, a double hook on the point can help anchor the cast in the water, especially as it's being lifted up to be dibbled at the

end of the retrieve. Rather than jump and skid on the water surface the weightier double tensions the leader and allows the top dropper to work to better effect. In addition, an intermediate line can also help anchor the line in a boisterous wind.

RETRIEVING – IT'S IN YOUR HANDS

Inching nymphs in a flat calm on Rutland Water, Rutland.

Unlike spinning and bait-fishing, where the line is retrieved by winding the reel handle to mechanically retrieve the line, the fly fisher uses his/her hands and fingers to re-gather the line once it's been cast. The ways in which the line is handled determine how the fly moves through the water, and there are a variety of ways to do this, which all produce slightly different effects.

The rod hand

The all-important index finger

The most important influence your hands have on the line lies not with the line hand but with the index finger of the rod hand. As the rod handle is gripped, the index finger traps the fly line against the cork. The index finger is very sensitive, and varying the pressure on the line will allow line to be pulled through the finger-grip or hold it tightly against the handle. In a sense it acts as a highly sensitive pressure switch, controlling the line flow, which is called on when casting, retrieving, hooking and playing a fish.

The line hand

The strip

The simplest form of retrieve starts with both hands together, gripping the line in the line hand (usually between

finger and thumb) and pulling down by extending the arm, releasing the line, returning the hand to the start position and repeating. Strips can be short (4 in/10cm) up to yard-long (1m) pulls, and range from a continuous movement to long intervals between each strip. The length of strip and its frequency can drastically alter the speed, action and movement of the fly. This is a common retrieve for fishing wet flies and lures.

Any retrieved line is released and allowed to fall on to the ground or water at the angler's feet.

The gather

When dry-fly fishing from a drifting boat, or upstream wet-fly fishing, any excessive slack line needs to be gathered in quickly so that the angler can make direct contact with the fly in order to effect a strike. If too much slack is outside the rod tip, a strike won't hook the fish, because lifting the rod fails to move the fly. You constantly need to gather in any slack line by stripping in line quickly through the index finger so that you 'stay in touch' with the fly.

Pull-and-pause

This is generally steady, longish (1ft/0.3m) draws on the line with a delay in between. This causes the fly to rise (on the pull) and sink (on the pause), and is a useful retrieve for drawing attention to nymphs or leaded nymphs and is very good for animating Tadpoles. For Tadpoles, a yard-long (1m) draw followed by a long, 15–20 second pause can be irresistible.

Figure-of-eight

1 The line is pinched between forefinger and thumb and the wrist cocks away from rod to draw line.

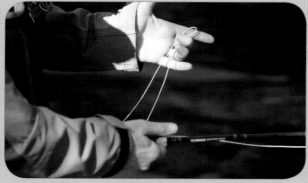

2 Fingers close around loop of line.

3 Wrist cocks back to rod and little finger draws in more line as hand closes.

4 Forefinger and thumb pinch the two coils of line as wrist cocks back away from the rod, drawing line again.

5 Wrist cocks back towards rod, hand closes, little finger draws in another loop.

6 The movement is repeated continuously in a slow or fast rhythm, each coil being held by thumb on forefinger.

Figure-of-eighting is one of the most common retrieves for the nymph fisher but is also used by the wet-fly and lure fisher and by the sea trouter. It produces continuous, smooth movement to the fly and can be made at anything from a very fast pace to a slow-motion crawl.

Also called the 'hand twist' retrieve, it entails pinching the line between thumb and forefinger, pulling the line whilst cocking the wrist back as if you were plucking a feather from a chicken, then curling down both the little and ring fingers to trap the line again at the heel of the hand. The thumb and forefinger release the line, the wrist rolls back to the start position, pulling more line, and the whole process repeats. As this occurs the retrieved line gathers in the palm of the line hand in figure-of-eight coils, one on top of the other. During this process the retrieved line can be held in coils in the palm of the hand or allowed to fall at the feet in loose coils.

DIRECT FIGURE-OF-EIGHT

The figure-of-eight retrieve can be made without the rod hand controlling the line at all, the line hand being in direct contact with the line feeding through the butt ring. This creates a super-smooth retrieve and is highly sensitive. It's an excellent retrieve for the sea-trout fisher, as it allows the take to be sensed through the line hand, and the fish tightened into by simply clamping down on the figure-of-eighted coils and lifting the rod tip.

Roly poly

1 Tuck the rod handle under the armpit and then strip directly down with both right...

2 ...and left hands alternately, as if milking a cow at high speed.

3 The line is constantly gripped by each hand alternately to maintain tension if a fish takes.

The roly poly is all about speed and smoothness. Commonly used by reservoir fishers using out-and-out lures such as the Blob, it's one of the fastest retrieves possible. Used to trigger the predatory instincts of trout, it can also be used for pike, bass and mackerel.

Static retrieve

The static retrieve is a common method of presenting nymphs, particularly Buzzers on stillwater, but the line is seldom completely 'static', as it drifts round on the current or breeze. Thus the angler fishing Buzzers 'static' shouldn't have a mind that's set in neutral, and should be constantly gathering line so he/she can control any slack, enabling a direct contact with the flies should a fish take. This might consist of a very slow figure-of-eight or gradual draw of the line through the index finger.

Retrieved line

What happens to the line that's retrieved?

Generally, line that falls at the angler's feet gathers in loose, slack coils and in the perfect position to be reshot. However, if there's vegetation or obstructions where the coils fall they'll invariably catch the line and it will tangle. The worst offenders in the vegetation stakes are rushes, thistles, bracken, filamentous algae and straps on fancy wellies! The same applies to a boat deck strewn with obstructions such as anchors, ropes, tackle bags etc; a clear deck means a clean shoot. A strong wind can blow loose line into the surrounding vegetation and wrap it around into the most sophisticated of knots. Also, if wading a fast-flowing river the retrieved line will belly downstream and create such resistance against the river's flow that your cast will fall short on

the next shoot. Such circumstances call for more advanced line-management systems.

1 A fistful of coils

If figure-of-eighting, the coils of line can be held in the line hand and cast directly from it. By opening the fingers on the shoot to release line, then clamping down again on to the coils as the line travels back on the back-cast, the line can be kept under complete control without tangling in surrounding vegetation or flowing away on a fast current.

2 A handful of coils

Another way to retain coils of line in the hand is to gather longer lengths of line and hold it in loops, first shown to me by Ally Gowans and demonstrated here (right) by Robert Gillespie.

↓ Figure-of-eighted coils can be shot straight from the hand.

1 For holding coils of line, the fingers of the bottom hand are key.

2 After five pulls on the line a loop is caught by the little finger.

3 Three more pulls and the ring finger takes a loop.

4 Two more pulls and a further loop of line is held by the middle finger.

5 Now the line between bottom hand and top is tensioned over the reel cage.

6 Once the stop is made on the forward cast the fingers open to release the coils of line for a long shoot.

3 A tray full of coils

Another method to hold line off the ground or water is to use a line-tray. This is a rigid – usually collapsible – container that straps around the waist of the angler to hold retrieved line in slack loops ready for the next shoot. Sea anglers often use a converted plastic washing basket for this role to prevent the line getting caught in the wind, tide, rocks or seaweed, and stillwater reservoir anglers often adapt their landing net so that it can be used as a temporary line tray, the pole being customised with a spiked end so that it can be stuck into position on the mud.

→ Using a line tray to keep the running line clear of vegetation.

WHAT ARE THE FISH EATING?

Pied wagtail with a beakful of newly hatched duns. The fly fisher needs to use any natural clues to make the most informed choice of artificial fly.

All fish are opportunists, so the food they feed on – and thus the flies we use to imitate them – relate to what's available to the fish at that particular time. With many species this will be a specific insect at a specific stage of its life cycle. Reading and searching for the giveaway signs or clues is very much like being a nature detective.

Become a waterside detective

Eyes on the water

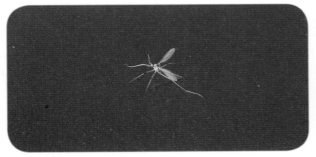

↑ A daddy-long-legs on the water.

The most obvious method of identifying what's hatching is to actually see it happen. Keep scanning the surface for adults emerging or flying past on the breeze. In a boat, keep an eye on the gunwales and seats – freshly hatched flies might hitch a ride there, or land-born insects might land in the boat. On a river, crouch really low on the bank so that you can look right across the water surface for signs of floating insects; their wings often catch the light, so look up and down the river to see if you can spot them. You should also check the inside of eddies along the banks, to see if any floating insects are collecting there.

Spiders' webs

Spiders, like fish, rely on trapping any insects for food, but they use their webs. A careful study of any structure close to the fishery – the jetty, the lodge, fences, bridges, even the boats themselves – will hold clues as to what was hatching just prior

↓ This spider's web at the boat jetty shows a sample of last night's hatch – lots of tiny adult buzzers (midges) and one much larger one.

to your visit. If midges, aphids, olive spinners, daddy-long-legs or yellow may duns are in the air, spiders' webs will catch them.

Detritus in the margins

Often, after a strong wind the remnants of a hatch will be pushed into the margins as a 'scum'. In the past I've seen signs of mass hatches of mayflies, caddis and midge pupae in the windward margins, comprised of both shucks and dead adults. It's clues like these that inspire fly choice.

Bird activity

Often bird activity will be your first indication that a hatch is taking place. The grey wagtail is a common bird to see flitting

↑ Swallows and swifts over the water indicate a hatch is taking place.

from the bankside to briefly hover over the water as it takes an insect, before returning to its bankside vantage point. Dippers, which can dive and feed underwater, indicate insects are on the move. Grebes dive for insects and small fish.

Seagulls often work a water's surface in flocks taking flying insects, as do swallows, swifts and house martins. Ducks will sometimes gather in a mass hatch to scoop up insects on the surface.

In the sea and on reservoirs terns are good indicators of small fish, whereas seagulls and gannets might indicate bigger ones, such as mackerel. Groups of cormorants diving will indicate shoals of either prey fish or larger ones.

In-stream investigation

Simply looking into the water can give you an indication of what insects are active – you may see swimming *Corixa* or

↓ A damsel nymph crawls ashore to hatch, just where the author was about to wade in. Other nymphs are likely to be doing the same.

damselfly nymphs. Turn over a few stones to identify what type of insects live in the water. Check the underside of a stone for olives, stoneclingers and caddis cases. Check when you move the stone for escaping *Corixa* and shrimp. Always replace the stone in exactly the same place after you've studied it.

For more accurate information, there are fine-mesh screens you can keep in your waistcoat pocket to stretch and hold across the flow to catch and analyse what's drifting in it.

Eyes on the land

Check the undersides of leaves on the bankside trees, which often harbour the adult flies of recent hatches, particularly mayflies, olives and caddis. Check the hedgerows for hawthorn fly. Keep a lookout in the fields for mass hatches of daddy-long-legs, aphids or drone flies, or on the heather for heather flies.

Signs of a hatch

If you suspect a hatch, you then need to identify the species. There are various characteristics of flight and behaviour that act as giveaway signs of a species:

↑ Mayfly hatch.

- Olives, stoneclingers and mayflies – look for broad, sail-like wings on the surface as the newly hatched dun floats.
- Sedges/caddis – these have an erratic, jinking flight, like a small moth. Often numerous – in the case of the grannom a hatch resembles a light snowstorm drifting on the breeze.
- Stoneflies – after hatching by crawling ashore, stoneflies rise in a hard-working, laboured climb, looking like a tiny biplane trying desperately to gain height.

↓ Adult stonefly: a flightless male with reduced wings.

↑ Caenis dun (*Caenis macrura*, left), seen on the right leaving the shuck and transposing into a spinner.

- Caenis – these miniature white 'mayflies' land on waders, hats, car bonnets etc in their hundreds, and transpose to emerge as full adults, leaving a tiny, white, empty skeletal shuck still gripping its shedding point.

↑ An adult chironomid.

- Chironomids/midges/ buzzers – a giveaway sign of a hatch is the 'plumes of grey smoke' hanging above hedges and trees as the adults mass and dance after hatching.
- Hawthorn fly, heather fly – these members of the terrestrial Bibio family were described succinctly by Neil Patterson as 'black-leather bikers with long pigtails hanging down their backs' (their pigtails being their legs).
- Black gnats – a crazy mass of tiny black 'ice-skaters' weaving erratically across the river, inches above the surface.
- Spinners – upwings dancing in the air – yo-yoing rhythmically, their tails trailing down – can suggest the onset of a spinner fall (but not always!).

Activity at the surface

Another giveaway sign of what the fish might be feeding on is how they move at the surface in order to take their food. Fish – like any animal in nature – are great conservers of energy, and will only expend excessive energy when the gains for doing so are justified. For instance, a pike will 'explode' at the surface to take a whole fish, having accelerated from its ambush point some distance away, as the energy it gains from eating the fish will far outweigh this energetic outburst.

Similarly, a grayling taking an aphid (greenfly) will simply rise up, sip it delicately from the surface, and tilt down again until the next one drifts by.

Attila Jandi

↑ This fish rising on Urigill, in north-west Scotland, was a good sign of a feeding fish, and the author changes to a dry fly.

← The dry fly worked!

Surface rise

A surface rise is the answer to the dry-fly fisher's prayers. The disturbance made as a fish's nose breaks the surface to take a floating fly may make a sound like 'gloop'. Having risen from deeper down, the fish takes the fly and returns whence it came.

Recommended flies: Hopper, Thoraxed B-WO, CdC Olive, dry Wickham's Fancy

Sip

Suggests small, inert flies which have no or little means of escape, *ie* they're dying or drowning – aphids, midges and spinners or drowned adults are prime candidates to be sipped or sucked down in a tiny whorl. This can be heard as a light kiss. Beware: a sip rise doesn't necessarily mean a small fish!

Recommended flies: Grey Duster, Black Gnat, Bob's Bits, Sherry Spinner.

↑Which one to cast to? A head-and-tail rise to the centre and a sip to the bottom of picture.

Head-and-tail

Head-and-tailing is a confident 'porpoising' rise, the fish's back and then tail breaking through the surface in a languid fashion, and suggests the fish is taking trapped pupae – generally midge or sedge – suspended just below the water's surface. In stillwater such fish will cruise in a straight line, rising regularly in the same fashion. These fish can be ambushed with a carefully placed fly cast well ahead of – but in line with – the rises. Note: sometimes this type of rise can be due the fish taking floating snails, which are difficult to spot in the water.

Recommended flies: Suspender Buzzer, Shuttlecock Buzzer, Klinkhamer Special, F-Fly.

Bulge

A flattening of the water surface caused by the fish's tail as it accelerates down, after turning on to and chasing a swimming pupa or small fish to take it. No part of the fish breaks the water surface. This suggests the pupae or fish it's feeding on are actively swimming away from the fish at speed.

In very shallow water this could be caused by fish grubbing on the bottom for shrimp, *Corixae* or caddis larvae.

Recommended flies: Shrimp, Corixa, Caddis Pupa, Hog Louse, Pheasant Tail Nymph, Jersey Herd, Dunkeld.

Boil

Caused by disturbance of the body turning close to the surface, suggesting the fish is taking slightly shallower prey than the 'bulging' fish. Again, sedge pupae, damsel nymphs or small fish can encourage such action.

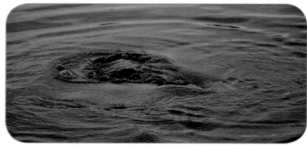

↑Boil.

Recommended flies: Sedge Pupa, Dunkeld, Damsel Nymph, Pearly Invicta.

Slash

An exaggerated boil that happens at the surface, causing a sideways splash. Caused by a desperate lunge of the fish to get at a food item before it escapes. This can indicate feeding on caddis pupae, olive and mayfly duns, hatching March browns, daddy-long-legs and hawthorn flies, as well as small fish, which will often also show themselves by

↓Slash.

leaping out of the water in unison at the same time of the attack. In the sea, shoals of mackerel and bass will attack baitfish shoals from beneath, causing a mass of slashing and splashing over a large area that looks as if a machine gun is spraying the surface of the water with bullets; rather than take cover, such a 'frenzy' is a signal to cast a baitfish pattern into the midst of the mayhem.

Recommended flies: Balloon Caddis, Poly May Dun, Goddard Caddis, Daddy-long-legs.

Slurp

A confident and greedy noise made by trout, carp and chub when sucking down a hatching – but trapped – caddis or daddy-long-legs.

Recommended flies: Balloon caddis, Daddy-long-legs.

Jump

Sometimes fish will try to drown a large adult insect by leaping in the water and landing on it. This can occur with daddy-long-legs, mayflies and damselflies. If this occurs to your artificial, leave it long enough – a few seconds – for the trout to recover, return and mop up the drowned individual (your artificial). On very odd occasions fish will leap out of the water and take an insect as it's flying – this is particularly so with damselflies. I've also witnessed wild brown trout leap out of the water, somersault in the air and swallow-dive directly on to my fly on the surface, taking the fly on its way down. That's talent!

Recommended flies: Balloon Caddis, Poly May Dun, Goddard Caddis, Daddy-long-legs, Adult Damsel.

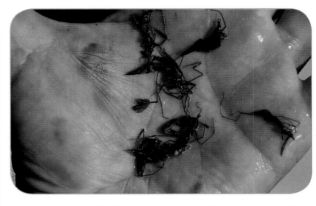

↑ The spooning of this fish reveals that it was feeding exclusively on daddy-long-legs.

Clues from the fish

The fish we've just caught can reveal a lot of interesting information about its recent feeding, which we can use to influence our fly choice.

Instant recognition

Sometimes fish will reveal what they're feeding on the instant they're landed. A pike might regurgitate its prey as it comes in, whilst a trout might reveal midge pupae snagged on its teeth whilst being unhooked. Similarly, a fish feeding hard on daphnia or sticklebacks may spew out some individuals into the net. If floating snails or cased

↓ A subsequent fish caught on a Foam-bodied Daddy.

caddis are being consumed in numbers then these can be felt through the soft belly of the fish, as if the stomach were a bag of marbles.

Spooning feeding

Using a marrow-spoon brings out the detective in a fly fisher, as it reveals a lot of interesting information about the fish

⬆ To use the spoon, simply hold the dead fish, ease the scoop into its mouth and push down the gullet into its stomach. Now simply rotate the fish so it's upside-down and withdrawn the marrow spoon to reveal what the fish had been feeding on. This one had been eating sticklebacks.

⬇ This trout was also feeding on sticklebacks, and had been for some time (note the partially digested ones). Also note the fly it was caught on – a stickleback imitation (a Jersey Herd) – of similar size, shape and colour.

we've just caught. If you're going to keep a fish, then spooning it will give you a fascinating and rewarding picture of what it was feeding on.

Analysing the spooning

Lying inside the spoon will be items on which the fish was recently feeding, those closest to the handle being what the fish was feeding on just before it took your fly. Look closely, and you'll see that the items on the tip of the spoon (which were further inside the stomach) look less distinct, being more broken up and partly digested, whereas those near the handle may still be fresh looking. Often some of these insects will still be alive.

We can assume that the partly digested items have been in the stomach for a few hours (depending on the water temperature) whilst fresh or living items were probably taken minutes or seconds before the fish took your fly. We can use this information not only to judge the type of food the fish was eating, but also to determine and match the size and colour precisely. Look closer still and you might be able to see exactly what stage of the insect's life cycle was being targeted by the fish. For instance, a first look might reveal olive duns or caddis adults. Now check closer to see if this is the full adult or whether it's only partly emerged, half-in, half-out of its shuck. The former tells us to use a dry fly, the latter to use a wet fly or an Emerger pattern.

When it comes to 'matching the hatch' the marrow spoon can prove invaluable.

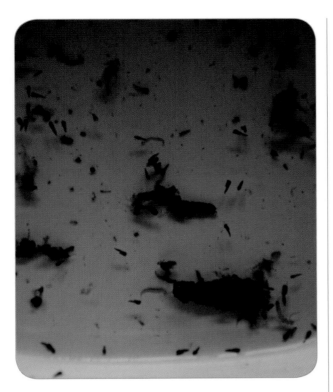

↑ This early season brownie was feeding on tiny midge pupae: almost a hundred of the 3–5mm dark pupae, along with one large 'welded stone' cased caddis, two smaller ones and a couple of free-swimming caddis. It also took a small Black Spider.

The pathologist

Some anglers, myself included, like to analyse the gut contents of any fish they decide to keep. It's always revealing and helps to build a better picture of what fish feed on. You can either empty the spoon contents into a white dish or saucer full of water, or open up the oesophagus and stomach of a gutted fish and wash out the contents. Separate the items, and then examine each forensically. This is a great source of inspiration for future fly choice, as size, colour, movement (some insects may still be alive) and other trigger-points become apparent to the observer.

Study any wings – clear, darkly veined ones suggest adults or spinners; trailing, collapsed grey shrouds are usually the wings of an emerger; light tan opaque cases are shucks. 'Welded' stones and sand tubes are caddis cases. Look for identifiable body parts – legs of a daddy-long-legs, beetle carapaces, wings of an adult stonefly etc. A jellied grey mass is likely to be daphnia. All these items are clues for what fly to fish.

Many years ago I caught some nice Rutland rainbows on a long-shanked Pheasant Tail Nymph. When I got home I opened up one fish's stomach and inside discovered 101 sticklebacks. I placed my Pheasant Tail Nymph against these tiny fish. It's size and outline was very similar to those sticklebacks. It convinced me of the use of a Pheasant Tail Nymph whenever I suspect trout are 'on' sticklebacks.

↓ This bass autopsy, taken from an East Anglian estuary, revealed a dozen crabs inside, some tiny but one of them at least 2in (5cm) across the shell.

PLAYING A FISH

A Blue River rainbow launches itself into the Colorado air.

You've hooked one! Fish on! But what do you do now?

First things first, although hooking a fish is called a 'strike' this suggests jerking the rod back to jab the hook home. Hooking a fish on fly – whether that's a dace or a salmon or a pike – is better described as a lift of the rod or as 'tightening' into the fish. Most often by the time the fly angler registers the take the fish has taken the fly into its mouth and is now turning away with it. All that's required now is for the hook-point to be set into the fish's mouth. It's more to do with timing than force. If this action is too harsh, then the sudden force exerted between rod and fish means either the leader will break or the hook-bend will open out. Both will result in the fish getting away.

Once hooked, the same rules apply. One of the reasons that a rod bends is to absorb the shock of a fish's powerful run, lessening the pressure on the leader and hook-bend. This is why it's essential to 'keep the rod up', *ie* as vertical as possible. This way the natural bend of the rod absorbs the pressure of the running fish – like a spring. Sometimes, however, this isn't enough, and a strong fish may require the angler to 'give line' to allow it to run. Giving line involves either letting line slip under pressure through the line hand, or it occurring directly 'off the reel', with the drag of the reel allowing the fish to pull line away if it exerts a certain amount of pressure. Both require judgement on the angler's behalf, and rely on the strength of the leader and hook – they're

↑ Welsh internationalist George Barron times his lift to perfection and tightens into a Brenig rainbow.

always the weakest link in the angler's system. The key point is that if the fish is dragging the rod tip down to a point where it's no longer bending freely, then line must be given.

At the same time, slack line is also the angler's enemy. A hook-hold can easily fail if it isn't held in position by a line constantly under tension (this is particularly the case with barbless hooks). This means that should a fish turn and run towards you, you need to recover line either by stripping it back or reeling in fast. The key is to keep a bend in the rod. A straightened rod signifies slack line.

Of course, there are times when the angler may have to make the decision to stop a fish from running – into a weed bed, out of the tail of a pool, under tree roots – and this is what will test his tackle to the utmost, and should only be done as a last resort. To maximise the effect, and 'persuade' a fish to turn, tilt the rod so it's horizontal, tighten the reel drag so it'll only give line under the maximum pressure from the fish, and hold hard, letting the bend of the rod absorb the run and the reel eke out line like a miser. This is where the angler can influence his 'luck' – by choosing a heavier breaking strain of leader and tippet, and also a stronger hook iron *before* casting to the fish.

Tips on happy landings

Strong current

If you're playing a fish in a strong current, like the neck of a pool, a river in spate or at a pool tail (where the water always speeds up), landing a fish becomes much more difficult. The key thing to do here is to get to a point where the current is slacker before the fish is ready to be landed. This usually means the edge of the river, but an eddy or a small bay is even better, and the inside of a bend better still. Whilst you're playing the fish, wade or walk to this spot so it can be landed as soon as it's ready.

1 A fish is hooked in the fast pool neck.

2 Instead of pulling the fish up through the current, walk downstream.

3 Here the current is much quieter...

4 ...and landing the fish is far easier.

Walking a salmon

When playing a salmon, the pool tail is often a concern (a salmon running downstream into another pool is fraught with a variety of problems), as is getting into a position where it can be successfully grassed or netted. Salmon, however, have this remarkable trait that, once the angler is in control after the initial run(s), allows it to be 'walked' upstream. To do this, simply wind in to maintain an even, firm tension on the fish downstream or directly opposite you, and then proceed to walk upstream, reeling in line just to maintain a constant tension, as if taking a dog for a walk. The salmon will swim slowly upstream 'on the lead' accompanying you. I've done this on pools on the Tay where I've 'walked' big spring fish almost 50yd (50m) upstream.

When the angler gets into the desired position to land the fish he can then exert more pressure on it, and the fight might kick off once again, albeit well away from the pool tail.

Jumping fish

Fish such as sea trout, trout, pike and sometimes salmon may launch themselves clear of the water when hooked. If this happens, it's awe-inspiring and spectacular, but there's no time to admire such acrobatics. The angler needs to be quick-witted. A good idea is to drop the rod-point towards the water surface, to allow the fish some slack line to 'cushion' the jump. In water the fish is 'weightless' due to its buoyancy, but in the air it's a dead weight (if it's a 10lb sea trout this is like having a 10lb lead weight attached to the end of the leader). If the force of it falling through the air over-taxes a tensioned line the leader will break, the hook will open out, or the hook-hold will fail. If a fish jumps then one thing is certain – it'll fall back down. So drop the rod tip!

By reel or by hand?

Some anglers like to play fish by simply pulling in the line and letting it slide through their line hand when giving line. Others, like me, like to play fish 'off the reel', using the drag of the reel to allow fish to take line under pressure and winding in again to gain line. Neither option is wrong. The hand-line version is less tidy, and is prone to tangling on the ground (and

 ↗ Some anglers, like Roger Dowsett, like to play fish 'by hand'.

→ Others, like Jonathan Simmonds, like to play fish 'off the reel'.

also within the line itself); the 'off the reel' option is less prone to tangling, but isn't so quick on line recovery if a fish runs towards you. Modern, large-arbour reels offer faster recovery than the traditional narrow-arbour ones. If playing fish 'off the reel' I find that, irrespective of the drag I've applied whilst playing the fish, easing off the drag just prior to the fish being landed insures against losing a catch by a fish bolting at the sight of the net.

In all cases of drag-setting, always be aware of too light a setting, as if line is stripped off fast this will cause overrun of the reel, which can lead to a reel jam.

Netting a fish

Once you're in control of your fish then you can start to think about landing it. The simplest, quickest and most reliable way is to use a net.

1 Sink the net, but wait until the fish is ready to be drawn over it. Most likely it'll bolt the first time it sees the net, and this is a likely time for your leader to break.

2 The fish is subdued and drawn towards the net.

3 Once over the net the net is lifted.

4 The fish securely inside.

Using a net

In order to use a landing net, the fish has to be brought within range of the net with the angler in control. There's no point in trying to net the fish until it's ready; in fact this is a key moment when a lot of fish escape. As they come close, fish are well aware of both the angler and his net and will bolt for safety, putting pressure on the line, the hook and the hook-hold. In order to prevent the agonising tale of 'the one that got away', the following skills are required, in this order:

- Patience – primarily to get the fish under control, to succumb and turn on its side ready to be drawn to the sunken net.
- Patience – this time to sink the net and not be tempted to scoop the fish into it. Let the rod do the work of drawing the fish over the net's rim.
- Patience – if the fish turns away let it run, then turn it and draw it in again.
- Patience – once the fish is completely over the net, simply lift it to engulf the fish in the mesh.

Notes on nets

There's evidence that landing nets have been used since Roman days. Since that time all styles and types have evolved in assisting the angler to secure that simple yet crucial step, when the hooked fish becomes a fish that's been caught.

The size of the net's frame reflects the quarry species; the net mesh today is always knotless to avoid damaging the fish's skin. Due to the fact that the net always needs to be at hand there are myriad ways of attaching it to one's person, including belt clips, holsters, snap-links, elasticised cords and zingers. Here I've listed my favourites, and explained why:

River net

A pan-handle shape with magnetic release on frame; fixes to

← Once unclipped, the elasticised retainer cord (which is attached to the angler) means the angler can drop the net and still use two hands to play the fish.

→ A net with an extending handle is useful in a boat.

→ Powerful magnet holds net securely yet enables it to be located in place quickly and without fuss.

↑ Magnetic release: quick, simple, efficient.

magnet on 'D' ring at back of neck. Keeps the net from dangling into thistles and barbed wire, yet is light enough not to cause aching after a day's fishing. An elasticised cord or nylon 'telephone cable' runs from handle to belt. For trout and coarse fish a light wooden river net suffices; for sea trout a larger net similar to above but fashioned in lightweight plastic is useful.

Boat net

When I first started fly fishing we didn't take a net, because my fishing buddy Dave Thorpe considered such a presumptuous move to be 'unlucky'. It was when I first hooked a trout from a boat at Eyebrook Reservoir that I realised not having a net in a boat wasn't unlucky at all, it was downright impossible! For landing fish from a boat you *need* a net, and a long reach is the primary requirement. Nets with extending handles are useful for both storing, transport and landing fish. A simple, rigid frame – a wide 'V' shape is best – avoids problems with tangling and 'failure to unfold'.

↑ A salmon safely in a gye net.

Salmon

The only net to use for salmon is a 'gye' net. You can never know how big a salmon you might hook, and if you do hook a good one then you certainly don't want to lose it. The gye has a big, circular aluminium frame, which has an aluminium extending handle ending with a plastic-coated handle. The handle slides through a mounting on the frame and across the centre of the net. An adjustable leather strap attaches to the handle via a metal ring. The other end of the strap ends with either a Velcro locking loop or a quick-release plastic tab. The strap holds the net on the back, handle pointing up, quick-release loop near the water. When a fish is under control and ready to be landed the line hand reaches back to feel for the quick-release, frees the loop, and the assembly can be slid into the water, net first. Holding the handle allows the net frame to slide down the extension, where a screw-in flange prevents the net head falling off. The net is now ready for use, unclipped and extended, all with just one hand.

TIP

A net can sometimes flow with the current and fail to form a 'bag' hanging from the frame. If this happens, place a pebble in the net to weight it down and stretch it. In a boat, set up your net so it's ready to hand before you leave the dock rather than having to find it, set it up and mess about with it whilst trying to control a fish on the line.

Landing by hand

More experienced anglers can learn to quickly land and release fish without the use of a landing net. The technique relies on playing out the fish then holding the rod tip up whilst reaching back with the rod arm to slide the fish across the water surface towards the outstretched line hand. The line hand then feels for and slides down the tensioned leader to effect the release without touching the fish.

1 The fish is played out and under control.

2 It's lead around the wading angler into the slower current at the river's edge, and then slid towards the angler...

3 ...who either grabs the hook by the shank to tweak it free, or reaches out and slides the fish's belly over the open fingers of his/her hand and lifts to secure the prize.

⬆ The fish under control is drawn to a gently shelving bank.

⬇ The wrist of the salmon's tail is grasped and the fish is gently slid up the bank until it's in water too shallow for it to swim.

⬆ It's possible to unhook a fish without removing it from the water.

Grassing or beaching a fish

Another way to land a fish is to either grass it or beach it. This involves finding a part of the river or lake that shelves gently into the water. The played-out fish is then slid across the surface of the water, by walking backwards with the rod tip up or reaching back over the bank with the rod tip, until it's lying on its side 'beached' in the shallows, either on the gravel, weed or flooded grass from whence it can be released. Weed or flooded grass are gentlest on the fish – be careful if beaching on gravel or sand so as not to abrade the fish's skin if it's to be released.

Handling and releasing your catch

Once the fish is landed it needs to be unhooked. The fish is now highly vulnerable to damage and suffocation. Fish cannot breathe air, and they have a layer of mucous (slime) which protects their scales, so the angler's primary thought should now be to unhook the fish as swiftly as possible while touching it as little as possible. If you want to keep the fish to eat, then despatch it as fast as possible.

Holding a fish isn't easy (the phrase 'as slippery as a fish' could not be more apt), but it comes with practice. The first rule is: don't aim to carry the fish anywhere. Place the net in the shallows and simply lift the fish gently up and out of the net; that way, if you drop it it'll fall into the net. Secondly, ensure you don't squeeze the fish; if you do, it'll struggle and writhe. I find that a loose grip is better and causes less reaction, and a loose grip with two wetted hands is better than one. Also, fish seem to struggle less if held upside down.

Unhooking a fish

Poor unhooking probably causes more distress and damage to a fish than any other action an angler can make. The best thing is to use a barbless (or de-barbed) hook, as these slip out very easily, often on their own after landing. With a barbless hook it's possible to bring a fish 'to hand', slide your hand down the leader, feel for the hook, grasp it by the shank and push and twist the hook as if you were screwing it into the fish's mouth. In most cases this'll release the hook-

➜ Forceps-grip the fly body and then ease it out of the fish's mouth by pushing down and back.

hold without the angler having to touch the fish. This is the quickest, least fussy and most proficient release.

If this doesn't release the hook-hold, grab your artery forceps, which again should be easily accessible, possibly clamped on to your waistcoat. With the fish lying in the net, in the water, maintain some tension on the line to open the fish's mouth and allow you to see the hook-shank. Feed in your artery forceps, clamp and lock on to the hook-shank, then press down and push back to release the barb.

Sometimes, you need to pick up the fish to support its head so the hook can be eased free. This requires a gentle but firm hold on the fish, but before you do this always wet your hands, as dry hands will remove the fish's mucous layer.

Killing a fish humanely

If you wish to keep a fish for the table, then your decision to kill it must be made the moment it's landed. Your 'priest' should be to hand at all times (perhaps in a known pocket in your waistcoat). Pick up the fish and hold it in your weaker hand, gripping it over the back and down the sides, behind the gills. Grip your priest loosely in your stronger hand and line it up on the fish's head, just behind the line of the eyes. Then tap the fish hard on the head with your priest, as if you were knocking in a nail with a hammer; as you do so you can lift the fish slightly with your weaker hand to meet the blow and maximise the impact. Be bold. Timidity isn't required here. It should take one, short, sharp blow to kill the fish outright. Once killed, unhook it.

RETAINING A FISH

If you're going to kill a fish make sure you keep it in good condition. An unprotected fish kept on a warm day will dry out and begin to lose condition very quickly. To keep it fresh, use a bass bag, constructed of woven cloth or canvas. The fish is popped into the bass bag and then the bag is soaked in the water. Don't leave the bag *in* the water, as the bass bag operates on the ancient Egyptians' principle of keeping water cool – evaporation on the outside causes cooling on the inside, thus the fish remains not only damp but also remarkably cool, even on a hot day.

↓ A bass bag is designed to be wetted throughout the day, keeping its contents cool through evaporation.

Releasing a fish

1 Once unhooked it's important to release the fish as quickly as possible, and for it to be out of the water for as little time as possible. If you're taking a photograph, aim to lift the fish out of the water just for the shot.

2 Hold the fish gently in the water by the wrist of the tail and support its belly just behind its pectoral fins, with its head pointing into the flow.

3 Give it plenty of time to recover; it may take a few minutes. When it kicks firmly, let it slide away.

FISHING FROM A BOAT

Looking for a rise on Loch Orbisary,
North Uist.

Fly fishers and boats go hand in hand. If you fish for trout, salmon or sea trout, pike, mackerel and pollack, you'll inevitably encounter casting and fishing from a boat. It's relaxing, accesses parts of water a wading angler can't reach and presents endless angling opportunities.

Managing a boat for success

Know your depth

Knowing the depth of water in which your boat is fishing is often vital to success. Sea anglers and pike anglers often use echo-sounders to read for depth and also to locate features such as ledges, rocks, 'structure' (wreckage, for instance) and baitfish shoals.

Traditionally, game fishers rely on their eye for reading the underwater terrain or accumulated local knowledge to gauge depth, which is one of the many skills of the gillie.

In many reservoirs the clarity of the water allows the eye (with the aid of polarised lenses) to judge depth, but deeper than this some anglers use other methods, such as measuring out the rope as it sinks down when lowering the anchor; or they may have a DIY wind-up tape measure with a sea-fishing lead attached to the end, which can be used as a plumb-line with a high degree of accuracy.

Using a gillie to strike gold

On many wild waters, particularly when fishing for salmon and sea trout, a gillie is worth his weight in gold. Not only does he know the 'lies' but he's also an experienced hand at controlling the boat – by pulling on or gently feathering the oars so that it's drifting over fishable territory for the majority of the time. Many salmon and sea trout lies are

so specific that the likelihood of catching migratory lake fish with a gillie is far greater than that of anglers who fish without one.

Apart from this make-or-break fact, the gillie is usually a great source of entertainment, encouragement and fishing experience. Enjoy your day!

↑ The para-drogue works like an underwater parachute. Note the C clamp on the gunwale, used to vary the position of the drogue rope to fine-tune the attitude of the drifting boat.

Drifts and drogues

A boat will drift side-on to the wind. If it is windy, then the boat can drift too quickly and overrun your flies. A drogue, or sea-anchor, can be used to slow the boat's drift. This allows the water to be covered more thoroughly, and the flies can be fished with more control, slower and/or deeper.

The simplest form of drogue is a small, square sheet of canvas with a hole in the centre and a cord attached at each corner. The four cords meet at a swivel link attached to a length of nylon rope. The drogue is attached to a rowlock and thrown overboard. It opens like an underwater parachute and slows down the boat.

Using a para-drogue

The para-drogue is a more sophisticated system, in that it can be collapsed immediately by pulling on one of the side-ropes, and also its position in the water can be altered in order to make fine adjustments to the angle the boat is drifting.

The para-drogue is a rectangular sheet of nylon with a pair of nylon lanyards linking the shorter corners on the left and right sides with a ring. A short length of rope connects each ring to the boat. Although it acts in exactly the same way as the simple parachute drogue, because it has left and

↓ How the para-drogue works under water.

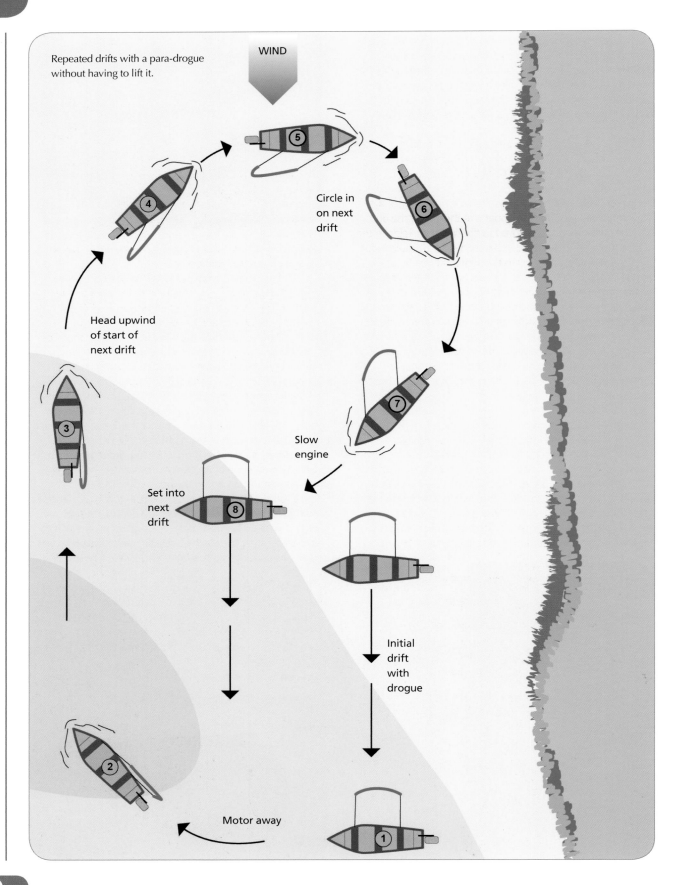

Repeated drifts with a para-drogue without having to lift it.

WIND

5

4

Circle in on next drift

6

Head upwind of start of next drift

7

Slow engine

3

Set into next drift

8

2

Initial drift with drogue

Motor away

1

right attachment its length and its position on the boat can be finely adjusted by attaching C clamps to the gunwale.

Careful positioning of the drogue can allow the boat to drift with more control. There's an element of drift-speed control too, as shortening the rope on the para-drogue means the boat can drift faster than on a long line, when the drogue 'bites' deeper into the water.

The para-drogue can also be deployed continually, without having to be hauled aboard, if a series of simple drifts are being made over open water. This technique can also be used with a single person in the boat, who needs neither to lift the drogue at the end of the drift nor throw it back in once the new drift is set. Assuming the boat is at the end of the drift and the para-drogue is deployed to the right-hand side to the engine, the engine is started and the boat simply motors out of the end of the drift, turns to the right, and heads back upwind on a straight line until it's just past the new set-in point. Then the boat curves in to the right and, when in line with the new drift, makes a neat but fairly wide 270° turn, always turning to the right to position the drogue on the same side of the boat, just as before, and the engine is cut. This way, the drogue will collapse as the boats starts to pull out of the drift, trail alongside the boat as it heads upwind, and redeploy once the boat's momentum has stopped, without tangling around the propeller.

Note This is a highly advanced technique, as the drogue ropes could easily become entangled in the propeller. Consequently it's for experienced boatman only and should be used only on open water, since it involves smooth turns of the boat. It shouldn't be attempted in areas of heavy boat traffic, or where any intricacies of steering or reversing are required. The key to this technique is that if the drogue is to the right of the engine, then the boat should only ever turn right. If the drogue is to the left of the engine, then the only turns made should be to the left.

TIPS

→ A longer rope allows the boat to slow down more.

- To slow down the boat, pay out more rope to allow the drogue to 'bite' deeper.
- When pulling in a drogue take care, its resistance is strong. Don't pull the drogue into the boat by the rope – grab, a corner and the parachute will automatically collapse and come in easily.
- In dire emergencies, which I've encountered on some wild trout lakes, a strong bucket with a nylon rope attached to the handle will act as a makeshift drogue.
- In rocky lakes, the drogue can tangle around a rock - be careful of using a drogue in such lakes in high winds.

Drifting without a drogue

A boat drifts broadside-on naturally, so a drogue isn't always required – sometimes the natural speed of the boat's drift is an advantage. At other times, such as over rocky shallows, a drogue is a hindrance and also unsafe, as it can get caught on the bottom. So a drogue shouldn't be thrown over the side as a matter of course.

Often the best approach to fly fishing is to cover (*ie* drift over) as much water as possible. With tactics that involve

No drogue required in this light wind whilst searching for fish.

faster retrieves, such as wet-fly fishing and lure fishing, this isn't usually a problem – if the boat is drifting faster, then the retrieve can be speeded up to counter that. The same principle can apply to static dry-fly fishing, only the slack line is gathered in more quickly.

However, as the wind gets up the boat's drift-speed increases to the point where it's drifting too fast for the angler to gain complete control of his flies, and the first sign of this is the boat overrunning the line or flies. Now is the time to deploy the drogue. Sinking lines, which require a number of seconds to get down to fishable level, or nymphing techniques, which require a slow retrieve with the line under complete control, are techniques in which the drogue is a valuable aid to enable the angler to fish more effectively. But only up to a point. In calm conditions, a drogue can be an unnecessary hindrance.

Another use for the drogue is to help to exploit specific rainbow trout behaviour, which is to patrol the water upwind in small groups or pods. This means that a free-drifting boat is a more effective way to find such roaming shoals. Finding the fish in the first place is the key to success. However, having connected with a fish on a drift and having marked the exact position of where the fish took the fly, the boat can be motored back round upwind to work the same drift, aiming to meet the same pod of fish again, only this time with the drogue deployed so the water can be fished over again with a more focussed approach. It's possible to fish such short drifts over and over again, constantly meeting fish.

In essence, drogue use boils down to adapting the boat to suit your fishing technique and ensuring you're fishing to maximum efficiency.

Anchoring

Sometimes fishing from a static platform, such as an anchored boat, allows for certain techniques to be used which are difficult to use from a moving boat, or the boat's position might be over a shoal of fish lying deep, or there's a prominent feature, such as a weed bed or a shelf, or it might be in a position where the fish are constantly coming towards and past the boat, such as trout patrolling upwind or saltwater fish moving in with the tide. Under such circumstances a static, anchored boat is very useful for fishing a fly deep or slow: sinking lines can be counted down; leaded flies can be inched along the depths of the bottom; a Booby can be twitched across the lakebed.

Alternatively, if fish are higher up in the water, but moving upwind, then nymphs or dry flies can be fished statically, or allowed to drift round on the wind – a deadly technique. Or the casts can be 'fanned' from this central platform. An anchored boat offers superb control of the flies over deep water and allows for a thorough search.

Double-anchoring

Deep nymphing on a floating line requires delicate line control, and can be made much easier if the boat isn't

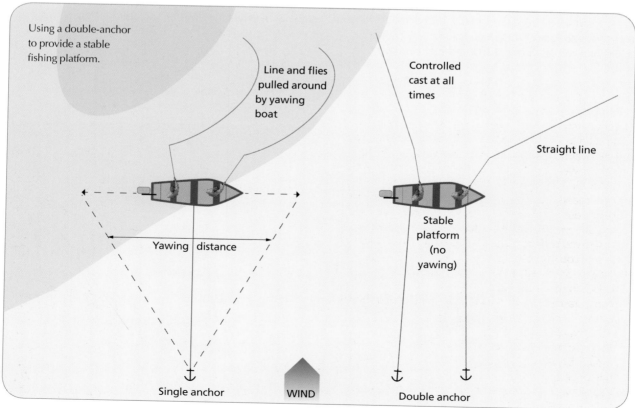

Using a double-anchor to provide a stable fishing platform.

Line and flies pulled around by yawing boat

Controlled cast at all times

Straight line

Yawing distance

Stable platform (no yawing)

Single anchor

WIND

Double anchor

⬆ This boat is anchored, allowing the two anglers to fish their flies just off the bank on to which the wind is blowing.

It's easy to drop anchor, but don't be tempted to stay anchored in the same place for too long if nothing's coming to the flies. Pulling up the anchor is harder work than dropping it, but keeping on the move, searching new areas, moving continually, is essential until you locate fish. An easier method is to drop anchor on a shortish line, fish the area, then let out another 15yd (15m) of anchor rope to fish a new area downwind, and keep repeating this process until all the rope is paid out. Once you've located fish you can stay there as long as you like!

yawing from side to side, as all single-anchored boats tend to do. The way round this is to take two anchors and position one in the bow and one in the stern. With the boat in position, drop both anchors simultaneously (this is easier with a trained boat partner!) and let out similar amounts of rope until the anchors bite. Secure the ropes to the respective bow and stern cleats and the boat will become a stable platform for fishing the most subtle of techniques.

Again, if searching for fish there's the option of simply paying another 15–20yd (15–20m) of anchor rope and allowing it to slide out from each cleat to access a fresh area downwind without having to lift and reset the anchors.

Boat safety

Unfortunately, angling, boats and drowning statistics go hand in hand. In the UK in 2012, 371 people drowned and, as ever, over half of the deaths occurred in inland waters.

- Always wear a life jacket. On many reservoirs in the UK this is the fishery rule, and in Ireland it's the law.
- Understand how your boat engine works in the dock, before setting out – the choke, pull-cord, gears, air-intake, fuel pipe and attachment – and make sure you can start it easily. Ensure you understand how to lift and set the engine.
- Ensure you take enough fuel.
- Take a pair of oars, and know how to use them.
- Check the bilge pump/bailer.
- Avoid standing up in an inland fishing boat; you should be able to cast, fish and manage the boat without standing up.
- Organise the boat for seats, tackle, rods, anchor and drogue before you set out. In particular, set up your rods before getting in the boat.
- Keep a weather eye open, particularly for high winds, lightning and dense fog.

- If you're uncertain about your location, the weather conditions, or concerned about the boat in any way, don't attempt to get back to the dock. Pull in to the most sheltered spot, pull the boat ashore and contact the lodge or boat-hire point.
- When under power, ensure the 'kill cord' is inserted under the relevant button on the engine and attached to your wrist or clothing.

⬇ An organised boat is a safe boat, as it means movement once afloat is kept to a minimum.

SALTWATER FLY FISHING

Colin MacLeod casting for golden grey mullet in the breakers of a sandy beach in north Cornwall.

Fly fishing in the sea, off coastlines all around Europe, has developed rapidly in the past 20 years. Modern saltwater-resistant gear has contributed to this, along with technological advances in casting and lines. However, for the most part it's the inventiveness, pioneering spirit and ability of fly fishers themselves that has been the significant driver of this exciting branch of the sport.

This was influenced by the Americans, who developed their own saltwater fisheries – for striper bass in the north-east, and for bonefish and tarpon in the south – back in the 1950s. The fish have always been there, and have always been angled for with bait and spinning gear: it's the attitude and innovation of fly anglers that's created this new fishery, with a massive potential for discovery and sport. Today any fly angler visiting the seaside on holiday should be able to find some fly fishing to suit him.

Where to start?

Firstly, as ever, one needs to know which species one is targeting, and this is influenced by the terrain of the coastline and the preferred habitat of the fish (see Chapter 1). Yet again, local knowledge is a valuable resource – the local tackle shop is a good place to start. The key information you require is:

- Where to fish exactly? (Take an Ordnance Survey map with you, and a pen).
- Which species are present?
- When's the best time to fish (ie the best state of the tide)?
- What baits do locals use?
- What are the dangers that might catch out a visitor? – the strength of the tides, shifting/quick sands, mud flats, cliffs etc.
- What time is high/low tide? (Local tide tables are generally available.)

If you can't access such information you can still work it out. The most likely spots for the coastal fly fisher are – depending on the species sought – estuaries, bladderwrack-covered rocks in sand (known as 'leopard bottom' due to its mottled, light-and-dark patches), deep water off cliffs, mussel shoals, a point on the edge of a bay, inside a reef, inside a bay, or even a beach (for golden grey mullet).

However, the crucial factor for the fly fisher is the wind. A strong wind blowing either into the angler or on to his casting arm makes for large waves and difficult casting conditions. More than anything else the strength and direction of the wind will influence where you fly fish.

The best fly fishing will come if the water is clear; the clarity of the water enables fish to see the fly easily. If the wind or flow of the tide stirs up the bottom to cause a silty suspension then fly fishing is going to be much more difficult (but not impossible). However, seeking areas of clear water is a good rule to start.

The next consideration is the timing of the tides. As a rule, when the tide is turning (ie slack water) fishing is slow. The tide needs to be flowing (in or out) to get fish moving, and on the feed for better fishing. It takes six hours for a tide to change completely (from low to high, and vice versa). During the first couple of hours, the tide runs slowly but then increases in flow and intensity to peak flows during hours three and four. During these peak hours of high current, everything – prey and predator – is on the move, and hunting peaks. On the sixth hour high or low tide is reached and the flow stops once again, before reversing.

The height of the tide varies too, depending on the phase of the moon, and every month at the time of the full moon there's a very high tide followed by a corresponding very low one. Again, an exceptionally high tide will flood areas not normally wetted, and might open up fishing opportunities only available for a few days a month. Similarly, an exceptionally low tide might offer access to grounds that can't be covered during 'normal' tides.

Which gear?

Having decided on your likely quarry you need to ensure the gear you've chosen to use is saltwater-proof. This applies particularly to reels and fly-rod fittings, which can corrode if allowed to be attacked by saltwater, but it also applies hooks, zips on clothing, scissors, boot cleats, aluminium fly boxes etc. Anodised reels and fittings should afford protection, but if you're in doubt, use stainless steel, plastic or nylon. Irrespective of the coatings, always wash down your gear with soapy, fresh water after using it in the sea.

Tactics for mullet

Colin MacLeod has pioneered a nymphing method for all three species of mullet, which are found in shallow, clear water areas that are relatively sheltered. The advantage of coastal mullet fishing is that standard trout gear suffices perfectly well, and his lightweight #5 or #6 outfit is perfectly matched to the mullet's environment, allowing these powerful fish to fully express themselves. He finds fluorocarbon makes his ideal leader material, and he uses 8lb BS as a minimum, constructing a leader 12ft (4m) in length featuring a single dropper located 3ft (1m) from the point fly. Fishing with two flies rather than three helps him to reduce tangles. A floating fly line is required, due to the shallow nature of the water being fished and for its ability to drift with the current. To avoid embarrassment, reels should contain at least 100m of backing.

Mullet flies

Flies may be the smallest piece of equipment but they're the most important. One of the main obstacles encountered when Colin began fly fishing for mullet in 2009 was the complete absence of recognised mullet patterns. The introduction of Ray Bramble's Red-headed Diawl Bach in 2010 was a game-changer, and suddenly mullet could be caught with consistency. A number of equally effective patterns created specifically for mullet soon followed and the once 'impossible' fish was now decidedly catchable. All flies are tied as size 12.

Red-headed Diawl Bach

A highly successful pattern for all three mullet species, offering a generic representation of the small invertebrates upon which mullet feed. Best fished by dead-drifting to an active shoal.

Flexi-worm

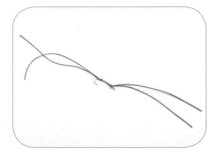

The colour red appears to attract mullet, and the wriggling, red Flexi-floss featured in this pattern has it in abundance. An effective pattern for drifting with on a current and for targeting mullet feeding in breaking waves. Passing sea trout can find this fly hard to resist. A good pattern for thick-lips, and Colin's most successful fly for golden grey mullet.

Flexible Fiend

A weighted version of the Flexi-worm, designed for drifting to fish sitting in deeper water or strong currents, possibly imitating a marine worm. Has produced thick-lips and golden greys (as well as bass, sea trout and a thornback ray) from fast, deep water.

Corophium volutator (mud shrimp)

A specific pattern representing the small shrimp which inhabit burrows in areas of mud flats. Features highly on the thin-lipped mullet menu. Best fished with short, sharp pulls to imitate a fleeing shrimp.

Flexi-shrimp

A robust, generic pattern that suggests all manner of small shrimps and invertebrates. Accepted by all three species and can be fished by dead-drifting or with a slow retrieve.

Ghostbuster

Designed to imitate marine woodlice (*Idotea*) on which mullet and bass dine with abandon. The pattern features a shellback of closed cell foam that enables the angler to target shoals feeding in extremely shallow water, with or without a current, where standard patterns would constantly snag the bottom. Has accounted for thick-lipped and golden grey mullet.

Spectra Shrimp

A pattern that more than rivals the Red-headed Diawl Bach as a catcher of mullet (and many other species!). Introduced in 2015, this fly has already provided Colin with personal bests of all three species of mullet and bass. The iridescent shellback seems to catch the mullet's eye. The Spectra Shrimp is unique in that it's worked with a pull-retrieve for mullet, which readily give chase to a smartly pulled fly under

↑ Spectra Shrimps.

the right conditions. The first thick-lip to fall for the pattern was an 8lb 12oz fish from a Welsh tidal river, which has been recognised as a UK record on fly.

Note With the exception of the Flexible Fiend, the flies are tied unweighted in order that they can be drifted on the gentlest of currents and fished in the shallowest of water. These patterns are now available from Selectafly.

Targeting thick-lipped mullet

Finding shoals of feeding mullet is the key to success, and there's no better place to begin your search than around the mouth of an estuary. The tactical approach typically takes place in water 6in to 1ft (15–30cm) in depth. Fishing the flooding tide from low often offers the best advantage, with mullet visibly exploring the shallows in search of food. Telltale signs for feeding fish include splashing, jumping and conspicuous 'V' shapes in the water as fish cruise the upper layers.

Wade quietly to take up position in advance of an approaching group and utilise any current available to dead-drift the flies in their direction. A Spectra Shrimp on the point with a Red-headed Diawl Bach on the dropper makes a lethal combination. Mullet actively feed on deceased shrimps and invertebrates transported by the current, therefore the flies are imitating dead organisms rather than living ones.

Monitor the end of the fly line closely for any indication of interest: mullet takes can be very gentle and lightning fast. Gently strip-strike to set the hook and utter a small prayer to the fishing gods. The ensuing tussle may well leave you trembling, and the high from catching your first mullet will last for several days.

Recommended flies include Spectra Shrimp, Red-headed Diawl Bach, Ghostbuster, Flexi-worm, Flexible Fiend, Flexi-shrimp and Red Tag.

Thin-lipped mullet in the harbour

Thin-lips also feed around estuaries and fall to the same approach used for thick-lips, but it's over areas of shallow mud flat that the most prolific sport takes place. Thin-lips move in over areas of mud on the edge of the flooding tide in search of *Corophium volutator* (mud shrimp) in water so shallow that their backs are exposed. The mullet suck feeding Corophium from their burrows and at times the mudflats can literally boil with feeding fish. Twitching a Corophium pattern in front of foraging fish can produce

↑ 5lb Hampshire thick lip.

→ Distinguishing feature of the thick-lipped mullet: the thick upper lip.

↓ The 8lb 12oz thick-lip which hammered a Spectra Shrimp on a Welsh tidal river. Recognised as the UK record for fly-caught thick-lipped mullet.

↑ A harbour thin-lip fooled by a Diawl Bach. The thin upper lip is clearly visible.

→ Thin-lips move in with the tide to feast on mud shrimp.

explosive sport, often within the confines of a small harbour where the close proximity of yachts, chains and anchor ropes adds to the contest.

Stalking golden grey mullet

Perhaps this species is most deserving of the accolade 'British bonefish' through its similarity to bonefish in appearance, habitat and blistering runs. Sight-casting to a pod of golden greys nosing through freshly flooded sand is as close as it gets to Caribbean-style fishing.

Golden greys primarily concentrate their feeding on the area where waves break against the shore, dislodging food in the process. Shoals often congregate around the mouths of rivers running into sandy bays as the tide begins to flood. Fish are commonly seen 'surfing' in on a wave, ready to pounce after the breaking wave stirs up shrimps, hoppers and other fare.

A typical cast for golden greys would consist of a 12ft (4m) leader with a Red Flexi-floss Bloodworm on the point and a Red-necked Diawl Bach or Flexi-shrimp on a single dropper. The most successful approach is to stand roughly 15yd (14m) from shore facing the beach. Cast the flies to

↓ Colin hooks a golden grey where the river enters the sea on the beach.

land on the beach, right on the edge of the breaking waves, and then slowly trickle the flies into the water. Takes are lightning fast and surprisingly hard and even a 1lb fish will run far and fast, jumping like a mini-tarpon along the way.

If surf conditions prevent stalking of the fish from behind then they can be approached from one side maintaining a low profile, as the angler will now be in the mullet's field of vision. Patience and a slowly retrieved Spectra Shrimp will often achieve the desired result. Recommended flies include Red Flexi-worm, Spectra Shrimp, Red-headed Diawl Bach, Flexi-shrimp and Ghostbuster.

Hunting bass

The sea bass was the first saltwater fish to be targeted seriously by the UK fly fisher, probably due to its aggressive nature and its willingness to hunt in shallow water. Bass will move in on the flooding tide to hunt for sandeels, crabs, shrimp and small fry.

As a result of their feeding habits, bass can be caught both on lures fished faster to imitate bait fish and sand eels, and slower-fished imitative flies, such as shrimps and worms.

↓ Sea bass.

↑ A nice bass taken on a Clouser at the inflow of a breached sea wall.

↓ Another bass is hooked, this time as the tide starts to recede (note the flow running back through the hole in the sea wall).

A floating line or a sink-tip (either mini-tip or full sink-tip) or intermediate is usually sufficient to get down to the fish, especially as a reliable fly for bass is the Clouser Deep Minnow, which has a bead-chain eye that allows it to attain depth even on a floating line. Good colours for Clousers are Chartreuse & White, Grey & White and Brown & White.

→ Deep Water Clouser is ideal for saltwater predators.

A good starting set-up would be a sink-tip with a 6–7ft (2–2.3m) 10–12lb BS leader with a fry pattern or Clouser Minnow attached. The Clouser has a bead-chain (or even heavier) eye, so the line and rod needs to be beefed up to an #8 or #9 for easy casting. Casting and stripping back the fly will provide realistic fish action, but the Clouser is such a good all-round attractor pattern that it can be fished slower and deeper by allowing the fly and sink-tip time to sink.

As the tide starts to flow the angler can treat the water just like a river. This is a good tactic if you expect bass to be swimming past you, for instance in an estuary, at the opening of an inflow or outflow or off a point. By wading out or by standing on a point and casting 'upstream' the angler can make an 'upstream' mend to buy more time for the sink-tip and Clouser to sink on a slack line. As the tide sweeps fly and line 'downstream', the line tightens and then swings it across the flow. All the angler needs to do is to introduce a few erratic strips to add life to the pattern as it fishes round.

Once 'on the dangle' it can be stripped back in and re-cast.

Positioning yourself so the flies will swing over a feature – such as a mussel bar or shallow reef – will improve your chances of meeting a hunting fish, as such a place would be exactly where the bass would expect to hunt down its prey.

This tactic can also be used for fishing two smaller wet flies, fished on an 8–10lb leader but with a dropper 3ft (1m) from the point. Use a silver-bodied fly like a size 6 or 8 Peter Ross, Teal, Blue & Silver or Silver Stoat's Tail on the point and a more suggestive fly (size 12) on the dropper – Hare's Ear, Mallard & Claret, Diawl Bach or even a Dunkeld. This is a good combination if you suspect sea trout might also be patrolling the shoreline.

Bass will move in close to shore, scattering fleeing bait fish as they attack, so can be contacted on beaches, off rocky points, in estuaries, around 'structure' (bridge pilings, tidal walls etc), at inflow points and at the edges of flooded marshland as the tide pushes towards its maximum height.

Another tactic worth trying is to fish a Popper. This tactic works especially well at dusk. A floating line is used, coupled with 9–10ft (3–3.3m) 10lb leader and a floating Popper or Gurgler attached using a loop knot.

The lure is cast out 'around the clock' from the angler's position and popped back across the surface with either long strips or short, intermittent pulls. The Popper is meant to imitate an injured or live fish on the surface and bass will

↓ The Popper's disturbance at the surface attracts bass.

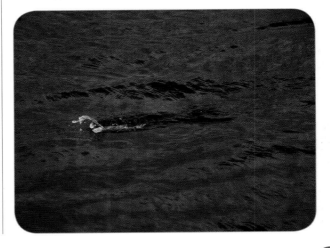

↑ Bass on a Red-headed Diawl Bach.

come up from depth to take it.

If surface activity of fleeing bait fish is noted within casting range then cover this with the Popper and expect action!

The Popper is also a good alternative tactic if you suspect bass feeding in shallow water, but your flies are continually catching on the bottom.

The saltwater nymphing advantage

Colin MacLeod's pioneering approach to saltwater nymphing with light tackle for mullet has also led to a number of exciting developments for other species.

Bass of a reasonable size regularly join mullet to engage

TIP

When looking for the shoals of small fish on which bass or mackerel feed, scan the coast for bird activity such as diving terns and gulls working at the surface. Such activity indicates the presence of bait fish shoals that will, in turn, indicate the possibility of bass or mackerel following underneath.

(Roger Hall)

---

in communal feeding, especially when an abundance of shrimp and marine slaters (*Idotea*) occurs. Dead-drifted Spectra Shrimps, Diawl Bachs and Ghostbusters will all be taken too.

In addition sea trout find a drifting red Flexi-worm irresistible, and Colin's first catch of the 2014 season was a flounder that unexpectedly fell to a Diawl Bach. More unexpected was the 7lb thornback ray which pounced on a Flexible Fiend as it tumbled along a deep trench.

Mackerel

This summer visitor to UK shores is one of the most voracious and hardest-fighting fish in the sea, distantly related to tuna, a much sought-after warm-water game species. Mackerel tend to be found mainly over deeper water and are best located and fished from a boat. However, the shore angler is always likely to encounter feeding mackerel at some time, so should be prepared in case a shoal comes in range, because they offer the chance of frenetic, high-octane sport.

Be prepared for the blitz

The best chance for the shore angler comes when fishing off rocks, particularly into deeper water but sometimes off a beach or in an estuary. However, mackerel move at a fast pace, and the shore-based angler is unlikely to have a shoal within range for long.

The first indication you may have of mackerel is a 'blitz' of fleeing fish. Mackerel attack a bait-fish shoal from below and tiny fish scatter across the surface like splinters. This is activity the fly fisher prays for. Cover it as much – and for as long – as possible. If you can, follow the marauding mackerel shoal (this is normally only possible along a beach). Cast the fly into the centre of this activity and strip it back.

If you have time to change flies, then switch to a White & Grey or White & Blue Clouser. If these don't work, fish them as fast as you can. If this still doesn't produce a result, change to something silver and smaller, such as a size 4 Teal, Blue & Silver.

The best time for shore-based mackerel fishing is during a 'weak' (neap) tide, *ie* when there's less height change between low and high tide. This occurs when there's either a waxing or waning half-moon. If the moon is new or full then the bigger, stronger tides will tend to keep the mackerel shoals further out at sea, in which case they can be tackled from a boat.

Mackerel from a boat

Remember those hand-lines you used as a child to haul up mackerel on a string of feathers? They would have had either a 4oz or a 6oz lead on the end to take the feathers down to the fish. If the mackerel are shoaling deep, and the tide is flowing, then both the current and the depth need to

↑ Deceiver: a good bait-fish imitation.

Pollack

There are three prerequisites for finding pollack – deep water, kelp and rocks. A typical pollack venue is a steeply shelving headland. I find pollack and lighthouses go together well. You can also catch pollack off rocky points. Another good place is off the steep sides of fjord-like sea lochs such as those in western Scotland or Norway.

The aim is to find a place where you cast easily into the drop-off, straight into deep water. Ideally you want your rock casting platform to be just above a steep drop into deep water, but BE CAREFUL. If waves are crashing into the rocks, don't go there: not only is there a danger of being swept away but fly fishing will be too difficult in any case; aim for a sheltered spot.

For pollack, a beefy outfit is required. At least a 9-weight. Firstly, the fly is likely to be weighted, so it's more difficult to cast distance, and secondly, the first thing a hooked pollack will do is make a power-dive back down to the rocks and into the kelp – it possesses this astonishing ability not only to effect its escape but also to leave your line fast in the kelp. The only way to prevent this 'Houdini act' is to lock up – give them not an inch of line – and lift them up as soon as they hit the fly. It's a genuine tug-of-war. If you let a big pollack dive you're likely to lose it. If you're fishing from rocks a longer rod is also useful as it can be held out over the water to hold fish and prevent them from diving into the kelp that's attached to the rocks under your feet.

When I first started hooking and losing pollack like this (on the Isle of Skye) I remedied the situation by using a 15ft salmon rod to hold and lift the fish out from far down under my feet. For this reason, I believe a 12–13ft #9 switch rod should make for a good rock-fishing pollack rod.

The reason you need to cast to distance from your position on the rocks isn't because the pollack are far out, it's because they're deep down. Once the line lands on the water it sinks down, like a pendulum, with the fulcrum at your rod tip. The longer you can cast, the deeper you can fish the fly. Cast as long as you can, and then let the fly and line sink deep. Count it down: 10 seconds, then retrieve; next try 20 seconds to sink the fly, then 30 seconds, and so on…until you either hit the bottom or hit fish. Retrieve the fly in steady, long strips to imitate a bait fish or sand eel. If a pollack hits the fly, hold tight!

be overcome by the fly fisher, and he has no 4oz weight to help him. Then there's the added problem of seawater's density: because it contains salt, objects are more buoyant than in freshwater, and this includes fast-sinking lines. A fast-sinker in a reservoir becomes a slow sinker in saltwater, so use the fastest sinking line in your armoury. A Hi-D Express line or a Rio Deep 7 is a good choice, teamed with either an 8- or 9-weight rod in order to cast the fly, which also requires weight in it: a Blue & White Clouser Deep Minnow is a good choice, but dressed with heavy brass or lead dumbbell eyes. Tie it on a short (5–6ft/1.6–2m) fluorocarbon leader of 15lb. This tactic is all about attaining depth…quickly.

Cast uptide and pay out any slack line to allow the fly and line time to sink as it drifts down with the tide. Once it tightens, strip back the fly in long pulls. If nothing takes, try to fish deeper. Do this by casting directly uptide, and strip off another 5yd (5m) of line from the reel and continue to pay out this slack to buy more time for your line to sink down before it tightens on the sweeping current.

If this still doesn't hit the fish's depth, repeat the procedure but strip off another 5yd of line and pay this out as the line sinks. Continue to increase the amount of paid-out slack line (you may even have to resort to paying out some backing) until a fish takes. Now your fly and line have reached the shoal's holding depth. Simply remember how much slack line you paid out to get to this fishing depth for the next and any subsequent casts.

The technique is the same whether the boat is drifting or at anchor, but it's easier if the boat's anchored, as a drifting boat has a tendency to overrun the sunken line if it's drifting fast.

If you're lucky enough to encounter surface activity with terns, gulls and gannets diving and bait fish scattering at the surface, there's no need (and there may not be time!) to switch lines, flies or rods. Simply cast into the frenzy and retrieve immediately to keep the fly near the surface.

Such activity may be prolonged, particularly in the evening. This is an opportunity to switch to a lighter outfit – say a 7-weight rod coupled with a floater, sink-tip or intermediate or sinking line – and a Deceiver Lure or even a sea trout Sunk Lure. Strip fast and prepare for fireworks when you hook one!

TIPS

- Pollack feed better in the dark, and often come closer to the surface at such times, so evenings and early mornings are good times for the fly angler seeking them.
- If fish are pecking at the fly, then change the pattern to a different size or colour.
- Black is a very good fly colour for pollack.

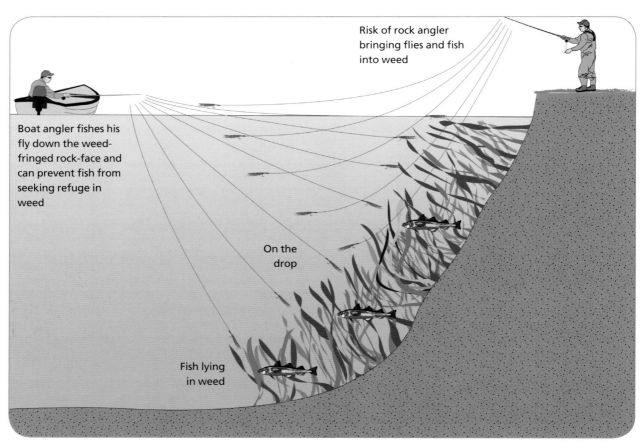

Risk of rock angler bringing flies and fish into weed

Boat angler fishes his fly down the weed-fringed rock-face and can prevent fish from seeking refuge in weed

On the drop

Fish lying in weed

↑ The boat angler can allow his flies to fish deep 'on the drop' along the edge of the kelp. However, the rock angler needs to be aware that any fish he hooks will be able to dive straight into the kelp. Using a longer, stronger rod helps prevent this happening.

↓ A pollack dives powerfully in deep water, just off the rocks.

When you land a pollack, keep it in the wet net or handle it with a soaking wet cloth, as their skin is easily damaged.

Pollack from a boat

A boat can access the rocky reefs and shelves in which pollack thrive. By anchoring uptide of the reef, or anchoring out from a cliff face, the fly line can be cast out – as long as possible – and allowed to sink into the deeper water (see 'Mackerel from a boat' above) in which the pollack patrol and is where they ambush their prey. Again, experiment with counting down the fly to ascertain the depth required to contact the fish.

An ideal position is if the boat can be anchored close to a rocky drop-off, where the fly can be cast out and allowed to free-fall down the shelf. The fly can be given an occasional twitch as it sinks down, but the aim is to allow it to free-fall as if it was an injured or dying fish. Some line can be pulled off the reel and paid out into the water (by swiping the rod tip from side to side) to maintain the fly's position as it sinks down just off the shelf-edge (normally it would be pulled away from the shelf as the line sinks in a pendulum curve from the rod tip; slack line at the tip helps delay the pendulum effect). Pollack live in and under the kelp attached to the shelf. The line between rod tip and fly will be fairly tight as the fly continues to sink deeper. If a pollack takes, it'll tighten further and pull on the rod tip. Strike and hold tight. The great advantage about this position is that the

→ Bladderwrack and kelp beds off Scotland's Western Isles. The tide here can rise many feet in a matter of hours.

angler can pull the pollack away from its kelp-infested sanctuary, rather than into it, as is common when fishing off the shore.

Safety at sea

- Always be aware of the height of the tide and the speed with which it can move. A rocky outcrop is always a prime position for a fisherman, but keep an eye on the low ground behind you as it floods on an incoming tide. Don't get stranded. Always ensure your way out and away from the water is clear.
- Know your local tidetables. Check the local weather report.
- Let other people know where you're fishing, and take a mobile phone with you in case of emergency. Keep the phone in a waterproof case.
- In remote spots always fish with a companion, and take a first-aid box.
- Wear proper footwear for grip. Rubber soles are good in mud, sand and gravel but are an accident waiting to happen on weed-covered rocks. Wear studded soles.
- Take a torch with you (for finding your route back and signalling) and if you're fishing off steep rocks, take a rope.
- Take a compass if fishing an estuary or bay. Mist and fog can be extremely disorientating and dangerous.

Fishing from a boat

Ensure everyone is equipped as above and for fishing in a freshwater boat (see Chapter 17) but in addition take:

- Two anchors.
- Ample rope.
- A compass.
- A VHF radio.
- Lights.

↓ Ensure your boat is well-equipped before going afloat.

PIKE FLY FISHING

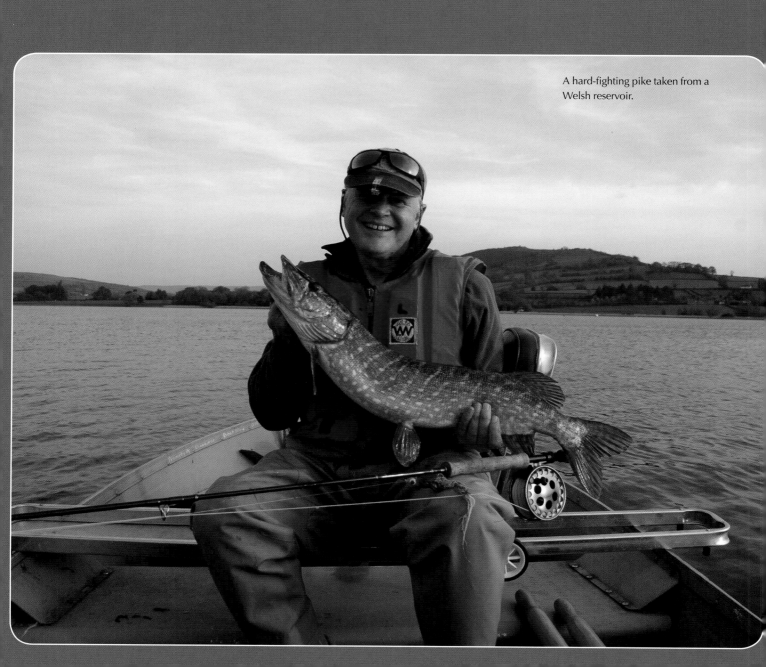

A hard-fighting pike taken from a Welsh reservoir.

Pike from both rivers and lakes have become a popular quarry for fly fishers in recent times, and this is unsurprising when we consider the sizes pike can attain and the dynamic sport they provide. Even 150 years ago it was well documented how flies could tempt large pike, often better fish than could be caught on bait. It appears that the sinuous, lithe movement of bait fish-style flies is an irresistible attractor for the predator, and stories abound from venues all over the northern hemisphere of fly fishers catching more pike than the traditional techniques of dead-baiting and spin-fishing.

Also, the take is often actually visible, which is very exciting…but remember to strip-strike rather than lift the rod.

Tackling up for pike

Due to the size and power of this predator, the bulk of the fly patterns and the wire trace necessary to avoid 'bite-offs', a tip-actioned 9ft #9 or #10 rod is advised. Smaller 'jack' pike (under 10lb) could be targeted with a #8 outfit, but most anglers would want to be able to cope with a big fish should one happen to take.

The fly line can vary from a floater through to a clear sink-tip, but the front taper should be short, allowing for good turnover of a hefty fly. A floating line is a good line to start with, but the clear sink-tip is one of the best presentation lines.

Leaders shouldn't be too long, and should be heavy enough to deal with big fish and to handle and turn over a section of wire trace plus the fly, so 20lb BS is recommended. A 6ft (2m) leader makes a good fishing and controlled casting length with a #9 rod.

A slow-sinker is sometimes useful for accessing pike that are lying right on the bottom in colder weather. In these conditions a short 4–5ft (1.3–1.6m) leader with a buoyant, foam-headed fly is a good tactic, the buoyant fly being allowed to dip, float and dive (in the style of the Booby – see Chapter 8) as it's pulled in a short strip-and-pause style.

A major hurdle for the pike fly fisher is overcoming the pike's teeth. It has

↓ A big fly, but lightweight to cast.

a set of triangular, razor-sharp teeth that line the mouth, and in the roof of the mouth are rows of tiny, backward-inclined teeth that are designed to grip the prey fish. Such is the efficiency of a pike bite that any fly attached to nylon is simply bitten through. This means that a length of wire is required to act as the connection between leader and fly.

Wired up for pike

Today thin, pliable trace-wire is available (20–25lb BS) that can be knotted, just as with nylon, and is very reliable. Use a non-slip loop knot to tie on your fly. To attach the wire to your leader use a double grinner. 18–20lb BS stiffish nylon is ideal leader material; pike aren't really 'leader shy'.

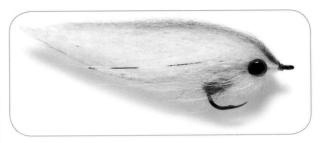

↑ Teardrop EP fibre flies maintain fish shape and action but remain light when casting, as the fibres shake off water during casting.

The best flies for pike are ultra-mobile flies such as fur-strip Zonkers, although in larger sizes these can prove difficult to cast when waterlogged. The Deceiver is also a useful fly, but teardrop-shaped flies of man-made fibres have the advantage of easily shaking off any water held within the fibres on being false-cast, and so make casting a much more simple affair, being much lighter. Add to this translucency, hints of flash, sinuous movement and that inherent bait fish shape, and they make an ideal choice for a bait fish imitation.

The fish pike eat regularly are roach, bream, perch, trout and their own young (big pike tend to control the number of smaller pike in a lake through their cannibalistic nature), so flies designed to imitate these species – light grey and light olive in the 'wing' with white on the underside – are a good start. A fly possessing big eyes is also useful. Flies 4–6in (10–15cm) long are a good size, but flies of up to 1ft (30cm) are also used, though casting them demands skill. Keep one or two in your box, just in case. Pike also have a preference for white and red flies.

Visible signs

Pike are highly sensitive to vibration, having special receptors in their lower jaw: small splashes and erratic movement can actually attract a pike. Hence the success of a noisy disturbance fly like the surface Popper. Best conditions are a fairly flat calm; twitch the fly and stop, and pull and pause, let it behave like a live thing. Make some noise with the fly.

In addition, pike can give themselves away. The most obvious sign of their presence is the launching of bait fish into

↑ Keeping back from the edge: pike can lie close in, and often take close to the bank.

the air as the pike attacks, the bait fish scattering from the point of the attack. A large boil or swirl in the water will signal the pike turning on its prey. This phenomenon can often be witnessed at dawn – one of the best times to catch a pike.

Pike often 'bask' in the sun, close in to the edges of water. If, when walking along the edge of a lake, you see a swirl and a resultant cloud of mud in the margin then this is evidence that a pike has just bolted from there…and won't be too far away. Sometimes, such fish of the margins magically appear into your window of vision, creeping into the shallows whilst you're fishing. These fish are inquisitive, and on the hunt, and are catchable.

When to pike-fish?

One of the advantages of pike is that they make a challenging quarry during the winter. However, they become more voracious as spring warms the water, and their peak feeding time is June/July. May and October are favourite times for pike fly fishers because the weed in which they dwell has either not developed or has died back, making pike more accessible to the fly at these times. (Be aware that May is the close season on English and Welsh rivers.)

Dawn and dusk are the best times to catch a pike. No one really knows what brings pike on to the feed, but this change in behaviour can occur at the flick

↓ A pike caught as the evening draws in.

of a switch, at any time of day. With pike this seems to be a collective behaviour – when they're on, they're on.

Lake and river… but where?

Pike can be caught in all types of water, and most anglers in the UK (apart from northern Scotland and the Scottish islands) will have a pike venue very close to their home.

Pike predate on other fish through ambushing them so can be located near the shoal fish on which they prey, but more critically near 'structure' that they can use as cover to get close enough to their quarry without causing alarm.

Thus pike are most likely to be found in and around:

- The edge of reed beds.
- The edge of lily and weed beds.
- Around sunken trees.
- The edges of weir pools.
- The junctions of a stream or backwater.
- The edge of a shelf or a drop-off.
- Boat jetty pilings.
- Slow river bends.
- Cutaway bays just off the river-flow.
- Deeper holes in the river.

Bear in mind that when pike are really on the feed they'll move out into open water, and will often hunt in packs around a big shoal of prey.

Approaching a lake

Drifting is better to cover more water and also to locate fish. Remember to cover the margins and weed edges with your fly – cast along the margin rather than far out – and keep moving. If you come across a group hunting in the same area, perhaps homing in on a bream shoal, it's best to stay in this place and wait for the pike to move in on them.

↓ A pike from the lilies.

Which lines?

In clear water it's best to use an intermediate sink-tip to hold the fly 1ft down – it prevents the fly from skating too. Pike in 10ft (3.1m) of water will 'look up' and take a fly that's swimming just 1ft down in the water. This set-up means you can cover a lot of water with a sink-tip.

Coloured water is a different story. You need to search the water more thoroughly, as the pike won't see your fly so easily. Now you need to let the fly sink after casting out, and be more thorough with both casting and retrieving to cover the water at all the depths and angles.

Deadly retrieves

The best retrieve for pike is quite slow with jerks so the fly acts like a dying fish. Sometimes faster retrieves work, especially in the summer, but don't be tempted to fish your fly too fast.

Pike often take 'on the drop', so always be alert. After casting, pull on your line to straighten it so you're in touch with your fly. If a pike takes, the line will draw away, indicating the take.

Fishing for pike can be a highly visual sport. Use polarised lenses to help spot pike following your fly. If fishing from a boat and a pike follows, don't be tempted to lift the fly to the surface (as you would for a trout) – the pike will spook, because it'll see the boat. Instead you can either stop retrieving and let the fly hang by holding the rod and line and very gradually raising the rod tip, or stop and let it sink to the bottom. If the pike doesn't take now then the key lies in your next move – suddenly jerking the fly into life again to galvanise the pike into taking it.

Use this sudden movement to tempt a following river fish too, or use the current to change the swing of the fly in a river. For instance, cast to far bank of the river, to the edge of the reeds where pike often lie. Let the current move your fly across the river, and if you spot a pike following let the fly swing right across until it's just off your own bank (on the dangle). Now give the fly a good pull to spark it into life. The pike should then take.

Fishing a Frog

There are various Frog flies and Poppers, complete with rubber legs, which are a great tactic to use in the weed beds as summer draws on. First, ensure the Frog fly has a weed guard. Use a floating line, and tie on the Frog fly to the wire trace using the non-slip loop knot.

Swimming Frog.

Cast so the fly lands on top of the weed or lily pad and then twitch it off with a short strip. Now use short, jerky

TIPS

- A pike that moves to a fly but doesn't take is very likely to make another attempt. A change of fly size or colour, or resting the area for a few minutes, can result in a more positive result.
- If you know fish are in the river or lake and you try to fish for them on one day and don't catch any, don't give up! They may have been off the feed.
- Be aware that if you can see a pike then it's likely it can see you. It can see you on the skyline if you're standing high on the bank. Often pike will follow the fly and take right under the rod tip, but they won't if they can see you. Keep crouching low as you retrieve.
- When a pike takes, don't lift the rod tip but strip-strike, ie make a long, positive draw with your line hand to make sure it's hooked.

strips to make your Frog 'swim' all the way back towards you. If a hungry pike is in the vicinity, it will hear the noise of the swimming frog and take it in a welter of foam. Concentrate on the take and remember to strip-strike. One take will make your day.

Handle with care

Although pike can be seen to be ruthless, merciless and powerful in nature they're actually quite delicate when out of the water. Various items of kit will assist a quick, efficient and healthy release.

↑Hold inside the gill-cover.

- Always be aware of a pike's teeth.
- Hold a pike by sliding your fingers from underneath the pike, inside the gill cover, on the inside of the gill rakers. Your fingers should come to rest on bone behind the pike's head.
- An unhooking mat provides protection to the skin, and is also padded so that they don't damage themselves.
- Large, 10–12in (25–30cm) forceps are required to remove the hook easily without your hands getting too close to those deadly teeth.
- A pair of long-nosed pliers is a useful tool if the hook-hold proves difficult or is deep.
- If you wish to weigh your pike use a weigh sling and scales.
- Work quickly and boldly to get the pike unhooked, weighed and released back into the water in the minimum amount of time.

Treat pike with care and respect and they'll swim away no worse for their encounter with you.

PRESENTATION CASTS

William Daniel makes an upstream cast with a nymph on the Upper Itchen, Hampshire.

Helpful casts

The way the cast is made can be to the angler's advantage. Rather than manage the line on the surface, which disturbs the water, these casts are fashioned in the air before the line lands.

Stillwater advantage

Presentation on stillwater is generally focussed not only on accuracy but also turnover. Getting the flies to turnover in a neat, straight line at the extremity of the fly-line tip on every

↑ As the forward cast is made...

↓ ...the line shoots and tugs on the reel, automatically kicking the flies over for good presentation.

cast is a skill, but the angler can 'cheat' by simply stopping the line fractionally before the end of the shoot.

- On the forward cast, the line is shot and allowed to fly out over the water.
- As the shoot starts to die, simply clamp down with the line hand to check the shoot abruptly.
- The cast will kick over, with the point fly stretching out the leader to its maximum.
- Depending on the amount of energy still in the shoot there may be an element of recoil on the line, which can also be used as a tactical river cast (see below).

River advantage

There are a number of casts for flowing water that can be made in different ways to gain tactical advantage. Slack line casts are crucial in river fishing. All such casts on rivers are to buy time for the flies to either sink or drift drag-free, or to delay bellying of the line in the current between angler and fly. The key to all these casts is to remember that the line always follows the rod tip, because it is, in essence, attached to it.

Recoil cast

As with the 'stillwater check' (see above), if this is made earlier in the shoot the energy in the cast will cause the line to kick over, stretch to its limit and then recoil to land on the water in a squiggly line. The advantage of this is that the squiggly line puts slack between the angler and fly and delays any effect of the current on the fly due to bellying of the line.

Single mend in the air

1 As the line shoots out the rod tip makes a late upstream sweep...

2 ...and back again before the line lands.

3 The result is a cast with an upstream mend over the faster, central flow.

4 This delays drag, as the current has to negate the upstream belly before it can drag the fly.

Due to the fact that the line always follows the rod tip, if, during the shoot, the rod tip makes a sideways deviation upstream and then back on to the tip's original track, this action will throw an upstream mend into the line before it lands. If the upstream deviation is made early in the shoot, the mend will be close to the fly-line tip, if it's made late, it will be closer to the angler. This is an ideal cast if casting across a faster current to slower water. The mend should be timed so that the upstream mend falls on the faster water flow.

Reach cast for extra drift

1 On delivery of the cast, the rod tip reaches upstream.

2 The rod tip tracks round as the current bears the line...

3 ...past the angler...

4 ...and far downstream before drag sets in on the fly.

This cast is useful on wide glides, and uses the full length of the rod and the extended casting arm to throw all the line upstream of the angler's position, thus allowing for a longer drag-free drift before the current acts on the line to 'belly' it and cause drag. The angler's body is turned to angle 45° upstream and the forward cast is directed at the same angle. However, on shooting the line the arm and rod tip extend upstream, as though the angler is trying to use his rod tip to point as far upstream as possible. The line should fall perpendicular to the flow, from the extended rod tip on one side of the current to the fly on the other. As the fly and line drift down the rod tip tracks round with the line, arcing round past the angler, and finishes with the angler reaching downstream to buy as much drag-free drift as he/she can.

Throw in slack with a Squiggle cast

A similar, but more exaggerated effect than the recoil cast. This is effected by the rod tip being moved from side to side as the line shoots out across the river, throwing a series of 'S' bends into the cast before it lands on the water.

1 Instead of driving the rod tip straight down, the wrist is waggled from side to side on the forward shoot. This not only introduces plenty of slack in the fly line but also causes loss of energy in the forward cast so that the leader collapses in a heap with plenty of slack too.

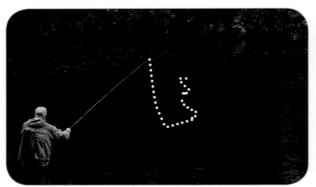

2 The current acts on the slack line, allowing the fly to drift drag-free.

3 A long drag-free drift results.

Parachute in some slack

A very useful cast for delaying dry-fly drag at the very tip of the fly line. It's used when casting across a flow to a lie that may be in current far slower than the mainstream, for instance an eddy on the far side of the current. Essentially the fly line transports the fly across the river and then, instead of turning over neatly, the cast collapses in a loose heap, the fly parachuting down on to the water. This is effected by stopping the rod high on the forward cast – at the 12 o'clock position – then smoothly, slowly lowering the rod tip rather than following through as normal. A good exponent can collapse almost all of a 9ft cast on itself, thus buying 9ft of delayed drag into the bargain.

Stopping the rod tip high and slowly lowering it causes the leader to land in a pile.

This cast can also be used for casting to a fish downstream. The slack-line cast is made in line with the rising fish, and the fly and line is allowed to drift right over its lie.

Sink deep with a dump cast

A useful cast for allowing leaded nymphs to sink fast. As the forward cast is made the rod is stopped suddenly in the 12 o'clock position. This causes the weighted fly/flies to kick over and pitch down vertically so that they all land in the same spot: point fly, middle dropper, top dropper and, lastly, fly-line tip. The flies land in a heap on a loose leader, not stretched across the flow of the river, so they sink unrestricted. The cast also drives the flies down from a height so that they pitch into the water with some force (rather than landing gently), which plunges them under even faster.

PERSUADING 'DIFFICULT' RISERS

If fishing for a 'difficult' fish with dry fly then it's worth working through a repertoire of different dry-fly casts. The refusals may be due to 'micro' drag (*ie* drag that isn't visible to the angler). Using different casts may mean one of them actually eliminates the micro-drag completely… and suddenly the 'difficult' fish takes your fly.

Casting in tight spaces

One of the great advantages of the Spey cast is that, because it's essentially a roll cast, it enables the angler to fish in places where an overhead cast isn't possible – such as a tree-lined river or a high bank etc.

Apart from being a widely used salmon-fishing cast, it's also well worth learning for the angler using a single-handed rod. Dry fly, wet fly and teams of nymphs can all be Spey-cast, using exactly the same casting principles.

↗ Spey casts are an advantage because they can be used to place the 'D' loop between hazards.

→ Here a single-handed double Spey puts the 'D' loop under an overhanging tree, and downstream of one tree branch.

↘ The cast is delivered from the tightest of spaces.

Casting in even tighter spaces

However, the 'D' loop of any Spey cast can still catch on impinging vegetation and obstructions on the bank unless the angler overcomes this added problem by careful placement of the 'D' loop. (For reasons of safety this switch in casts can only be made if there's no, or very light, wind.)

For instance, if an overhanging tree branch is just downstream of the angler's position, then switching from a double-Spey cast off the right shoulder to a Circle C cast off the left shoulder changes the whole angle and position of the 'D' loop, steering it clear of the obstruction.

↗ Hemmed in by trees, a high bank and line-grabbing old branches presents a casting challenge.

→ Careful placement of the line from the Circle C cast also means bankside obstructions can be avoided.

⬂ Here the line is placed well out over the stream.

⬆ The rod tip sweeps back to make a cast off the left shoulder, the 'anchor' well out in the stream.

➔ The 'D' loop forms clear of the branch obstruction...

⬊ ...and the line is delivered at an ideal fishing angle.

FLOAT TUBING

Float tubes offer a relaxing way to fish, and access to the parts of lakes others cannot reach. This one is in the Outer Hebrides.

The ability to get into places on a lake that no one has ever fished before is the ultimate goal of every angler – who knows what leviathans lurk in such places? The float tube allows an individual that ability. The term 'float tubing' almost certainly originated from an inflated lorry inner tube in which the angler sat, suspended, using divers' flippers on his feet to move around. Otherwise known as a belly boat or a kick boat, float tubes are far more sophisticated these days. Each have their own advantages. The V boat is the best of the designs as it allows for swifter travel across the lake, due to its streamlining, and will drift side-on to the wind.

The author's pontoon boat (right) is lightweight and less speedy across the water, but it's easy to carry. This enables him to walk into remote waters with his float tube, or change location in a lake by getting out, taking off his fins, putting the tube on his back and walking to a different area before launching again.

↑ Pumping up the float-tube on location using a hand pump.

↑ Although providing highly efficient power in the water, flippers (or 'fins') are very awkward to wear on land, and it's actually best to walk backwards when wearing them to avoid tripping over!

In addition to the float tube the angler requires:

- A life jacket.
- Chest waders.
- Wading boots.
- A pair of fins.
- A floating (wooden) pan net with clip-on lanyard.

Float-tube tactics

Float tubes can provide access to areas that are rarely fished, particularly on lakes that don't have boats on them. They also drift far slower than a boat, so offer the chance to fish targeted areas thoroughly.

The four techniques described below demonstrate the versatility of the float tube and ways in which it can be used tactically.

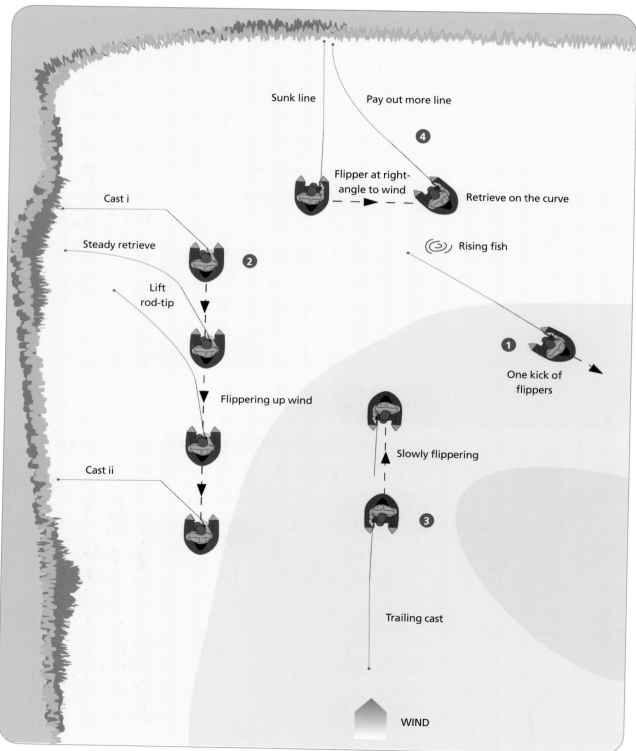

Sunk line

Pay out more line

4

Flipper at right-angle to wind

Retrieve on the curve

Cast i

Steady retrieve

2

Rising fish

Lift rod-tip

1

One kick of flippers

Flippering up wind

Slowly flippering

Cast ii

3

Trailing cast

WIND

1 The Buzzer lift

On stillwaters, when fish are cruising upwind and showing occasionally, sipping down hatching midge pupae (buzzers), there's a tactic unique to float tubing that the author calls 'the Buzzer lift'. This involves fishing a team of three flies on a floating line with a 12–14ft (4–4.6m) 6lb BS leader with, for instance, a size 14 Olive Buzzer on the first dropper, a size 12 Black Buzzer on the second dropper and a size 10 or 12 Black-thoraxed Pheasant Tail Nymph on the point.

If a rising fish is spotted, turn the tube and cast so the flies land 5–6yd (5–6m) upwind and across the path of the fish. Ensure the flies turnover properly, and straighten the line. A fish may take the flies as they gradually sink; if it does the line will simply tighten. However, try and judge when the fish is in close proximity to your flies and make one power kick on the fins. This will cause the sunken nymphs to rise in the water, right in front of the fish. Irresistible.

2 'Turning flee'

This relates to an old Scottish gillie's tactic of trying to get a fish for his 'gentleman' if all else failed. The tactic works because: a) wild loch fish like to lie just off the shoreline; and b) flies retrieved on a curve are a deadly presentation for predatory fish.

The float-tuber can replicate this scenario by finning into the wind at a constant speed and casting towards the shore. The cast would be a typical wet-fly cast: 12ft (4m) of 6lb BS with, say, a Bibio on the top dropper, a Claret Spider on the middle and a Kingfisher Butcher on the point. Short pulls on the flies can also help, as can raising the rod tip as the flies are drawn closer to get the bob-fly walking through the water in a convincing, escaping-fly manner. Due to its manoeuvrability, the float tube can hug the shoreline 20yd (18m) out for great distances and has the potential to catch a good bag of fish, whilst keeping you fit at the same time!

3 Back-dragging

Trolling by any other name, but a good technique for catching or locating a fish. Simply trail the line behind the tube as you fin hard to another fishing place. If you use a sinking line with a Viva lure or Black Tadpole attached, let the line sink to the bottom and then use your fins to allow the fly to trickle along the bottom of the lakebed. Fish will often tap at the fly before taking it – be ready to lift into it. Although low on skill levels, this can catch you a fish on those really hot summer 'dog days' when catch rates are low and nothing is showing.

4 Deadly curve

Mike Duxbury uses a technique that we call the 'Deadly curve'. For this tactic, a sinking line is used along with a lure – Woolly Bugger, Gold-head Damsel etc – and cast directly downwind. Then the tube is finned perpendicular to the cast, say 10yd/10m to the right, paying out more line as the fly and line sink. Now the retrieve commences in long pulls and the fly will rise from the bottom and swing round on an upward curve, which predatory fish find so irresistible. If nothing happens, cast downwind again then fin 10yd more to the left and continue to cover new water.

↑ Whatever tactic you employ – dry fly, nymph, wet fly or lure – there's no doubt that floating around a lake on a warm summer's day, fly fishing, is a very pleasant (and effective!) way to spend a day. This 19lb 1oz rainbow from Loch Tay took a size 12 Pearly Invicta, cast from a float-tube to just 3yd from the shore.

SAFETY TIPS

- Never take a float tube on a river.
- Ensure your tube has twin airbags rather than just one.
- Wear a life jacket.
- Lake water is cold: wear thermal layers underneath breathable waders, or wear neoprene waders.
- Always fin out into the wind so you'll be blown bank on to the shore if you get into trouble.
- Float tube remote waters in pairs.
- If working on your terminal gear (ie changing a fly), hook the other flies on the leader into a fly patch; don't let them dangle in the water – they'll almost certainly catch on your flippers.

- When launching, position the tube at the edge of the water and have your rod ready to hand before you put on your flippers.
- Launch by walking backwards into gently shelving water.

TENKARA FISHING

Dave Southall hooks a good fish on the tenkara outfit in the Austrian mountains.

Tenkara is a traditional Japanese, fixed-line style of fly fishing that evolved to provide the best possible presentation on the complex flows of the turbulent mountain streams of that country. Similar styles were used in the UK up till the late 1800s and are still used in the mountain streams of the Valsesia region of Northern Italy. It's a technique that's simple to set up, easy to use and is a good introductory method to fly fishing on small rivers. Here, keen tenkara exponent Dave Southall outlines the method.

Long rods, short lines

Tenkara rods are long (3–5m/10–16ft) with thin, flexible tips to facilitate the casting of very light lines. They're made from carbon fibre and are telescopic, usually in about eight sections. They aren't designed to catch really big fish, and a 4–5lb BS tippet is the maximum strength normally recommended, although big fish have been successfully landed, including salmon.

A good starter rod for those new to tenkara is one of 3.5–4m long with a 6:4 action (most flexible in the top four-tenths).

The lines, which are attached to the rod tip by a short length of braid called the lilian, vary in length from a metre shorter than the rod up to about twice the rod length, to which is then added about a metre of tippet. Most tenkara practitioners choose to use level, high visibility (bright yellow, orange or pink) fluorocarbon lines of between 0.285 and 0.330mm diameter.

⬇ Fishing a tiny pocket in an Austrian alpine stream with all the line off the water.

FLOW

Superior presentation

When dead-drifting flies, the ability to hold all the line off the water surface is the key reason why tenkara gives far superior drag-free presentation and causes far less fish-scaring disturbance than even a one-weight fly line. The optimum set-up in this respect is undoubtedly a light, level line plus tippet about the same length as the rod. In addition the normal, short casting stroke, stopping the rod tip high at the ten o'clock position, facilitates a fly-first presentation, with the aim of ideally preventing any of the main line from landing on the water.

Limitations

The advantages of tenkara cannot be overstated. However, it does have some limitations. First, the range that can effectively be fished is limited. Second, since it's impossible to give line to a hard-fighting fish, considerable skill and – in some cases – luck is required should a really big fish be hooked.

↑ Austrian rainbow trout caught from a tiny pocket amongst a maelstrom of white water.

↓ Tenkara suits the mobile angler on small streams.

↑ Brown trout from a tiny Derbyshire brook.

Landing a fish

Using a line plus tippet longer than the rod requires hand-lining the fish in. The rod must be swept back over the shoulder and the non-rod arm swept in a wide arc to catch hold of the line; then the fish must be carefully drawn towards the angler by pulling the line through the fingers of the hand that's holding the rod whilst being ready to let the line slip back through the fingers should the fish start to pull too hard. This can be inelegant, and until the technique is mastered it can be the cause of lost fish.

Flies for tenkara

Any dry fly can be used, but some practitioners only use one fly pattern, usually a well hackled Sakasa Kebari, similar to the soft hackle spiders used on northern rivers in the UK, but generally with a reversed hackle that's angled forward to facilitate extra movement and simulate life.

A wide range of subtle movements can be applied to the flies to give them 'life' and induce a take. With slight taps on the butt of the rod with the forefinger the delicate rod tip can be made to vibrate, which makes the fly twitch as it drifts, whilst slightly more movement of the rod tip can generate more distinct pulses of the fly.

Where can you fish tenkara?

Many modern tenkara fishers don't confine themselves to using traditional flies or to fishing solely in fast, mountain, pocket-water streams. Tenkara can be effective on large lakes, big slow rivers and tiny brooks. It's also a superb way to fish with dry flies, for Czech and French/Euro nymphing and for fishing the 'duo'.

↑ Partridge & Orange Sakasa Kebari.

↓ Tenkara gear is ideal for small upland streams, and is highly portable.

ACCESSING FISHING

A cast for sea trout in the Scottish hills.

No matter where you live, fly-fishing potential will never be far away. As we've seen, fly fishing is no longer the exclusive domain of the game angler. As well as wild salmon, sea trout and trout, techniques for many other types of water and species of fish exist. From the prime salmon river to the urban canal holding big pike or rudd, all waters possess exciting potential for the fly fisher. In order to discover what riches lie near your home or your holiday destination, refer to the local fishing guidebooks and leaflets that are usually produced. Otherwise, visit your local tackle shop; they're often an invaluable mine of information.

How to find fishing

For wild-game angling – unless you live close to it – consult the relevant magazines, websites and other avenues of expert opinion to discover places that suit your needs. Apart from the price of the fishing, this may also include the type of accommodation or other family requirements. Primarily the game fly fisher needs to plan his visit by firstly the type of water – is it suitable for fly fishing? For instance, some stretches of salmon water can be highly productive, but not so conducive to fly fishing. Timing is the next consideration: when are the best runs of migratory fish? For trout, consider when the best hatches occur on that particular water.

A local club is always a good route through which you can obtain fishing relatively cheaply. Much of Britain's network of coarse fishing rivers, canals and lakes is controlled through such clubs. Some allow day-ticket access

↑ Locating a pool on a public salmon river in northern Norway.

to the water for visitors, but most local members pay an annual fee for access.

Guides

Another route to fishing is through hiring a guide – probably the quickest route to successful fishing. A network of guides now operate throughout the UK, Ireland and Europe, the principle stemming from the USA originally. A local guide will have access to local fishing, know the best spots, the best times to go and the best tactics, and many have qualifications for instruction in both casting and fishing.

Time for lunch on the Borselva river, northern Norway.

Gillies and boatmen

Most gillies or boatmen, who can be hired locally, aren't instructors as such, but their knowledge and experience is invaluable for both fishing success and safety, especially when it comes to knowing a particular water and where the fish lie. A boatman's skills also lie in controlling the boat for efficient, successful fishing. Their knowledge of the water also ensures safety, as some waters can be particularly dangerous.

Licences and permits

The requirement, price and place of purchase of tickets/permits and rod-licences for fishing need to be noted. No rod licence is required in Scotland but is a legal requirement to fish in inland waters in England and Wales. No rod licence or permit is required to fish in the sea in the UK or Ireland, but in Denmark, for instance, a licence is required for a nominal fee. While no licence is needed for trout, pike and coarse fishing in the Republic of Ireland, a rod licence is required in Northern Ireland. In both Northern Ireland and the Republic of Ireland, licences are required for salmon and sea trout fishing. The French licensing system means the possession of the local licence allows access to all fishing within that Department of France.

Within this system of government-run fisheries are lakes, stocked waters and private stretches of river that are run by individuals, syndicates and clubs. Payment for a ticket or membership fee allows access. Some private concerns combine accommodation with available fishing.

← A boatman uses a single oar to steer his anglers over a known salmon lie on Lough Currane, Ireland.

↓ Permits to fish, rod licence (which is compulsory for fishing in England & Wales) and a Norwegian disinfection certificate, which is necessary on some fisheries to prevent spread of invasives and disease.

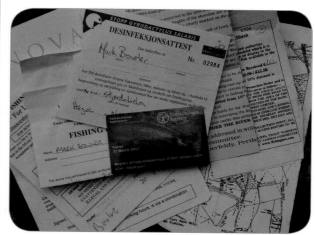

Specialised wheelchair access boat on Eyebrook Reservoir, Northamptonshire.

Disabled access

Apart from platforms, many lakes and some river beats are now equipped with special Wheelyboats, which allow wheelchair access for disabled anglers.

Finding an instructor

In the UK and Ireland there are various bodies for instructors and guides: the AAPGAI (Association of Advanced Professional Game Angling Instructors); APGAI (Association of Advanced Game Angling Instructors); REFFIS (Register of Experienced Fly Fishing Instructors and Schools); GAIA Level 1 & 2 (Game Angling Instructors Association), SGAIC (Scottish Game Angling Instructors Certificate) and STANIC (the Salmon and Trout National Instructor's Certificate), now defunct. In Europe and the USA the more common instructor would be FFF-qualified (the international Federation of Fly Fishers).

It's important to remember that all instructors, gillies, boatmen and guides rely on the fact that you'll enjoy your day. A good instructor won't be examining or testing you, he'll be aiming to make your day as enjoyable, interesting and successful as possible. After all, that's why we go fly fishing.

Instruction on one of *Fly Fishing & Fly Tying's* salmon school residential courses on the Annan, Scotland.

A 19lb salmon for Heidi Williams - her first fish - on the *Fly Fishing & Fly Tying* salmon school.

GLOSSARY

Adipose – a small, fleshy vestigal dorsal fin specific to a game fish.

AFFTA number – American Fly Fishing Trade Association industry standard for fly-line weights.

Arbour - the internal drum of the fly reel around which the fly line and backing are held.

Backing - thin, extra line which is attached to the reel end of the fly line in case a hooked fish runs further than the length of the manufactured fly line.

Baitfish - collective term for any small fish on which larger fish predate.

Breaking strain - a measurement in pounds or kilos estimated to be point at which the line will break.

NATIONAL FISHING/ FISHERIES BODIES

Angling Trust
Governing body for angling in England & Wales and protecting the rights of anglers.

Atlantic Salmon Trust
UK-based charity with Atlantic-wide interests, championing the salmon and sea trout

Salmon & Trout Conservation UK
Charity campaigning for conservation, protection and sustainable management of the aquatic environment.

North Atlantic Salmon Fund
A fund-raising campaign to restore Atlantic salmon stocks nationally and internationally.

Riverfly Partnership
Network of organisations, representing anglers, working to protect the water quality and riverfly populations, and their habitats.

Wild Trout Trust
Charitable organisation dedicated to the conservation of wild trout and their habitat.

Butt leader – a heavy (thick) piece of monofilament to act as a junction and to assist in energy transfer between fly-line and leader.

Casting loop – the shape of the fly line as it travels through the air, as viewed from the side (ie tight loop [narrow]; open loop [wide]).

Cyprinid – family of freshwater fish, including carp, roach, etc.

Dead drift – to drift completely naturally on the current or on the water surface unaffected by the pull or support of the leader or fly line.

'D' loop – the crescent shape of fly line formed between rod-tip and water surface when making a roll cast.

Drag (fly) – The affect of the current or wind acting on the fly line or leader causing it to pull the fly unnaturally.

Drag (reel) – tensioning device on the reel drum which can be varied to make it easier or more difficult to pull off line.

Dropper - a length of monofilament which projects at an angle from a knot in the leader.

False cast – a forward cast which is prevented from landing on the water, and is then used in the back-cast, prior to shooting the line.

Hackle - a splay of feather fibres, usually at the front of a fly.

Leader – the monofilament link between the fly and the tip of the fly line.

Leader-to-hand – also called Euro-nymphing and French leader, a means of casting and fishing the flies using only monofilament (ie, without the use of a fly line).

Lie – a position in the river where a fish holds station.

Lining a fish – casting a line over a fish's head (and scaring it).

On the drop – a fly (or flies) cast out and allowed to free-fall through the water column.

On the swing – a team nymphs (usually buzzers) fished on a floating line and allowed to swing across the breeze.

Presentation – the way the fly, leader and fly line alights on the water.

Shooting line - extra line taken through the rod rings, due to momentum of the forwad cast.

Spate – a high water level, or flood, in a river after rain.

Spey-cast – a redirected Roll Cast, where the fly line uses the water as an anchor-point

Switch rod - a short double-handed rod.

Turnover – the path of the fly as it is delivered to the target by the leader through the energy given to it by the fly line.

Spent flies - dead or dying adult aquatic insects after returning to the water after mating, or to lay their eggs.

Tapered leader - a leader – either manufatured or hand-tied – which graduates in line diameter from the butt (thick) to the tippet (thin).

Terrestrial - a land-borne insect which lands in the water.

Tippet – fine diameter monofilament attached to the fly.

Washing line - a technique where the flies hang down off the leader which is supported at one end by the fly line and a buoyant fly at the other.

⬇ Wading with a guide in the lakes of the Camargue, southern France, sight-fishing for carp.

RECOMMENDED READING

Fly Fishing & Fly Tying magazine
www.flyfishing-and-flytying.co.uk
Fred Buller and Hugh Falkus. *Falkus and Buller's Freshwater Fishing* (1988).
Bob Church. *Reservoir Trout Fishing* (1977).
Brian Clarke. *The Pursuit of Stillwater Trout* (1975).
Oliver Edwards. *Flytyers Masterclass* (1994).
Hugh Falkus. *Sea Trout Fishing* (1983).
— *Salmon Fishing* (1984).
Dominic Garnett. *Fly Fishing for Coarse Fish* (2012).
John Goddard. *Trout Flies of Britain and Europe: The Natural Fly and its Matching Artificial* (1991).
Malcolm Greenhalgh. *Trout Fishing in Rivers* (1987).
— *Lake, Loch and Reservoir Trout Fishing* (1987).
T.C. Ivens. *Stillwater Fly-Fishing* (1973).
Chris James. *Still Water Fly Fishing For Trout* (1994).
T.C. Kingsmill Moore. *A Man May Fish* (1979).
Derek Knowles. *Salmon on a Dry Fly* (1989).
Peter Lapsley. *River Trout Flyfishing* (1988).
— and Cyril Bennett. *Pocket Guide to Matching the Hatch* (2010).
Derek Mills. *Salmon and Trout: A Resource, its Ecology, Conservation and Management* (1971).
Bruce Sandison. *Trout & Salmon Rivers & Lochs of Scotland* (2009).
John Symonds. *How to Flyfish from Newcomer to Improver* (2014).
— and Philip Maher. *Fly Casting Skills for Beginner and Expert* (2013).

Want to know more?

Get your monthly fix of fly fishing